THE FUTURE
OF RITUAL

THE FUTURE
OF RITUAL

Writings on Culture and Performance

Richard Schechner

London and New York

First published 1993
by Routledge
11 New Fetter Lane, London EC4P 4EE

Simultaneously published in the USA and Canada
by Routledge
29 West 35th Street, New York, NY 10001

Typeset in 10/14pt Garamond, Linotronic 300, by Florencetype Ltd, Avon
Printed in Great Britain by T.J. Press, Padstow, Cornwall

British Library Cataloguing in Publication Data
A catalogue record for this book is available from the British Library.

Library of Congress Cataloging in Publication Data
Schechner, Richard
The future of ritual: writings on culture and performance /
Richard Schechner.
p.   cm.
Includes bibliographical references and index.
1. Theater and society.   2. Performing arts—
Philosophy.   3. Rites and ceremonies.   4. Play.   I. Title.
PN2039.S38   1993
792'.01—dc20   92-16123

ISBN 0-415-04689-0

To my son Sam
To my daughter Sophia

Contents

Acknowledgments

My writings usually exist in versions or variants. My writing isn't finishable. My strategy is to rehearse, rework, revise. I publish at various stages of working, not being too neat about precisely when a constellation of ideas gets into print. Just about everything in this book has shown up before one way or another. Nor is *The Future of Ritual* definitive. Some stuff will appear again, maybe changed. Of everything it must be said, there is no final saying.

"Playing" (Chapter 2) was my 1987 keynote address to The Society for the Association for the Study of Play (TASP). My talk was revised as the inaugural essay in the Society's journal, *Play and Culture* 1 (1), 1988.

"The street is the stage" (Chapter 3) was written to keynote the 1990 Celebration of Literature conference at the University of South Florida, Tampa. Substantially revised, it appeared as "Invasions friendly and unfriendly" in *South African Theatre Journal*, May 1992, and in *Critical Theory and Performance*, edited by Joseph Roach and Janelle Reinelt, 1992. The version published here is further revised.

"Waehma . . . at New Pascua, Arizona" (Chapter 4) arose out of a set of three conferences in 1981 and 1982 on ritual and performance conceived by Victor Turner, me, and a team of planners (see Schechner and Appel 1990). After seeing the Yaqui Deer dances in November 1981 I returned to Arizona at Easter time in 1982, 1985, and 1987 for the Waehma celebrations at Pascua Pueblo. A short version of "Waehma at New Pascua" appeared in Ano 6, no. 11 of a special issue of *Gestos* on theatre edited by Juan Villegas and Diana Taylor. The essay is also in *Performance and the Renewal of Community: Easter in Northwestern Mexico and Southwestern United States*, edited by Rosamond B. Spicer and N. Ross Crumrine, 1992.

"Striding through the cosmos" (Chapter 5) is the most recent of my articles – ultimately to culminate in a book (I hope) on the Ramlila of Ramnagar, India. A short version of "Striding" is in *Living Banaras: Hindu Religion in Cultural Context*, edited by Bradley Hertel and Cynthia Humes, 1992.

"Wayang kulit in the colonial margin" (Chapter 6) began as my reaction to a 1988 performance of wayang kulit (Javanese leather shadow puppets) at the University of Michigan where I was a visiting humanities fellow. In 1989 I developed the themes during talks at Northwestern University and the University of Iowa. The article was published in *TDR, The Drama Review* 34 (2), summer 1990: 25–61.

"The future of ritual" (Chapter 7) has undergone many transformations. A version of it was published as the inaugural essay of the *Journal of Ritual Studies* 1 (1), 1987: 5–34. Other fragments appeared in my essay, "Victor Turner's last adventure" (itself in two versions): *Anthropologica* 27 (1–2), 1985: 190–206 and my introduction to Victor Turner's *The Anthropology of Performance* (1986).

A prefatory note

Who knows what would have been done if things had been done differently? We leave tracks, and that's that.

Without Carol Martin this book would not be. And without my students and faculty colleagues at the Department of Performance Studies, Tisch School of the Arts, New York University, this book would not be what it is. Special thanks to David Oppenheim, Barbara Kirshenblatt-Gimblett, Peggy Phelan, Brooks McNamara, and Mick Taussig. And to my friend, the movie actor Michael Kirby. The editors of *TDR*, *The Drama Review*, especially Mariellen Sandford, have helped me focus my thinking and writing. People too numerous to list helped me accomplish my research and artistic work in India, China, South Africa, Taiwan, and elsewhere. To all these, I say thank you.

Finally, the texture of my life is woven of my children, Sophia and Sam, who are always present in what I do. *The Future of Ritual* is dedicated to them.

1

Introduction
Jayaganesh and the avant-garde

The best way to . . . understand, enliven, investigate, get in touch with, outwit, contend with, defend oneself against, love . . . others, other cultures, the elusive and intimate "I-thou," the other in oneself, the other opposed to oneself, the feared, hated, envied, different other . . . is to perform and to study performances and performative behaviours in all their various genres, contexts, expressions, and historical processes. What the book was, the performance has become: index and symbol, multiple truths and lies, arena of struggle. And what is performance? Behavior heightened, if ever so slightly, and publicly displayed; twice-behaved behavior. Even in con games, spies, and stings where performances are cunningly masked and folded into the expected, these are enjoyed by a secret audience, the producers of the deceptions. And no matter how sinister and destructive the deception, when it's made public people get a special kick out of learning all about it. Gordon Liddy of Watergate harvested fat fees lecturing at colleges about his crimes. Performances can be celebratory; performances can terrorize. Many trials and public executions are both. The night the Rosenbergs were electrocuted some people wept, others were enraged, and still others danced in the streets. Performance is amoral, as useful to tyrants as to those who practice guerrilla theatre. This amorality comes from performance's subject, transformation: the startling ability of human beings to create themselves, to change, to become – for worse or better – what they ordinarily are not.

A Jewish Hindu named Jayaganesh

In the summer of 1976 I was living in Churuthuruthy, a small town in Kerala, southwest India. I'd come to India in January of that year with The

Performance Group (TPG) – a New York-based experimental theatre company which I founded in 1967 and directed until 1980. After I left, TPG completed its metamorphosis into the Wooster Group. For three months TPG toured across north India from New Delhi to Lucknow, Calcutta, Bhopal, and Bombay performing Brecht's *Mother Courage and Her Children* (see Schechner 1983:31–54). When the tour was over, several people struck out on their own.

I'd been to India before in 1971–2 so I knew some of what I wanted to see. During the spring Chaitra Parva celebrations, I went to Purulia, Seraikella, and Mayurbhanj in eastern India to observe the three forms of chhau dance theatre. Then I spent time in Calcutta viewing traditional and new jatra, modern theatre, and experimental theatre, especially Badal Sircar's Satabdi group. While in Calcutta I made plans to travel to Vrindaban and then Ramnagar (near Banaras) to study Raslila and Ramlila. The mid-summer was reserved for an extensive trip to the south. I was especially looking forward to my weeks in Kerala, where I would take some classes in kathakali and observe the training and performance practice at the Kalamandalam in Churuthuruthy.

Kerala was very attractive to me as a performance theorist and theatre director. Kathakali, teyyam, and kutiyattam – closely related genres of theatre and ritual – were thriving in proximity to each other. Kutiyattam continued an ancient practice of Sanskrit theatre in association with the Hindu temples. Teyyam was an exorcistic, extremely robust folk ritual theatre. It was performed near simple shrines often incorporating old and numinous trees and rocks. Kathakali, especially as practiced at the Kalamandalam, was rapidly modernizing its ways of training and performing. Professional troupes performed in venues ranging from tourist hotels to village squares. Performances were taking place not only in Kerala but also in the metropolitan cities of India and overseas. The great form itself, originating in the seventeenth century, renewed in the 1930s, was undergoing further changes as every living art does.

I wanted to understand through observation and experience as much of the village–temple performance complex as I could. But I found myself shut out from the interiors of many temples because I was not a Hindu. This exclusion was one more reminder that I was, and would always be, an outsider. I saw performances in theatres and village squares, rode careening intercity buses and chicken-choked local ones, walked the ridges of the steamy rice paddies where farmers worked their patient, hulking, black water buffaloes, and sat at many a roadside stall slurping hot, sweet, milky Indian tea trying to make myself understood to Malayalam speakers. I was welcomed in academic and artistic institutions where English was the lingua franca. But I wanted more. I was hungry for what was happening inside such Kerala temple complexes as Guruvayur, Vadakkumnatha, and Sri Padmanabha. Inside the temples, I wanted to inspect and study the kuttampalams – theatres constructed according to the *Natyasastra*, the ancient Sanskrit text on performance. I wanted to experience kutiyattam, a vestige of Sanskrit theatre, performed in a kuttampalam. I might even live in a temple for some days, as I had done in the spring of that year at Sankat Mochan, Banaras's Hanuman temple.

I decided to convert.

Well, not exactly.

In the matter of conversion, I was uneasy about what I was taking on, what I was giving up. Before entering the Ramakrishna ashram near Trichur, Swami Sakrananda, the President of the ashram, interviewed me concerning my intentions. I told him my purpose was to see temple dances and ceremonies close up, to study architecture, especially as it pertained to performance, and to participate in temple rituals. "Are your motives religious or aesthetic?" the Swami inquired. I hemmed and hawed, finally slipping the knot by asking him, "How can you separate the two, especially here in India?"

On 6 July 1976, the eve of my Upanayana ceremony – the tying of the sacred thread that would signify I was "twice-born," a high-caste Hindu – I wrote in my notebook:

> I think about my initiation into Hinduism. I am not cynical about it. And this lack of cynicism stirs contradictions. Am I "betraying" my Jewishness? I am attracted to Hindu philosophy, especially the *Bhagavad Gita*, and what I know about the *Upanishads*, and Hindu art, of course. And I want to go deeper – is this the way?

That night I rehearsed my initiation by copying into my notebook the ten pages of ritual text, written partly in Sanskrit and partly in English, whose recitation constituted the main portion of the ceremony. In the name of Sri Ramakrishna (an Indian ecstatic saint of the nineteenth century, teacher of Vivekananda), "I pray[ed] to be blessed with Upanayana initiation with due solemnity for the attainment of the four aims, Dharma, Artha, Kama, Moksha. . . . I embrace[ed] with deep sraddha [faith] the Sanatana Vaidika

Dharam. . . . I accept[ed] all the Vedic Rishis and incarnations and acharyas as guiding saviours in my life," and so on.

What was I doing? Why was I writing all this out?

Was I attempting to tame the ceremony, own it, reduce it to a discourse I could master?

The next morning the initiation was performed. I repeated the many mantras I was instructed to enunciate. The sacred thread was laid over my left shoulder. Sandal paste was applied to my forehead. I was given my Hindu name. At the end of it all, I received a small "Conversion Certificate," featuring a passport photo and text, in full:

> This is to certify that Mr Richard Schechner, New York City, a Jew by faith, has been converted into a Hindu and named Jayaganesh as per his request after performing purificatory rites at this Ashrama on 7–7–1976.
> SIGNED
> Swami Sakrananda,
> President,
> Sri Ramakrishna Ashrama
> P.O. Puranattukara,
> Dt. Trichur, Kerala

The ceremony itself, far from erasing my doubts, magnified them. Immediately before accepting initiation, I wrote:

> Actually, now that the time for my initiation grows close, I ought to set down the motives for this act. Were I not denied entry into temples because temples are reserved for Hindus, I would not have chosen this path. I do not use the word "conversion" because it is repugnant to me. I am frightened because I want my Jewishness to remain "intact." Thus I go into this with my fingers crossed, winking at my Jewish self. It would be easier and smoother if it were sheer cynicism, if I could just say to myself, "Well, you want to see/study these things; this is the only way."

After my initiation, I felt easier in the temples, though wicked in my heart. Threaded in my new Hindu identity, I was "authentic," almost.

As I entered Sri Padmanabha's inner sanctum, deep in my pocket I held tight to my Conversion Certificate. I learned also of the objective power of ritual – the efficacy of ritual acts despite the duplicity, or worse, of those undertaking them. To this day I keep my sacred thread, as I have preserved the teffilin given to me at my bar mitzvah. As I, a 58-year-old man, write these words, I wonder at the secret spectacle of my Keralan incarnation: a New York man of 42, dressed Indian-style, fretting as only an atheist Jew can over his hypocritical conversion, moving through a crowded temple courtyard – what was this Jayaganesh doing if not performing himself performing his Hinduism?

The five avant-gardes or . . .

What the avant-garde has become during the past 100 years or so is much too complicated to be organized under one heading. There is an historical avant-garde, a current avant-garde (always changing), a forward-looking avant-garde, a tradition-seeking avant-garde, and an intercultural avant-garde. A single work can belong to more than one of these categories. The five avant-gardes have emerged as separable tendencies because "avant-garde" meaning "what's in advance of" – a harbinger, an experimental prototype, the cutting edge – no longer describes the multifid activities undertaken by performance artists, auteurs, directors, designers, actors, and scholars operating in one or more of the various "worlds" the planet has been partitioned into. At this point, even as I use them, I voice my objection to these outdated categories. The end of the cold war dissolved the opposition between the first world and the second. The collapse of Soviet hegemony over Eastern Europe and even the territories of the USSR itself was not a spasm temporally limited to 1989–91 or spatially localized in Europe. A steady and long-term infiltration of possibilities and alternatives accompanied, forced, and highlighted the failure of Soviet communism to deliver the goods or permit an open play of ideas. Similar historical processes are at work eliding and topsy-turvying other apparently stable systems, including Europe, China, and that most stable of them all, the USA. If by "new world order" George Bush means American hegemony (as he surely does), he is mistaken. The third and fourth worlds are everywhere. The pressures on America from the south are steadily increasing. There is a large and growing south in the USA, the UK, France, and other northern European countries. Change is coming both to China and the USA, forced on them by circumstances working themselves through in historical rather than journalistic time. As for the third world, it is characterized by tumult and often uncontrollable transformations. The task for cultural workers is to express as clearly as we can both the emotional and the logical sense of the changes taking place. We need to find ways to celebrate individual and cultural differences, even as people work towards economic and political parity. Is such a differential egalitarianism possible?

The historical avant-garde took shape in Europe during the last decades of the nineteenth century. It soon spread to many places around the world. The plays of Ibsen, and the naturalistic style of presenting them, for example, affected the modernization of Japan and the liberation of China from the Qing Dynasty. But the first great modern avant-garde, naturalism, soon evoked its opposites in an explosion of heterodoxies: symbolism, futurism, cubism, expressionism, dada, surrealism, constructivism . . . and many more with names, manifestos, and actions that came and went with such speed as to suggest their true aim: the propagation of artistic difference. Along with this was a political agenda, one of sharp opposition. Poggioli is near right when he detects in the historical avant-garde a "prevalence of the anarchistic mentality . . . an eschatological state of mind, simultaneously messianic and apocalyptic" (1968:99–100). Avant-gardists were on the left because the right was in power. When the left came to power, in the USSR for example, experimentalists were treated like kulaks, ripe for repression and extermination. Look what happened to Mayakovsky and Meyerhold, who, among a host of others, were reclassified from "revolutionary comrades" to "enemies of the people." Stalin protected remnants of bourgeois culture, Stanislavski among them, and fostered the dullest kind of "socialist realism." Decades later, marching under the authority of Mao Zedong's "little red book," China's cultural revolution, orchestrated by Jiang Qing, actress and Mao's second wife, razed Chinese culture, both traditional and avant-garde. What Jiang produced were "model operas," brilliant but wooden performances expressing her own political and aesthetic values.[1] At present, categories like "left" and "right" have lost much of their meaning; they are useful only in very particular historical circumstances, not as general principles.

Regarding the historical avant-garde, Michael Kirby is on the mark when he says that

> "avant-garde" refers specifically to a concern with the historical *directionality* of art. An advanced guard implies a rear guard or at least the main body of troops following behind. . . . Some artists may accept the limits of art as defined, as known, as given; others may attempt to alter, expand, or escape from the stylistic aesthetic rules passed on to them by the culture.
>
> (1969:18–19)

What Kirby identifies as the avant-garde's "impulse to redefine, to contradict, to continue the sensed directionality of art" (1969:18–19) is the energy source and connecting link holding together the disparate movements of the historical avant-garde.

The historical avant-garde was characterized by the twin tendency to make something new that was also in opposition to prevailing values. Since Romanticism, these values have been seen as social and political as well as aesthetic. The Romantics introduced the idea that artists lived their lives in terms of their art – that experience, display, and expression were inextricably linked, each one functioning in terms of the others. "Action," whether poetic, personal, or political (trying to affect the way society was organized) became key. Wordsworth's description of poetry (in the 1800 "Preface" to his *Lyrical Ballads*) as the spontaneous overflow of powerful feelings . . . "emotion recollected in tranquillity" was soon replaced by Shelley's call for direct radical action. This affection for radical thought, rhetoric, and action in opposition to accepted values was at the heart not only of the historical avant-garde's politics, but also of its bohemian lifestyle.

Even the *ancien régime* was not hated as much as the new dominant class, the bourgeoisie. Not only was the middle class in power, and to avant-gardists therefore the cause of what was wrong with society, it was also uncultured, grossly materialistic and greedy. Ironically, some of Shelley's heirs, in their hatred of bourgeois values and manners, adopted aristocratic airs. Paris's Left Bank and New York's Greenwich Village were famous as places where artists, dandies, and radicals (not mutually exclusive categories) lived their eccentric and libidinous lives, making art, mocking the bourgeoisie, and plotting revolution. Middle-class people considered the artists to be neurotic, childlike, and savage – a trinity formulated by Freud (in many ways an apologist for the Victorianism to whose practices his "talking cure" adjusted errants). From the bourgeois perspective, artists were thought "naturally" to be impetuous and irresponsible when it came to money, sex, and politics.

After the Russian Revolution of 1917, the conjunction of revolutionary thought and art grew stronger. Meyerhold was the most visible of a large cohort who wanted to find a place for experimental performance in what he believed was a new and progressive social order. For a time, until the paranoid "man of steel" Josef Stalin turned it off, light came from the East in the form of biomechanics, constructivism, Russian futurism, montage, multimedia, and vibrant performance styles combining the most recent technological innovations with traditional popular entertainments, such as *commedia dell'arte*, circus, and the cabaret. And just as Germans fleeing Hitler in the 1930s and 1940s fertilized the artistic and intellectual life of Great Britain and the Americas, so Russians (Czarists as well as progress-ives) vitalized Western European and American theatre, film, and visual arts.

The "current avant-garde" (second of the five types of avant-garde) is by definition what's happening *now*. Of course, "now" is always changing – it will be different when this writing is published from what it is as I write in New York in November 1991. Today's current theatre avant-garde includes reruns of the historical avant-garde as well as the practices of formerly experimental artists whose work is by now "classical" in terms of its predictability, solidity, and acceptance. You know what to expect from Robert Wilson, Laurie Anderson, Elizabeth LeCompte, Meredith Monk, Lee Breuer, Richard Foreman, Merce Cunningham, Pina Bausch, Rachel Rosenthal – and a bunch of younger people working in roughly the same ways as their predecessors and mentors; people like Anne Bogart, Julie Taymor, Bill T. Jones, and Martha Clarke.

The work of the current avant-garde is often excellent, virtuosic in its mastery of formerly experimental and risky materials and techniques. This mastery, coupled with a second and third generation of artists working in the same way, is what makes the current avant-garde classical. Over time, the historical avant-garde modulated into the current avant-garde: what were once radical activities in terms of artistic experimentation, politics, and lifestyles have become a cluster of alternatives open to people who wish to practice or see various kinds of theatrical art. The current avant-garde offers no surprises in terms of theatrical techniques, themes, audience interactions, or anything else. Like naturalism before it, "avant-garde" has become a style, a way of working, rather than a bellwether. But unlike naturalism, the current avant-garde is not "mainstream," not what most theatres do. It is simply a menu of options drained of the fervor of their original impulses.

The current avant-garde certainly may be considered a "new establishment." As Graham Ley wrote, "The continuing admiration for a select group of experimental practitioners prompts the question of whether we can have a theatrical avant-garde that would seem to be so well-established" (1991:348). Ley identifies certain qualities of the current avant-garde that are antithetical to what drove the historical avant-garde. Chief among these are the heavy doses of money – most of it from government, big business, and foundations (where the robber barons and their descendants buried their pots of gold) – underwriting almost all of the established current avant-garde biggies from Robert Wilson and Peter Brook through to Grotowski and the Wooster Group. (Ley does not exclude me from the list of the subsidized, due to my long employment by first Tulane and then New York

University.) Not only do well-known avant-gardists feed from various patrons (as did artists in the days before the marketplace), subsidy is what further generations of theatre, dance, and other artists expect as their birthright. One has to go to popular entertainments – pop music, sports, movies, and TV – to find arts conditioned by the rough-and-ready economics of the market. However "vulgar" these entertainments, they are also often both lively and innovative, especially in the development of physical techniques (lighting, sound, ways of including the audience, "special effects"). The current avant-garde is not only dominated by a group of oldsters (of which I am, for better or worse, one), but it is also quite clearly an established style of performance, one that in many ways is not distinguishable from orthodox theatre and dance. What innovation comes from the current avant-garde, is mostly emanating from performance art, where people are exploring such things as explicit sexual art and the combining of the extremely personal with the political.

Another wing of the current avant-garde is the activist political theatre – heir to the guerrilla and street theatre movements of the 1960s. This work is avant-garde because there has been free trade of techniques, persons, and ideas between the avant-garde and political theatre from the days of Meyerhold, Brecht, and dada. People and groups like the gay activists of ACT UP (AIDS Coalition to Unleash Power) who use guerrilla theatre to demand more AIDS research and treatment, the radical environmentalists of Greenpeace, and the "theatre of the oppressed" of Augusto Boal are in the forefront of this kind of theatre. There are very active political theatres in Latin America, Africa, and Asia.[2] ACT UP and Greenpeace work along two lines simultaneously: to get their message across graphically to the general public by using sudden, often disruptive, and dramatic means: and to instill solidarity among their members – nothing brings a group together faster or with more enthusiasm than collectively taking action in an atmosphere of risk. When ACT UP members lie down in the streets simulating the dead and dying of AIDS, or when a Greenpeace ship intercepts a polluting or nuclear arms-bearing vessel, not only does the media catch the event and broadcast it, but group members are also invigorated, reaffirming in public their belief in their cause and each other. In this way, the activist political theatre is a religious and ritual theatre, a theatre of "witnesses" in the Buddhist, Christian, and Hindu sense. Indeed, the strategies of Gandhi live in the work of political theatres everywhere.

Boal's techniques, originating as opposition to Latin American fascists –

Boal himself fled Brazil in the late 1960s and was later forced from Argentina; he is now based in Paris and back in Rio – are somewhat different from those of ACT UP, Greenpeace, and other guerrilla theatre operations. More than wanting to unmask, attack, and ridicule systems and people he feels are oppressive, Boal wants to empower the oppressed. To do this, he has developed, over nearly twenty-five years of work, a non-Aristotelian form of improvisational participatory performance. Boal has written extensively about his work. And his Center for the Theatre of the Oppressed in Paris regularly issues publications.[3]

Political performance, formalist theatre, personal expression, meditative performances . . . and on through a long list of styles, objectives, social and political contexts, and venues: for a long time, since the late 1970s at least, the trend has been away from hegemony toward a situation where there are a number of styles, each of which is an alternative to all the others. Instead of fiercely contentious "isms" struggling against the mainstream and each other (a characteristic of the historical avant-garde), the current avant-garde is one where producing organizations and particular venues celebrate their receptivity to various styles. So, for example, in New York, the Brooklyn Academy of Music's (BAM) "Next Wave" festival is actually a compilation of many different kinds of nonnaturalistic theatre and dance, none of it really new, none of it about to replace everything that came before. BAM has no ideological or artistic program beyond presenting what Harvey Lichtenstein and his cohorts think is "hot." BAM titles its annual avant-garde festival the "Next Wave," an absurd appellation for artists most of whom have been on the scene for decades. Or take the 1991–2 season at the Public Theatre arranged by the organization's new artistic director, JoAnne Akalaitis, a Mabou Mines founder. Works range from solo pieces by people of color ("curated by George C. Wolf"), to performance art, to productions of Shakespeare, Ford, and Lorca, to Anne Bogart directing the Mabou Mines company in Brecht's *In the Jungle of Cities*. The former dominant mainstream – Broadway, the West End, regional theatres – for their part freely borrow techniques and people from the current avant-garde. Such willy-nilly eclecticism, a monoculturalist's nightmare, is the way things are going to be for a long time.

But it's not enough to divide the avant-garde in two, the historical and the current. Since at least the last great burst of new activity in performance, the late 1950s through the mid-1970s – the time of happenings (later to become performance art), environmental theatre, guerrilla theatre, ritual arts – there have been two strong themes within the avant-garde: the forward-looking and the tradition-seeking. Those who are forward-looking advocate and celebrate artistic innovation and originality. This branch of the avant-garde is heir to the historical avant-garde, on the lookout for new ideas and techniques – multimedia, video hookups and interactive telecommunications, megasound, laser light shows, cybernetics, and hyper or virtual time/space. The works of Robert LePage, Laurie Anderson, John Jesurun, and the Wooster Group come to mind. Naim June Paik and many performance artists are forward-looking in the way I am specifying; or those who showed their works at one of the PULSE shows (People Using Light, Sound, and Energy) in Santa Barbara, California. Often this kind of work fuses the avant-garde with popular entertainments because so much of pop culture is not only technologically driven but also where the money is.

The forward-looking avant-garde enacts a future that is both amazing and apocalyptic. The very technology that is celebrated is also feared; it obliterates even as it liberates. The film *Total Recall* very clearly shows this. In the movie the boundary between inner fantasy life and outer "real" life is blurred. As in Indian tales where the dreamer wakes up into his own dream, the Schwarzenegger character in *Total Recall* doesn't know if his vacation to Mars – a violent, grotesque, and erotic place – is happening inside his mind or in ordinary time/space. The movie ends with the hero and heroine barely escaping death as they witness the violently explosive terraforming of Mars. The old, desiccated planet is transformed into a new, fertile Edenic world. Unfortunately, this exciting denouement becomes pure Hollywood when it's stripped of its ambiguity and it's made clear that it's no dream; it's really happening.

The tradition-seeking avant-garde, so strongly present in Grotowski and Barba but visible as well in "roots" movements and "shamanic" performances, rejects fancy technology and cybernetics, preferring the "wisdom of the ages," most often found in nonWestern cultures. Jerzy Grotowski's journeys, both actual and conceptual, are paradigmatic of this tendency in the avant-garde. Grotowski's theatre education in Poland and the USSR was nothing unusual. He got his certificate in acting from the Krakow theatre school in 1955; from August 1955 until 1956 he studied directing in Moscow at the State Institute of Theatre Arts, where he became a "fanatic disciple of Stanislavsky" and "discovered Meyerhold" (Osinski 1986:17–18). Then in the summer of 1956, he traveled through central Asia where, it seems, he experienced an epiphany. In Grotowski's own (translated) words:

During my expeditions in Central Asia in 1956, between an old Turkmenian town, Ashkhabad, and the western range of the Hindu Kush Mountains, I met an old Afghan named Abdullah who performed for me a pantomime "of the whole world," which had been a tradition in his family. Encouraged by my enthusiasm, he told me a myth about the pantomime as a metaphor for "the whole world." It occurred to me then that I'm listening to my own thoughts. Nature – changeable, moveable, but permanently unique at the same time – has always been embodied in my imagination as the dancing mime, unique and universal, hiding under the glittering of multiple gestures, colors, and the grimace of life. (In Osinski 1986:18)

Grotowski returned to Poland where he studied directing and became involved in the anti-Stalinist movements then gaining strength.

But his interest in things Asian and traditional continued. In 1957 he gave public lectures on "The philosophical thought of the Orient," including discussions of yoga, the Upanishads, Buddhism, Zen-Buddhism, Advaita-Vedanta, Taoism, and Confucius. In 1957 and again in 1959, Grotowski traveled to France where he saw works of Jean Vilar and Marcel Marceau, whom he greatly admired. All the while, Grotowski was directing Western works ranging from Ionesco's *The Chairs* and Chekhov's *Uncle Vanya* to an adaptation for radio of Mark Twain's *The White Elephant*. In 1959, Grotowski and critic–dramaturg Ludwik Flaszen took over Opole's Theatre of 13 Rows where they and their colleagues developed what was to be known as "poor theatre" (see Grotowski 1968, Kumiega 1985, Osinski 1986). This style of performing – emphasizing the actors' psycho-physical abilities, refusing theatrical sets, redefining audience–performer interactions according to the needs of each production, constructing a textual montage from many sources (rather than interpreting a drama written by a single author) – was based on rigorous training founded at least initially on yoga and other principles Grotowski derived from his studies of Asian theatre and philosophies, combined with a deeply Polish Catholic and Hassidic mystic practice. In fact, Grotowski felt the similarity between these traditions, a similarity that Eugenio Barba some years later dubbed "Eurasian theatre" (Barba:1988). The stripped-down stage, the ritualized nature of the encounter between performers and spectators, the startling confrontation of extremely personal expression and totally composed face and body "masks," all were modeled to a degree after what Grotowski knew of Asian theatre, ritual, and thought. Grotowski's most audacious and experimental inventions are founded on tradition. What Artaud intuited and theorized, Grotowski researched and practiced.

In the late 1960s, Grotowski "left the theatre." He stopped directing plays. He began a series of research projects taking him to and putting him in touch with many artists and ritual specialists from different cultures in an attempt to find and express in specific theatrical ways – dances, songs, gestures, utterances, words – universals of performance. These research projects have had several names: theatre of sources, objective drama, ritual arts. The work is not yet complete and is probably uncompletable. It has taken Grotowski to Asia, the Americas, the Caribbean (and possibly other places too: Grotowski often travels incognito). Grotowski has not been silent regarding his work after poor theatre; and often enough he sounds classically avant-gardist:

Art is profoundly rebellious. Bad artists *speak* of rebelling; real artists *actually* rebel. They respond to the powers that be with a concrete act: this is both the most important and the most dangerous point. Real rebellion in art is something which persists and is competent and never dilettante. When I began working with the Theatre of Sources (it was still the period of participatory theatre) it was quite clear that in certain traditional human activities – which may be called religious – from different cultures where tradition still existed, it was possible to see, in some cases, participatory theatre without banality. It soon became clear that not all the differences can be reduced, that we can't alter our own conditioning, that I shall never be a Hindu even if I am consecrated by the Hindus. One can, however, move toward what precedes the differences. Why do the African hunter from the Kalahari, the French hunter from the outskirts of Saintes, the Bengali hunter, and the Huichol hunter from Mexico all adopt the same body position when they go hunting, with the spinal backbone leaning slightly forward, and the knees slightly bent in a position that is sustained at the base by the sacrum–pelvis complex? And why can only one kind of rhythmic movement derive from this position? And what use can be made of this way of walking? There is a very simple, very easy level of analysis: if the weight of the body is on one foot and you move the other foot, you don't make any noise and you can also move very slowly without stopping. In this way certain animals remain unaware of your presence. But this isn't the important thing. What is important is that there exists a certain primary position of the human body. It's a position which goes back so far that it was probably the position not only of homo sapiens, but also of homo erectus, and connected in some way with the appearance of man. An extremely ancient position connected with what some Tibetans call the "reptile" aspect. In the Afro-Caribbean culture this position is linked more precisely with the grass snake, and in the Hindu culture linked with the Tantra, you have this snake asleep at the base of the backbone. We are now touching on something which concerns my present work [1985]. I began asking myself, at the end of the period of the Theatre of Sources, how people used this primary energy, how, through differing techniques elaborated in the traditions, people found access to this ancient body of man. I have traveled a lot, I've read numerous books, I have found numerous traces.   (Grotowski 1987:30–5)

It is not necessary to summarize Grotowski's work over the past twenty-five years to note two things. It remains in the vanguard of experimental work concerning performance (if not strictly theatre in the Western sense); and it is deeply traditional in a way that Grotowski himself, among others, is defining.

Eugenio Barba, Grotowski's longtime colleague and the founder–director of Odin Teatret, one of Europe's leading experimental theatres, challenges Western orthodoxy with Asian practice.

Why in the Western tradition, as opposed to what happens in the Orient, has the actor become specialised [. . . instead of being able to act, dance, mime, and sing?]. Why in the West does the actor tend to confine herself within the skin of only one character in each production? Why does she not explore the possibility of creating the context of an entire story, with many characters, with leaps from the general to the particular, from the first to the third person, from the past to the present, from the whole to the part, from persons to things?   (1988:126)

Barba proposes an experimental theatre of roots.

Here the term "roots" becomes paradoxical: it does not imply a bond with ties to a place, but an ethos which permits us to change places. Or better: it represents the force which causes us to change our horizons precisely because it roots us to a center.   (1988:128)

The roots movement is not only of the West. Re-examining and redefining tradition is a characteristic of the avant-garde in India, Japan, and elsewhere. Suresh Awasthi writes:

I am taking the risk of giving a label – "theatre of roots" – to the unconventional theatre which has been evolving for some two decades in India as a result of modern theatre's encounter with tradition. . . . Directors like B. V. Karanth, K. N. Panikkar, and Ratan Thiyam have had meaningful encounters with tradition, and, with their work, reversed the colonial course of contemporary theatre. . . . It sounds paradoxical, but their theatre is both avant-garde in the context of conventional realistic theatre, and part of the 2,000-year-old *Natyasastra* tradition. (1989:48)

Awasthi points out that the "theatre of roots" must be seen against the backdrop of more than a century of Western naturalistic theatre which is the mainstream in India. Some qualities of the "theatre of roots" – rejection of the proscenium stage, closer contact between spectators and performers, integration of music, mime, gesture, and literary text – are identical to the experimental theatre program practiced by environmental theatre workers in the West. Of course, this would be so: many of the Western experiments were modeled on the kinds of performances directors like me studied and/or saw in India or elsewhere. That this same avant-garde impulse should now be affecting modern (that is, orthodox or mainstream) Indian theatre is only to be expected.

In Japan, butoh, a word which used to mean "ancient dance," now refers to an intense, physically extreme, and rebellious avant-garde performance art developed by Kazuo Ohno and the late Tatsumi Hijikata. Butoh is practiced by Kazuko Shiraishi, Min Tanaka, Natsuo Nakajima, and several groups (Dai Rakuda-kan, Muteki-sha, and Sankai Juku are the best known). Described by Bonnie Sue Stein as "shocking, provocative, physical, spiritual, erotic, grotesque, violent, cosmic, nihilistic, cathartic, [and] mysterious" (1986:111), butoh is closely linked to noh and kabuki as well as other traditional Japanese arts.

Butoh is an anti-traditional tradition seeking to erase the heavy imprint of Japan's strict society and offering unprecedented freedom of artistic expression. . . . Nakajima said, "We found that we were making the same discoveries as noh actors made, using some of the same terminology, but we had never learned these forms." (Stein 1986:111)

The images and actions butoh performers create are striking. Ohno in his eighties still performs the movements of a young coquette, her face painted white, her lips scarlet. "He drapes himself across the edge of the stage in the serpentine curves of traditional femininity, then kicks his foot high like a carefree young lover. To the slow koto music, he skips, flutters, and poses" (Stein 1986:107). Or Sankai Juku's nearly naked performers, their bodies powdered white, who dangle upside down far above the street, held aloft by ropes tied around their ankles. In Seattle in 1985, a rope broke and a Sankai Juku dancer plunged to his death. But risk is what butoh is about. Often performing outdoors in extremely harsh weather, forcing their bodies against rocks or into icy seawater, their teeth blacked out or painted, butoh performers awaken Japan's shamanic heritage, demonic mythology, and folk theatre. Butoh performers are also disruptive bohemians, canny city-based artists consciously playing out their subversive countertext mocking Japan's hyperorganized social life.

Examples like "roots" from India and butoh from Japan could be multiplied from all around the world. There is no area, be it Micronesia, the Pacific Rim, West Africa, the Circumpolar Region, or wherever, which does not have artists actively trying to use, appropriate, reconcile, come to terms with, exploit, understand – the words and political tone vary, but the substance doesn't – the relationships between local cultures in their extreme particular historical development and the increasingly complex and multiple contacts and interactions not only among various cultures locally and regionally but on a global and interspecific scale. Fitfully, unevenly, and with plenty of cruelty, a planetary human culture is emerging which is aware of, if not yet acting responsibly toward, the whole geobiocultural system. Founded on certain accepted values which express themselves abstractly as mathematics and materially as technology, this planetary culture is engaging more and more scientists, social activists, and artists concerned with mapping, understanding, representing, and preserving the earth as an integrated geobiocultural system.

When I say "accepted values" I don't mean these are God-given or inherent in nature or experience. They are constructed and imposed. These imposed values – mathematics and its expression in technology – can be used for good or bad. What constitutes good and bad is, of course, what philosophers, religious and spiritual people, and artists want to find out – and impose. No matter what is written or spoken at any given time – the Bible, the Koran, the Upanishads – history teaches that the question of good and bad is always open. Inquisitors used the Bible, bloody Muslim zealots the Koran, and the architects of the Indian caste system the Upanishads. Which leads me to the fifth kind of avant-garde, the intercultural. For whatever reasons – leftover colonialism, American imperialism, the hunger of people everywhere for material goods, the planetary spread of modernism,[4] the ubiquity of a "cosmopolitan style" in everything from airports to clothes – artists of the avant-garde are producing works on or across various borders: political, geographical, personal, generic, and conceptual. In a world where so-called universal values each day run up against deeply held local values and experiences, the result is clash, disturbance, turbulence, unease about the future, and hot argument about what the past was.

As intercultural performance artist Guillermo Gomez-Pena says:

> I physically live between two cultures and two epochs. . . . When I am on the US side, I have access to high-technology and specialized information. When I cross back to Mexico, I get immersed in a rich political culture. . . . When I return to California, I am part of the multicultural thinking emerging from the interstices of the US's ethnic milieus. . . . I walk the fibres of this transition in my everyday life, and I make art about it. (1991:22–3)

This kind of uneasiness marks many in the intercultural avant-garde. It is not mostly a question of the artist not knowing where she lives. It is about belonging to more than one culture, subscribing to contradictory values, conflicting aesthetic canons. Salman Rushdie well knows the contradictions between Western liberal and Muslim fundamentalist values as they apply to literature and life. Rushdie has said he'd like to belong both to the Western and Islamic worlds. And within every nation many people are living diffi-cult, sometimes exciting, multiple lives. The "nation" no longer describes how or even where hundreds of millions of people live. As Sun Huizhu, aka William Sun, a leading young Chinese playwright who since the crushing of the democracy movement in Tiananmen Square in June 1989 has been unable to return to his native Shanghai, says:

> I would like to call on artists to pay more attention to an increasingly important reality. More and more people of different cultures are interacting and having problems in their interactions. As intercultural artists – often as ambassadors to other cultures – can we artists do something to address this issue and help solve some of those problems?[5]

Engaging intercultural fractures, philosophical difficulties, ideological contradictions, and crumbling national myths does not necessarily lead to avant-garde performances. Intercultural performances occur across an enor-mous range of venues, styles, and purposes. What is avant-garde is when the performance does not try to heal over rifts or fractures but further opens these for exploration. For example, I would say that Peter Brook's *The Mahabharata* was intercultural but not avant-garde, while Gomez-Pena's solo performances as *Border Brujo* or the *Warrior for Gringostroika* defini-tely are. The difference is that Brook wants to elide difference; he is look-ing for what unites, universalizes, makes the same. The conflicts in his Euro-Indic epic are philosophical, personal, familial, and religious – not intercultural. Brook assumes – as the English who own Shakespeare do – that certain works operate at the "human" rather than cultural level. His *Mahabharata* does not interrogate the epic or subvert it; nor are spectators to regard with anything but liberal approval the "international cast" Brook assembled to enact not only the epic story but also the universalist doctrine that under the skin all humans are the same. Don't get me wrong. I support nontraditional, color-blind, culture-blind casting (see Schechner 1989b). But in the case of Brook's *Mahabharata* such casting could have been the occasion for an exploration of the tensions between nonracialist universalism and the ethnic, nationalist, religious, and racial jungle of current world politics and personal relations.

. . . Or none?

Of what use is dividing the avant-garde into five? These categories clearly overlap. The current avant-garde includes work that is forward-looking, tradition-seeking, and intercultural. But despite the rudeness of the division, the operation reminds us of how complex, how multiple, the avant-garde has become. We can also see how very far the current avant-garde is from the historical avant-garde. The current avant-garde is neither innovative nor in advance of. Like a mountain, it just is. Although the term "avant-garde" persists in scholarship as well as journalism, it no longer serves a useful purpose. It really doesn't mean anything today. It should be used only to describe the historical avant-garde, a period of innovation extending roughly from the end of the nineteenth century to the mid-1970s (at most). Saying something is avant-garde may carry a cache of shock, of newness, but in the West, at least, there is little artists can do, or even ought to do, to shock audiences (though quite a bit can offend them). And why try to shock? There are no surprises in terms of technique, theme, or approach. Everything from explicit sex shows, site-specific work, participatory performance, political theatre and guerrilla theatre (of the kind Greenpeace or ACT UP now do), to postmodern dance, the mixing of personal narratives with received texts, the deconstruction of texts, the blurring of boundaries between genres and so on, has been done and done again many times, over the past forty years. And if the scope is opened to 100 years, what in today's performance world can be said to be new? But the question is not, "Can anything new happen?", but "Who cares? Does it matter?" Who today could write manifestos comparable to the febrile outpourings of Artaud, palpitating with hatred, rage, and hope? Who would want to? Is anyone waiting for an Artaud to come around again?

I doubt it. A Rubicon has been crossed. Events today are recorded, replayed, ritualized, and recycled. And if Artaud were to show up, he would be accepted, put in his proper place. The limitless horizons of expectations that marked the modern epoch and called into existence endless newness have been transformed into a global hothouse, a closed environment. I do not agree with Baudrillard that everything is a simulation. But neither do we live in a world of infinite possibilities or originalities. A long neomedieval period has begun. Or, if one is looking for historical analogies, perhaps neo-Hellenistic is more precise. A certain kind of Euro-American cultural style is being extended, imposed, willingly received (the reactions differ) by many peoples in all parts of the world. Exactly what shape this style will take, what its dominant modes of thought will be, are not yet clear. But it will be a conservative age intellectually and artistically. That does not mean reactionary or without compassion. Nor is the kind of conservatism I am talking about incompatible with democratic socialism. It is a conservatism based on the need to save, recycle, use resources parsimoniously. It is founded on the availability of various in-depth "archives" of many different prior experiences, artworks, ideas, feelings, and texts. This stored and recallable prior knowledge is being used to avoid repeating certain kinds of events as well as to promote certain new kinds of events. Local violence increases, no one seems to care how many die if the bloodshed, starvation, or plague is "limited" (not in danger of becoming pandemic). What those in control fear is global violence, a threat to the established order not simply emergent but already firmly in place. The world's peoples are reminded daily of what will happen if global violence – to the environment, to populations, to species – is not brought under control. At the same time, entertainment expands its scope to include almost anything that happens that is technically witnessed and can be edited and played back. Art comes in several mutually reinforcing varieties: that which passes the time of those with enough money to buy tickets; that which excites without satisfying the appetites of its consumers; that which shows off the wealth, power, and taste of its patrons; that which is acquired as an investment. Popular entertainment follows roughly the same path.

To recycle, reuse, archive and recall, to perform in order to be included in an archive (as a lot of performance artists do), to seek roots, explore and maybe even plunder religious experiences, expressions, practices, and liturgies to make art (as Grotowski and others are doing) is to ritualize; not just in terms of subject matter and theme, but also structurally, as form. Ethologists and psychologists have shown that the "oceanic feeling" of belonging, ecstasy, and total participation that many experience when ritualizing works by means of repetitive rhythms, sounds, and tones which effectively "tune" to each other the left and right hemispheres of the cerebral cortex (see d'Aquili *et al.* 1979; Eibl-Eibesfeldt 1979; Fischer 1971; and Turner 1983). This understanding of ritual, as a process applying to a great range of human activities rather than as something tethered to religion, is a very important development. The relatively tight boundaries that locked the various spheres of performance off from each other have been punctured. It is doubtful if these boundaries ever really functioned, in fact. Certainly they didn't in popular entertainments and religious rituals. The boundaries, in fact, are the ghosts of neoclassical and Renaissance readings of the Aristotelian "unities." Keeping each genre in its place is a last ditch regressive action mounted by some critics and academics.

The four great spheres of performance – entertainment, healing, education, and ritualizing – are in play with each other. This playing (and it can be a very serious matter) is the subject of this book. What used to be a tightly boundaried, limited field has expanded exponentially. Each of the performance spheres can be called by other names. Entertainment includes aesthetics, the arrangement and display of actions in ways that are "satisfying" or "beautiful" (according to particular and local cultural canons). Education includes all kinds of political performances designed to exhort, convince, and move to action. Healing performances include shamanism, the ostensive display of hi-tech medical equipment, the bedside manner, and all kinds of interactive psychotherapies.

As the writings in this book show, I am of at least two minds regarding all this. I am enthusiastic about the expanding field of performance and its scholarly adjunct, performance studies. Performative analysis is not the only interpretation possible, but it is a very effective method for a time of charged rhetorics, simulations and scenarios, and games played on a global scale. It has always been a good method for looking at small-scale, face-to-face interactions. The public display of these "for fun" may be taken as an operative definition of drama. But only a small number of artworks relate creatively and critically to the worlds around them. These are what used to be the avant-garde, but which today, as I've been saying, barely owns its name. A century from now the world may be running on new fuels, the automobile may have passed away, human settlements may exist on the moon and elsewhere – and on through a list of as yet barely imaginable changes and technological improvements. The basic tendency of all these changes has already been set. That tendency is to use without using up; to reserve the ability to repeat; to test through modeling, virtual experience, and other kinds of mathematical and analogical rehearsing.

Where does that leave Jayaganesh?

The writings in this book all relate to aspects of what I have called the "broad spectrum" of performance (see Schechner 1988b, 1989c, 1990). The broad spectrum includes performative behavior, not just the performing arts, as a subject for serious scholarly study. This book is one contribution to this big project. How is performance used in politics, medicine, religion, popular entertainments, and ordinary face-to-face interactions? What are the similarities and differences between live and mediated performances? The various and complex relationships among players – spectators, performers, authors, and directors – can be pictured as a rectangle, a performance "quadrilogue." Studying the interactions, sometimes easy, sometimes tense, among the speakers in the quadrilogue is what performance studies people do. These studies are intensely interdisciplinary, intercultural, and intergen-ric. Performance studies builds on the emergence of a postcolonial world where cultures are colliding, interfering with, and fertilizing each other. Arts and academic disciplines alike are most alive at their ever-changing borders. The once distinct (in the West at least) genres of music, theatre, and dance are interacting with each other in ways undreamt-of just thirty-five years ago. These interactions are both expressive of and part of a larger movement culturally.

The chapters in this book examine various cultural and artistic perform-ances as Jayaganesh Richard Schechner experienced them, thought about them, and was able to put his thoughts into written words. These perform-ances were often more social, political, or religious than artistic. They were meant to effect and cause life, not reflect or express it. Even playing – discussed in chapter 2 – is more often serious and dangerous than it is relaxing or frivolous. Live performance increasingly happens not as art but as religious practice, political demonstration, popular entertainment, sports match, or intimate face-to-face encounter. Such was the brave and tragic confrontation between the young and the old in Tiananmen Square in May–June 1989 when Deng Xiaoping played Creon to a multitude of Antigones and Haemons (chapter 3). Or in Pascua Pueblo near Tucson, where a village of Yaquis annually don their Chapayeka masks to play out again their relationship not only to Jesus but also to their friends and family and to the whole outside world (chapter 4). Or the Ramlila of Ramnagar, where for one month a mid-size city is reconfigured so that celebrants can participate with the Hindu gods as they enact their epic adventures (chapter 5). What will happen to such performances, especially as they are repositioned by writers like myself? The question of what happens when scholars intervene in wayang kulit, a Javanese shadow puppet theatre, is discussed in chapter 6. I write in chapter 7 about ritual and violence, playing and pretending – themes erupting from my earliest published essays of more than twenty-five years ago, and still unresolved.

The writings that make this book are shadow plays of my having been in this place or that, in such and such a frame of feeling and mind. Maybe I was led to that ashram in Kerala by my desire wherever I went and worked (in a rehearsal hall as well as in a village) to transform myself. Is there any other way to understand experience? Or maybe the conversion was Jayaganesh's confession that such a transformation cannot take place. What is possible is what's left: experiences retold as stories, stories rendered as discourse.

Notes

1. Actually, the model operas were very good, both technically and in some of the values they espoused. Jiang Qing was extremely concerned about the status of women in China. Her operas showed women in positions of leadership, acting courageously in battle, and taking on responsibilities too often denied them. The model operas also uplifted the peasants and other poor. Traditional Chinese theatre ("operas") features the brave exploits and romantic adventures of aristocrats and scholars (mandarins). What Jiang was working against was the taste of the vast majority of Chinese. And her methods – whatever her idealistic, ideological pronouncements – were dictatorial, oppressive, and murderous. The fact that she was a woman didn't make her any more popular. An actress early in her life, the cultural revolution gave Jiang the chance to unleash an extremely destructive narcissistic ego. One can think only of one contemporary parallel, Ronald Reagan, whose recumbent actor's ego, once brainwashed and under control, presided over a wholesale (if sometimes legal) looting of America as well as a disastrous unwinding of many beneficial social programs.
2. For examples from Zimbabwe see McLaren 1992; for Korea, the Philippines, and India see Van Erven 1987, 1988, and 1989.
3. See Boal 1980, 1983, 1985, 1990a, 1990b, 1990c, and 1991.
4. For a discussion of the differences between "modernization" and Westerniza-

tion" see chapter 6, "Wayang kulit in the colonial margin."

5. Sun made this statement during a five-day conference on intercultural performance held in Bellagio, Italy in February 1991 under the auspices of the Rockefeller Foundation. Gomez-Pena was also there, as were sixteen other artists and scholars from the Americas, Asia, Africa, and Europe. It became clear during the meetings that intercultural performance was both an experimental enterprise and an unsettling issue. Papers and proceedings from the conference will be published in 1994.

2

Playing

Why define?

If the old dichotomies dividing play from work, seriousness, and ritual are too rigid and/or culture-bound; if the classic distinction fencing child play off from adult play is improper; if play need be neither voluntary nor fun; if both flow and reflexivity characterize play; if ethological and semiotic studies asserting that play's functions are learning, exploration, creativity, and communication are really as much about nonplay activities as about play; if psychoanalytic studies linking play with the expression and reduction of anxiety and aggression are also as much about nonplay as about play; if the negotiated time/space between infant and parent is not the foundation of child and adult play activities, including art and religion; if play is not always transitional or liminal or liminoid; if all definitions of play are "ideologies" – cultural projections and impositions – how can we talk about whatever there is to talk about?

Maybe scholars should declare a moratorium on defining play. Maybe, as Victor Turner said in one of his last writings, play is undefinable. "As I see it," Turner wrote, "play does not fit in anywhere particular; it is a transient and is recalcitrant to localization, to placement, to fixation – a joker in the neuro-anthropological act [*sic*]" (1983:233). But having said that much, Turner couldn't resist having a go at it. He subtly shifted his reference from "play" to "playfullness" – a switch as decisive as that from "ritual" to "ritualizing":

> Playfullness is a volatile, sometimes dangerously explosive essence, which cultural institutions seek to bottle or contain in the vials of games of competition, chance, and strength, in modes of simulation such as theater, and in controlled disorientation, from roller coasters to dervish dancing. . . . Most definitions of play involve notions of disengagement, of free-wheeling, of

being out of mesh,with the serious "bread-and-butter," let alone "life-and-death" processes of production, social control, "getting and spending," and raising the next generation. . . . Play can be everywhere and nowhere, imitate anything, yet be identified with nothing. . . . Play is the supreme *bricoleur* of frail transient constructions, like a caddis worm's case or a magpie's nest. . . . Its metamessages are composed of a potpourri of apparently incongruous elements. . . . Passages of seemingly wholly rational thought jostle in a Joycean or surrealist manner with passages filleted of all syntactical connectedness. Yet, although "spinning loose" as it were, the wheel of play reveals to us (as Mihaly Csikszentmihalyi has argued [1975]) the possibility of changing our goals and, therefore, the restructuring of what our culture states to be reality.

(1983:233–4)

Turner concluded that play is an activity – or set of activities – that are categorically uncategorizable, the "anti" by means of which all other categories are destabilized. But even Turner's panegyric is full of contradictions. Isn't love-play or foreplay necessary to procreation? Doesn't play educate? And isn't the play of ritual clowns – like the playing of the superbowl – carefully orchestrated rather than "free-wheeling"?

The problem is not so intractable if "play acts" are measured against six templates: structure; process; experience; function; ideology; and frame. Let me offer capsule definitions of each template:

1 *Structure*: viewed synchronically, what are the relationships among the events constituting play acts?
2 *Process*: viewed diachronically, how are play acts generated and what are their phases of development?
3 *Experience*: what are the feelings or moods of those participating as players, directors, spectators, and observers? A spectator is often directly involved in the play act – such as fans who root for their teams or their favorite performers – while an observer is, for example, a scholar who in studying a phenomenon attempts to maintain a non-involved distance from it.
4 *Function*: what purpose or purposes do play acts serve?
5 *Ideology*: what values do play acts enunciate, propagate, or criticize either knowingly or unknowingly? Are these values the same or different for every player, director, spectator, and observer?
6 *Frame (or net)*: how do players, directors, spectators, and observers know when a play act begins, is taking place, and is over? Is being

"over" the same as "concluding" or "finishing"? What metaplaying is framing the playing?

Play acts, players, spectators, and observers can be independently analyzed in terms of each of these templates. It is possible to be playing but not be in a play mood; to be playful but not playing; to be playing and neither know it nor be in a play mood (as in *Candid Camera*, a scam or sting, or as the butt of a practical joke); to study play without playing or feeling playful, etc. Furthermore, play acts often serve multiple, contradictory purposes simultaneously. The processes generating play acts can be nonplay or not playful, as in the production of many dramas, films, and sports. It is possible for spectators to be in a play mood, while the players themselves are neither in a play mood nor playing – as in gladiatorial games. Moods are especially labile and can shift suddenly and totally. A serious injury can change the tone of a football game, both for players and spectators, but once the wounded are carried from the field, the mood changes back to the playful.

I don't know how many possibilities the interplay of these six categories might yield, but I do know that playing fast and free with play acts without framing them as more analyzable subcategories has precipitated much confusion in the name of theory. I also know that such framing for the purpose of analysis is also analyzable. As a theatre director (manipulator of playing) I know that we all live in mirror-mazes, or echo chambers: playing the game is learning how to shut out some of the multiplicity of converging, convecting actualities in order to "make sense."

In short, definitions are necessary for discourse: to separate the genres of play from playing, from how it feels to be playing, from what play does for individuals and/or society, from the ideas encoded in play, from the signals players and spectators use to communicate that playing has begun, is interrupted, or ended.

A coherent theory of play would assert that play and ritual are complementary, ethologically based behaviors which in humans continue undiminished throughout life; that play creates its own (permeable) boundaries and realms: multiple realities that are slippery, porous, and full of creative lying and deceit; that play is dangerous and, because it is, players need to feel secure in order to begin playing; that the perils of playing are often masked or disguised by saying that play is "fun," "voluntary," a "leisure activity," or "ephemeral" – when in fact the fun of playing, when there is fun, is in playing with fire, going in over one's head, inverting accepted procedures and hierarchies; that play is performative, involving players, directors, spectators, and commentators in a quadrilogical exchange that, because each kind of participant often has her or his own passionately pursued goals, is frequently at cross-purposes.[1]

I cannot here unpack this unified theory-to-be. Instead, I will make one comment and then go on to look at three key aspects: multiple realities, dark play, and generating performances.

Security is needed at the outset of play more than later on. Once play is underway, risk, danger, and insecurity are part of playing's thrill. Usually there is a safety net, or a chance to call "time out," or appeal to an umpire or other nonplaying authority who takes care of the rules. But in informal play, and in what I call "dark play," actions continue even though individual players may feel insecure, threatened, harassed, and abused. This pattern of moving from safety to danger is true of performance workshops, which need to commence in an atmosphere of "safety" and "trust" but, once underway, are places where very risky business can be explored. On a larger scale, the whole workshop–rehearsal phase of performance needs protection and isolation, a well-defined safety net, while the finished performance can move from place to place on tour, overcome many particular distractions heaped on it by audiences, and in general "take care of itself."

Maya–lila: playing's multiple realities

In the West, play is a rotten category, an activity tainted by unreality, inauthenticity, duplicity, make believe, looseness, fooling around, and inconsequentiality. Play's reputation has been a little uplifted by being associated with ritual and game theory. The defense department takes play seriously when it stages war games and simulations. The reason why play – or, more properly, playing – is a rotten category is because the multiple realities of playing are situated inside a pyramidical hierarchy of increasing reality leading from unreal make believe to "just the facts, Ma'am."

In 1945 Schutz called the multiple realities of "dreams, of imageries and phantasms, . . . [of] art, . . . of religious experience, . . . of scientific contemplation, the play world of the child, and the world of the insane . . . finite provinces of meaning," enclosing them each within its own "cognitive style" (1977:229). He explicitly denied what makes multiple realities so powerful, the systematic quality of their transformability, and claimed:

There is no possibility of referring one of these provinces to the other by introducing a formula of transformation. The passing from one to the other can only be performed by a "leap," as Kierkegaard calls it, which manifests itself in the subjective experience of a shock. (1977:230)

I agree to the extent that reality comes bundled in discrete "packets" of energy and/or information (as physicists would say). But the absence of smooth continuity does not disallow systems of transformation from one reality to another – developing such systems is precisely the work of art (and often the work of science and religion too). It may, in fact, be the main occupation of humankind. Sometimes the passage between realities is experienced as a leap or shock and sometimes as a smooth, even imperceptible, flow. Schutz prioritized "the world of working in daily life [as] the archetype of our experience of reality. All other provinces of meaning may be considered as its modifications" (1977:230). Useful as his insights are, I don't agree with Schutz's prioritizing of realities. Playing, not "the world of working in daily life" is the ground, the matrix, birthing all experience's exfoliating multiple realities. Or, to express the same idea in a different metaphor: being is playing and "working daily life" is just one reality cookie-cut, or netted, out of playing. Working daily life is not prior or privileged; it is a culture-bound, time-bound reality and as such can appear to be "the archetype of our experience" only as the result of careful netting.

Contrast this Western archetype of reality to *maya* and *lila* – Sanskrit terms for illusion and play. Maya and lila are hard words to translate because their meanings shift according to whether one is emphasizing the delights of the world, *samsara*, or the desire to end all desire, freeing one's self from the wheel of birth–death–rebirth, *moksha*. According to O'Flaherty, maya originally

> meant *only* what was real; through its basis in the verbal root *ma* ("to make") it expressed "the sense of 'realizing the phenomenal world' . . ." to "measure out" the universe [,] . . . to create it, to divide it into its constituent parts, to *find* it by bringing it out of chaos. . . .
> Magicians do this; artists do it; gods do it. But according to certain Indian philosophies, every one of us does it every minute of our lives.
> This concept of *maya* as a kind of artistic power led gradually to its later connotation of magic, illusion, and deceit. . . . It often means not merely bringing something into existence . . . but manipulating the existent forces of nature or invoking the "power to create and achieve the marvelous." Thus *maya* first meant making something that was not there before; then it came to

28

mean making something that was there into something that was not really there. The first describes the universe in the Vedic world-view; the second, the universe in the Vedantic world-view. The first is *samsaric*; the second *moksic*. In both cases, *maya* can often best be translated as "transformation."

. . . A similar cluster of meanings radiates from it [maya] as from the English derivatives of the Latin word for play (*ludo*) – de-lusion, il-lusion, e-lusive, and so forth – and from the word "play" itself – play as drama, as swordplay or loveplay, as the play of light that causes mirages, as the double image implicit in wordplay (as Johan Huizinga pointed out so brilliantly in *Homo Ludens*). These word clusters delineate a universe full of beauty and motion that enchants us all. All Indian philosophies acknowledge that *maya* is a fact of life – the fact of life; but some (the *moksha*-oriented) regard it as a negative fact, to be combated, while others (the *samsara*-oriented) regard it as a positive fact, to be embraced. (O'Flaherty 1984:117–19)

Lila is a more ordinary word meaning play, sport, or drama; it is etymologically related to the Latin *ludus* and from there to English ludic, illusion, elusive, and so on. Gods in their lilas make maya, but so do ordinary people, each of whom shares in the identicality of individual atman with the absolute brahman.[2] Maya and lila create, contain, and project each other: like a snake swallowing its own tail.

Maya–lila is fundamentally a performative–creative act of continuous playing where ultimate positivist distinctions between "true" and "false," "real" and "unreal" cannot be made. Psychoanalyst D. W. Winnicott, in attempting to describe the process of playing that begins in infancy, declares

that the essential feature in the concept of transitional objects and phenomena . . . is *the paradox, and the acceptance of the paradox*: the baby creates the object, but the object was there waiting to be created and to become a cathected object. . . . We will never challenge the baby to elicit an answer to the question: did you create that or did you find it? (1971:89)

Such a paradox concerns *the whole world*: did we humans create it or did we find it? As I wrote elsewhere,

Winnicott's ideas mesh nicely with Van Gennep's, Turner's, and Bateson's, in whose "play frame" (1972: 177–93) "transitional phenomena" take place. The most dynamic formulation of what Winnicott is describing is that the baby – and later the child at play and the adult at art (and religion) – recognizes some things and situations as "not me . . . not not me." During workshops–rehearsals, performers play with words, things, and actions, some of which are "me" and some "not me." By the end of the process the "dance goes into the body." So Olivier is not Hamlet, but he is also not not Hamlet. The reverse is also true: in this production of the play, Hamlet is not Olivier, but he is also not not Olivier. Within this field or frame of double negativity choice and virtuality remain open.   (Schechner 1985:110)

In theatrical terms, maya–lila is the presence of the performer enacting the "not" of her role: the Ophelia who is not there, who never was there. Ophelia can only exist in the playing field between rehearsal, performers, performance, dramatic text, performance text, spectators, and readers. Or in the monsoon season performances of Raslila in India, where little boys (swarups) enact/become young Krishna, his beloved Radha, and all the *gopis* (cowherding women) who dote on Krishna, wanting to dance with him.

> With his haunting flute he [Krishna] summons the women of Braj away from their mundane occupations to come out to the forest and dance with him the mating dance, the dance of love, the *ras*; and as the peacock rotates so that his plumage will be visible to every eye, so Krishna multiplies himself to be available with an equal intimacy to every girl he summons. (Hawley 1981: 14)

In ancient Greece, Dionysus drew the women of Thebes onto the slopes of Mount Cithaeron, as Krishna drew them to the forests surrounding Brindavan. But Dionysus induced jealous frenzy for there was only one of him and so many of them, while Krishna multiplied himself limitlessly, satisfying each of the gopis who desired him. And during Raslila in Brindavan, there are as many boy Krishnas, Radhas, and gopis as are desired by the audiences who in looking at these boys see gods.

> The roles of Radha, Krishna, and the cowherd girls (*gopis*) are sanctified and dignified with the title of *svarup*, which means that the Brahmin boys who adopt them are thought to take on the very form of the personages they portray once their costumes are complete. The term applies quintessentially to Radha and Krishna, and once the two don the crowns appropriate to their roles, they are venerated as the divine couple itself.   (Hawley 1981: 13–14)

These appearances are the same in principle as the Christian Eucharist, but so much less abstract, so immediate in the flesh-and-blood presence of the swarups and the acts of devotion shown to them by the thousands who gather to catch a glimpse, a *darshan*, of the divine. As gods the boys don't stop being little boys, the two realities are mutually porous. The boys/gods swat at flies, doze, giggle, or look longingly for their mothers; but they acquire sudden dignity while dancing or when reciting the lines whispered into their ears by ever-attentive priests/directors. This kind of performing-being-playing is not unique to Raslila. It constitutes an essential quality of a number of Indian performance genres.

Maya–lila is important to all aspects of Indian life, but especially decisive in theatre–dance–music. According to the *Natyasastra* (second century BCE–second century CE), the Sanskrit text dealing specifically with performance, theatre came into being as an entertainment for the gods but is enjoyed also by all classes of people. At Ramlila – an epic cycle of north India telling the story of Rama, an incarnation of Vishnu – long poles are erected, on top of which effigies of the gods-as-spectators look down on the action involving gods, men, animals, and demons. Vishnu and Lakshmi, played by two swarups, watch Rama and Sita played by two others. But Vishnu is Rama and Lakshmi is Sita, so these gods–boys double their existence, manifesting themselves before delighted, often wildly ecstatic, crowds. And from time to time the ever-observing gods intervene in the action. This is maya producing, through lila, multiple realities and comparably complex ways of participating in the drama.

Maya is the multiplicity which the world is: creative, slippery, and ongoing. Not to be too fancy about it, keeping the world existing takes a continuous playful effort on the part of Brahma or whatever god – including none – is accomplishing the acts of creation. The cosmos itself – from the highest heaven to the Raslila or Ramlila grounds to the most ordinary of daily activities – is an immense playground. This playground is not necessarily or always a happy place. Shiva, also called *nataraj*, king of dance(rs), dances existence into being and also dances it into destruction and chaos at the end of each *yuga* or aeon.[3] Shiva's dancing creates and destroys maya and is his lila. Asserting that existence is a continuous dance is not a soft-headed metaphor for the Indians; nor is it inconsistent with contemporary theories of particle physics or cosmology as astronomers playfully construct them. For example, an article in *Science* (20 February 1987) reports:

> An analysis of localized inflation [of "black holes"] suggests that empty space may be spawning universes by the billions, without us ever knowing; was our own universe created this way? What would happen if we could somehow reproduce the conditions of the Big Bang in the modern universe? More precisely, what would happen if a sample of matter were somehow compressed into a tiny region of ultrahigh density and temperature – say 10^{24} K? . . . In one solution, for example, the outside universe simply crushes the hot region into a standard black hole. However, there is a much more interesting solution in which the hot region does indeed inflate – but in a totally new direction that

is perpendicular to ordinary space and time. It becomes a kind of aneurysm bulging outward from the side of our familiar universe. In fact, it quickly pinches off and becomes a separate universe of its own. . . . This newborn cosmos [could then] expand to a scale of billions of light-years, producing galaxies, stars, planets, and even life. (Waldrop 1987:845)

This construction of things is very maya–lila.

Krishna, whose very name means blue-black, dark like the underside of a thundercloud, is not always or only a being of ecstatic dancing; he also has his time of bloody play, represented most clearly in the *Bhagavad Gita*, probably India's single most sacred text. To remind you of the story: the great armies of the Pandavas and Kauravas are assembled on the field at Kurukshetra. The Pandava warrior Arjuna wants to see the full array. Barbara Stoler Miller's translation takes up the story:

"Krishna," [Arjuna says,] "halt my chariot between the armies! Far enough for me to see these men who lust for war." . . . Arjuna saw them standing there: fathers, grandfathers, teachers, uncles, brothers, sons, grandsons, and friends. . . . Dejected, filled with strange pity, he said this: "My limbs sink,/my mouth is parched, . . . The magic bow slips from my hand, . . . I see no good in killing my kinsmen in battle!" (Vyasa 1986:23–5)

Krishna then recites his great song. "You grieve for those beyond grief. . . . Never have I not existed nor you, nor these kings; and never in the future shall we cease to exist' " (31). Step by step this Krishna, no longer the *bala* (boy) Krishna of Brindavan, but a great awesome Krishna, and a trickster, leads Arjuna along the path of his *karma*, toward doing that which he must do. In the tenth of his eighteen teachings, Krishna catalogs all that he is.

"Listen," [he tells Arjuna,] "as I recount for you in essence the divine powers of myself. Endless is my extent. . . . I am indestructible time, The creator facing everywhere at once. . . . I am death the destroyer of all, the source of what will be, the feminine powers: fame, fortune, speech, memory, intelligence, resolve, patience. . . . I am the great ritual chant, the meter of sacred song, . . . the dice game of gamblers, . . . the epic poet Vyasa among sages." (91–4)

Vyasa is the author of the *Mahabharata* of which the *Gita* is a part. In the eleventh teaching Krishna allows Arjuna a theophany:

"I see the gods in your body, O God, and hordes of varied creatures. . . . I see your boundless form everywhere, the countless arms, bellies, mouths, and eyes. Lord of All, I see no end, or middle or beginning to your totality. . . .

32

Throngs of gods enter you, some in their terror make gestures of homage. . . .
As moths in the frenzy of destruction fly into a blazing flame, worlds in the
frenzy of destruction enter your mouths. You lick at the worlds around you,
devouring them with flaming mouths; and your terrible fires scorch the entire
universe, filling it, Vishnu, with violent rays. Tell me – who are you in this
terrible form?" [. . . Krishna replies:] "I am time grown old, creating world
destruction."   (99–103)

Theophany is one of Krishna's favorite kinds of dark play.

One day when the children were playing, they reported to Yasoda [Krishna's
mother], "Krishna has eaten dirt." Yasoda took Krishna by the hand and
scolded him and said, "You naughty boy, why have you eaten dirt?" "I
haven't," said Krishna. "All the boys are lying. If you believe them instead of
me, look at my mouth yourself." "Then, open up," she said to the god, who
had in sport [lila] taken the form of human child, and he opened his mouth.

Then she saw in his mouth the whole universe, with the far corners of the
sky, and the wind, and lightning, and the orb of the earth with its mountains
and oceans, and the moon and stars, and space itself; and she saw her own
village and herself. She became confused and frightened, thinking, "Is this a
dream or an illusion [maya] fabricated by God? Or is it a delusion in my own
mind? For God's power of delusion inspires in me such false beliefs as, 'I
exist,' 'This is my husband,' 'This is my son.' " When she had come to
understand true reality in this way, God spread his magic illusion [maya] in the
form of maternal love. Instantly Yasoda lost her memory of what had
occurred. She took her son on her lap and was as she had been before, but her
heart was flooded with even greater love for God, whom she regarded as her
son.[4]

In 1972 in Madras I saw the great bharatanatyam dancer, Balasaraswati,
perform Yasoda as a solo dance. When Balasaraswati–Yasoda shook her
forefinger sternly demanding that Krishna open his mouth, I laughed; but
when she looked in, I saw/felt what she did, and I shuddered with terror and
joy. And when she asked her son/god Krishna to close his mouth, shutting
out from her all knowledge of the absolute, I too felt relief.

In even more complicated ways, the Ramlila of Ramnagar is a performance of the interrealities coexisting on different scales simultaneously. The
town of Ramnagar is itself, plus the seat of the maharaja of Banaras, sponsor
of the Ramlila, plus all the places where Rama's adventures take place, plus a
model of India during its presumed golden age of Ramraj (when Rama was
king), plus Ayodhya, the capital of Rama's kingdom, plus a pilgrimage
center where for a month "god lives here" (as spectators say). On the

thirtieth day of the thirty-one-day cycle, the maharaja invites the gods to dinner. As in Raslila, when the swarups wear their costumes and crowns, they are presumed actually to be the gods they represent. Mounted on splendidly decorated elephants, illuminated by continuous flares of fireworks, they arrive at the Fort, the maharaja's palace.

Thousands of common folk – usually excluded from the Fort's inner courtyard – crowd in as the maharaja and his whole family greet the gods. As a devotee of Rama the maharaja washes their feet, as host he feeds them. But even as he performs these acts, they, the boys, are being honored by the king of the place. In other words their divinity as swarups does not cancel out their existence as boys and subjects. And the maharaja is a king, I might add, who has not been "real" since 1947 when India, upon gaining independence, abolished all principalities within her borders. Still, the people of Banaras and Ramnagar treat Vibhuti Narain Singh as their king and more, hailing him with shouts of "*Hara, Hara, Mahadev!*" – "Shiva, Shiva, great god!"

Thus maya–lila generates a plenitude of performances: interpenetrating, transformable, nonexclusive, porous realities. All of these are play worlds that are the slippery ground of contingent being and experience. That is, from the Indian perspective, playing is what the universe consists of. To be "at play" is to recognize that all relationships are provisional. Ultimate reality, if there is such, is *neti*, literally "not that." To any and every specification of what such an ultimate reality might be, the answer is neti, not that. The only realities that can be experienced – personally, socially, scientifically, philosophically – are the interpenetrating, transformable, nonexclusive, porous, multiple realities of maya–lila. The Indian tradition of maya–lila rejects Western systems of rigid, impermeable frames, unambiguous metacommunications, and rules inscribing hierarchical arrangements of reality. But if reality and experience are networks of flexible constructions, dreams of dreams, unsettled relationships, transformations, and interactions, what then of "ordinary play" – children manipulating their toys, adults playing ball, and so on? These exist in India, as they do in the West, but they can suddenly, shockingly open to whole worlds of demons, humans, animals, and gods, as Yasoda found out when she looked into her son Krishna's mouth.

The contrast between Western and Indian approaches to playing can be summarized as follows:

PLAYING

West: Positivist	India: Maya–lila
Creation is finishable work: "On the 7th day God finished the work. . . . And God blessed the 7th day and declared it holy because on it God ceased from all the work of creation."	Creation is never finishable. Cycles of creation and destruction. Continuous creation.
There is a hierarchy of reality or truth.	Multiple realities. If there is an ultimate reality, it is *neti*.

Therefore playing is:

Deprivileged and low status.	Privileged, the divine process of creating.
With art and religion, not serious or real.	With art and religion, serious, real, and often fun.
Best when nonviolent, or when violence is pretended, limited, or tightly framed.	Creative–destructive: Siva's *tandava* dance, the violence of Krishna in the *Bhagavad Gita*.
Female and infantile, an activity of the powerless.	Female and male, the activity of gods, of the most powerful.
Loosened gender roles.	Transformative gender roles.
Represses the erotic or represents it pornographically.	Celebrates the erotic, representing it ecstatically.
Framed off as not really real.	Multiple realities transformable into each other.
Metacommunication declaring "now I am playing" or "now I am not playing."	Intentional blurring of playing–not playing boundary.
Temporary.	Permanent.

The maya–lila notion of playing describes volatile, creative–destructive activities that are transformative, less bounded, less tame, and less tightly framed in time and space than Western play. In Hindu–Vedic terms, what is beyond play is not knowable: the atman (self)/Brahman (absolute) is unthinkable, undescribable, unexperienceable, but obtainable. To achieve *moksha* or *nirvana* or *samadhi* is to be released from the round of birth–rebirth, from maya–lila, from playing. But daily experience – the life people lead – is a flux that includes not only the grind of farming, child-bearing, and money-making but also – and on an equal basis – the categories and experiences represented by art and religion. Intense belief, ecstasy, dreaming, and fantasy are creditable among peoples living immersed in maya–lila belief systems. These are the very categories and experiences mainstream modern Western thought devalues as make believe, nonordinary, and/or unreal.

Dark play

Let me bring just a little of this home by touching on what I call "dark play." Dark play may be conscious playing, but it can also be playing in the dark when some or even all of the players don't know they are playing. Dark play occurs when contradictory realities coexist, each seemingly capable of canceling the other out, as in the double cross, or as in the Indian tale of "the Brahmin who dreamed he was an untouchable who dreamed he was a king" but who could not determine who was the dreamer and who the dreamt because each of his realities tested out as true (O'Flaherty 1984:134–5). Or dark play may be entirely private, known to the player alone. Dark play can erupt suddenly, a bit of microplay, seizing the player(s) and then quickly subsiding – a wisecrack, a flash of frenzy, risk, or delirium. Dark play subverts order, dissolves frames, breaks its own rules, so that the playing itself is in danger of being destroyed, as in spying, con games, undercover actions, and double agentry. Unlike the inversions of carnivals, ritual clowns, and so on (whose agendas are public), dark play's inversions are not declared or resolved; its end is not integration but disruption, deceit, excess, and gratification.

For all this, dark play need not be overtly angry or violent. And what might be dark play to one person can be innocuous to another. In a 1985 seminar on play,[5] I invited graduate students to write out, anonymously if they chose, examples of dark play from their own lives. I quote some of the responses:

Female: When I am feeling especially depressed or angry about the world and my life, I will play a form of "Russian roulette" with the New York city traffic: I will cross the streets without pausing to see if it is safe to do so or not – without checking the lights or the traffic. . . . At the time of "play" there is a thrill in abandoning precautions and in toying with the value of life and death.

Female: At approximately 9 pm six of us piled into a small Dodge Dart with a large quantity of alcohol and pot. It was early Spring after a very cold winter in Buffalo and rather spontaneously we decided to drive to Kentucky and see that famous Kentucky blue grass. . . . I remember lots of singing, drinking, smoking, laughing, and then being awoken at dawn by one of my friends as we were crossing an old wooden bridge that said, "Welcome to Kentucky." We drove for only a short while and stopped at a small shop off the road. . . . We asked the elderly woman behind the counter where we could find Kentucky blue grass. . . . We pressed her rather rudely. . . . Eventually she just shrugged her shoulders and said, "Well I guess all this grass is blue grass." We found this hysterical . . . and proceeded to joke and laugh and taunt, demanding that blue grass must be blue and this grass is green. When we exhausted ourselves . . . we returned to the car and drove. . . . We came to a railroad track and soon after a freight train came by. Two of us decided to hop it and asked the others to pick us up at the train yard in Cleveland. . . . But due to our general state of ludicrousness and silliness, not to mention tiredness, we soon fell down on the ground, rolling, crying with laughter and exhaustion, and let the train pass us by. Our friends picked us up, turned the car around, and headed back towards Buffalo. After having breakfast we stopped at a liquor store and refueled on alcohol. We figured we should return home in the same way we had left it – somewhat out of control. And so we did, arriving back approximately 22 hours after we had left, very drunk, stoned, and triumphant.

Female: I was 16 years old and on vacation at Yosemite with my father. I climbed out over the guard rail to get a better view of the waterfall. When I realized that my father was crying for me to come back, I went to the very edge and did an arabesque. I continued balancing on one leg until he got onto his knees, crying, begging for me to come back. Ten years later, in the Sierra Nevada range I repeated the same act in front of my husband who shouted at me to think of our daughter as a motherless child. My initial inspiration for dancing on the edge was in both cases the thrill of the beauty and the danger of the dance. My father's and husband's anxiety sharpened the experience for me – the further I got away from them the closer I came to communion with some Other.

Female: I was on vacation with a friend who is not my boyfriend. During a bus ride I was teaching him a song when an old man turned to us, interested in where we came from, etc. Instantly the two of us made up a romance story of where we met, why we were there on vacation, and what we were planning to do – none of which was true. Since we both felt we were being approached as "a couple" we reacted to it as such, having a lot of fun doing so.

Male: I can achieve a flow experience by listening to music, rocking approximately in time with it, and letting my mind wander in free association. What makes this play dark is that I rock in a chair that is not a rocking chair but an over-stuffed chair. It is my body that rocks instead of the chair. My whole body enters into the flow. . . . I have maintained this activity since very early childhood. I recommend it highly – and anonymously.

Leaving aside psychological interpretations of motives, personal gains, anxieties, desires played out, and so forth, what do these examples show?

First, they subvert the metacommunicational aspect of the play frame. In all cases, only some of those involved knew that playing was going on. The New York City car and truck drivers, the little old lady behind the counter in Kentucky, the father and husband, the man on the bus are performers in the playing but they do not know they are playing. In fact, the metacommunication is just the opposite: "I, or we, are not playing," the players say to the nonplaying participants. These nonplayers – innocents, dupes, butts, anxious loved ones – are essential for the playing to continue; the reaction of the nonplayers is a big part of what gives dark play its kick. In the last example there are no coplayers and anonymity is important to the player. In three cases there is a high degree of physical risk. Crossing blindly through NYC traffic, driving drunk and stoned, and dancing on mountain ledges is playing where losing might mean dying.

Yet, I don't think any of these players are pathological. Why would they want to so endanger themselves? In only one case is there a clear instance of make believe, the con game on the bus. Rocking in a stuffed chair is an example of secret, intimate dark play. I suspect there are many more instances of this sort of secret dark play originating in early childhood and continuing right through to old age. People are cautious about sharing these kinds of solitary activities. Masking is very important – sneaking off, not being recognized, playing out selves that cannot be displayed at work, or with family. The thrill and gratification of such play is to perform anonymously, in disguise, or in a closet what one cannot do publicly "as myself."

Taken together, these examples indicate that dark play:

1 is physically risky;
2 involves intentional confusion or concealment of the frame "this is play";

3 may continue actions from early childhood;

4 only occasionally demands make believe;

5 plays out alternative selves. The play frame may be so disturbed or disrupted that the players themselves are not sure if they are playing or not – their actions become play retroactively: the events are what they are, but by telling these events, by reperforming them as narratives, they are cast as play.

Generating performances

I won't discuss finished performances of theatre, dance, sports, rituals, and popular entertainments. Not that these aren't of interest to play theorists, but I want to focus on some aspects of the processes for generating performances. I find in these processes a recurrent theme connecting dark play, Western ideas of play, and the maya–lila theory. This theme is "provisionality," the unsteadiness, slipperiness, porosity, unreliability, and ontological riskiness of the realities projected or created by playing. Playing – whether of divine beings or cosmic forces as in maya–lila, or in the preparatory phases of constructing a performance (the training–workshop–rehearsal phases), or in instances of dark play either privately acted out or publicly displayed – is unfinishable. The *structure* of play – one of the six templates I laid out at the beginning of this chapter – shapes and interrupts the process of playing, imposing end points requiring further starting points. Playing left to itself would go on forever. Playing – the processual template – is a continuous bending, twisting, and looping of . . . that for which I can find no appropriate name, so "action" will have to do.

In preparing performers to perform, rigorous exercises reshape their bodies. This is as true of kathakali as it is of football, of ballet as it is of shamanism. As Eugenio Barba put it:

We use our bodies in substantially different ways in daily life and in performance situations. In everyday life we have a body technique which has been conditioned by our culture, our social status, our profession. But in a performance situation, the body is used in a totally different way. . . . This extra-daily technique is essentially based on an alteration of balance. We can say that balance – the human ability to maintain oneself erect and moving through space – is the result of a series of muscular relationships and tensions within our organism. The more our movements become complex – by taking longer steps than usual or by holding our heads more forwards or backwards than usual [or slowing down, or speeding up, or leaping, throwing, and falling, etc.] the more our balance is threatened. . . . change of balance results in a series of organic tensions which underline the corporal presence, but at a stage which precedes intentional individualized expression (the pre-expressive stage).

(1986:115, 117)

How pregnant Barba's observations are. Each genre deforms and reforms the body by introducing disequilibrium, a problem to be solved by a new balancing specific to the genre: ballet's way of unbalancing–rebalancing is not football's is not a Huichol shaman's is not noh drama's, and so forth. But each form *needs to play dangerously with the body*, to deconstruct and reconstruct it according to its own plan of action. The body is deconstructed – opened, made provisional, uncreated, enters Brahma's night – so that it can be re-created according to plan. The plans are not fixed. They change, sometimes slowly sometimes suddenly. Ballet's body, and football's, and so on, are each a maya–lila of human possibility. And as many genres as exist, untold others could exist: of natural balancing there may be limits, but no such limit hinders the invention of new unbalancing–rebalancing cycles according to not-yet-known codes. As with the body, so with thoughts and spirit: this bending and reshaping is the essence of yoga and of maya–lila.

The deconstruction–reconstruction cycle begins with the body but does not end there. In other writings (Schechner 1973, 1985), I've detailed how that process plays with performers' personal life experiences, materials brought into or uncovered by workshops and rehearsals, or even discovered during public performances. Barba's insight is a general principle: disequilibrium intentionally introduced into apparently stable systems forces the search for new balance. The steady-state of tradition's invented body–mind, becomes "daily," while introduced disequilibrium provokes the invention of new "extra-daily" techniques which, in their turn, become daily. Specific examples are readily available, not only in expected venues like the Western avant-garde, but in apparently unlikely places like Japanese noh theatre or native American ritual performances.

Conclusions

Playing is a creative, destabilizing action that frequently does not declare its existence, even less its intentions. I do not reject Bateson's play frame entirely – there are situations where the message "this is play" is very important. But there are other kinds of playing – like dark play – where the play frame is absent, broken, porous, or twisted. One need not accept as empirically true the maya–lila universe of multiple, contradictory realities to recognize in it a powerful performance theory. Maya–lila is not simply a version of "all the world's a stage" (a weak metaphor trivializing both art and daily living), but a dynamic system with no single fixed center, no still point or absolute referent. In this, maya–lila theory harmonizes with both contemporary science (physics and astronomy) and poststructuralist literary theory (deconstruction). Or, as O'Flaherty has it, "the illusion of art is of the same nature as the illusion of life" (1984:279).

Indeed, art and ritual, especially performance, are the homeground of playing. This is because the process of making performances does not so much imitate playing as epitomize it. From this perspective, the Batesonian play frame is a rationalist attempt to stabilize and localize playing, to contain it safely within definable borders. But if one needs a metaphor to localize and (temporarily) stabilize playing, "frame" is the wrong one – it's too stiff, too impermeable, too "on/off," "inside/outside." "Net" is better: a porous, flexible gatherer; a three-dimensional, dynamic, flow-through container.

Playing is a mood, an attitude, a force. It erupts or one falls into it. It may persist for a fairly long time – as specific games, rites, and artistic perform-ances do – or it comes and goes suddenly – a wisecrack, an ironic glimpse of things, a bend or crack in behavior. It is "banana time" – the transformation of work into play:

> So a serious discussion about the high cost of living could be suddenly transformed into horseplay or into a prank; or a worker might utter a string of "oral autisms." The expression of themes was thus temporary, somewhat idiosyncratic excursions into the reality of play; and each protagonist experi-mented in his own way, and to some extent at his own pace, with these transitions from the reality of work to that of expressive behavior. . . . The interspersal of "themes" among serious actions held the participants perpetu-ally on the edge of a liminal phase – on the border of reality transformation – since none could be certain exactly when one of their number would effect the passage into an unannounced and unexpected expressive frame. . . . Faced with the vista of a multitude of diverse, locally fashioned worlds of meaning, the researcher must return to intensive observation and participation to catch the emergent symbolic and organizational modes through which persons con-struct their life-experiences with one another. I prefer to believe that, rather than being a cause for despair, this is a recognition of the immense capacity of human beings to come to terms with, and to express, the manifold predica-ments of their social existence.   (Handelman 1976:443–5)

41

Handelman is on to something. But it's wrong to think of playing as the interruption of ordinary life. Consider instead playing as the underlying, always-there continuum of experience, as the maya–lila theory says. Ordinary life is netted out of playing but playing continuously squeezes through even the smallest holes of the worknet – because there is no such thing as absolute opacity, there are no totally blank walls. No matter how hard people try, play finds its way through – banana time is always with us, even in the operating theatre or on death row. But what of horrors like the Holocaust? It is as difficult for a Jew to think of Auschwitz "as play" as it was for Arjuna to consider the slaughter of the Kurukshetra war as Krishna's lila. And consider this: the very efficiency of the Nazi death camps was as extreme an example as can be actualized of "work" as the systematic erasure of playing. But, on another level, were there not jokes told in the concentration camps? Or games of various kinds played? Does thinking there were deflect or lessen the dread historicity of the Holocaust, doing disrespect to its victims and survivors? The realities of illusion can become paths into dark worlds of demons, witches, curses, black magic, illness, torture, and death. It is not easy for modern positivists to project themselves into such realities of other cultures, or back to the Salem witch trials of seventeenth-century America, or even to keep remembering the Holocaust.

Work and other daily activities continuously feed on the underlying ground of playing, using the play mood for refreshment, energy, unusual ways of turning things around, insights, breaks, openings and, especially, *looseness*. This looseness (pliability, bending, lability, unfocused attention, the long way around) is implied in such phrases as "play it out" or "there's some play in the rope" or "play around with that idea." Looseness encourages the discovery of new configurations and twists of ideas and experiences. Thus the imbalancing–rebalancing process that Barba calls attention to occurs on the mental as well as physical, psychophysical, spiritual, and metaphysical levels.

Playing occurs on several levels simultaneously. The basic ground of existence is maya–lila, an ongoing construction–deconstruction, destroying–creating. Like the theophany of Krishna, this deep play is impossible to look at (for very long) – it is as terrifying as it is exciting, as blinding as it is beautiful. In order to live our daily lives – lives of work and play in the ordinary sense – humans have constructed/invented "cultures" (see Wagner 1981). The genres of play – play, games, sports, art, and religion – are part of these cultures: they are play within culture within maya–lila. But however powerful the play genres, however "total" the work life, the basic ground of existence, maya–lila, leaks through and permeates both daily life and the play genres. So, am I proposing that maya–lila exists outside of or before cultures? Am I attempting to reintroduce some kind of transcendent force or energy? That question can't be answered yes or no, because maya–lila swallows its own tail (tale). Each culture, each individual even, creates its/her/his own maya–lila even as it/she/he exists *within* and *stands on* maya–lila. Maya–lila is not reducible to the logic of either/or choices. It is an "empty space [that] may be spawning universes by the billions, without us ever knowing" (Waldrop 1987:845).

What I can say is that it's much too limiting, too tight, too certain to build play theories around notions of play genres, identifiable "things." Of course there are play genres: efforts to contain, enslave, tame, use, and colonize playing. But presently, we need to stop looking so hard at play, or play genres, and investigate *playing*, the ongoing, underlying process of off-balancing, loosening, bending, twisting, reconfiguring, and transforming – the permeating, eruptive/disruptive energy and mood below, behind, and to the sides of focused attention. (Why not "above"? I really don't know, it's probably just cultural prejudice.) The questions we need to ask are: how, when, and why is playing invited and sustained? How, when, and why is playing denied or repressed? Is playing categorically antistructural – that is, does it always take the opposite position or role to whatever is happening at the time it erupts or is invited? Is playing autonomous – that is, will it "just happen" if nothing else blocks, cancels, or represses it?

Notes

1. See Sutton-Smith (1979:297) for his discussion of the "play quadralogue." Sutton-Smith says, it follows then that

> if language is always a *dialogue*, a situated act, and not merely a text, that all expressive forms, of which play is only one, are a *quadralogue* [sic]. They always involve at least four prototypical parties: the group or individual that stages (or creates) the event, as actors and co-actors; the group that receives this communication (the audience); and the group that directs the race or conducts the symphony (directors).

I count only three groups in Sutton-Smith's list, but to these I add a fourth, the commentators – critics and scholars – who may not even be present at the event but whose discourse affects not only future performances but the ways in which past events are received.

2. Atman is the "soul," the Self with a capital S, the imperishable whatever-it-is identical to brahman, the transcendent, universal, single absolute which a person can experience, or enter, but not describe or relate. Atman–brahman is beyond maya–lila, a cancelling out of maya–lila in a way roughly equivalent to the way antimatter anihilates matter.

3. According to Hindu mythology as told in the *Puranas*, the existence of the world is divided into four aeons, or yugas. The Indians, loving mathematics, calculated these precisely in terms of both divine and human years (one divine year = 360 human years). The Krita yuga lasts 1,728,000 human years and is a period of perfection; the Treta yuga lasts 1,296,000 years and is a truthful age; the Dvapara yuga lasts 864,000 years and is a time of diminished good; and, finally, the Kali yuga (our own time), lasts 432,000 years and is a period of darkness and calamity. One Mahayuga equals all four yugas (4,320,000 years); and 1,000 Mahayugas (4,320,000,000) is a day of Brahma.

> At the close of this day of Brahma, a collapse of the universe takes place which lasts through a night of Brahma, equal in duration to his day, during which period the worlds are converted into one great ocean. . . . At the end of that night he awakes and creates anew. . . . A year of Brahma is composed of the proper number of such days and nights, and a hundred of such years constitute his whole life. (Wilkins 1975:354)

When Brahma's life ends, the elements of the universe dissolve.

4. From the *Bhagavata Purana* translated by O'Flaherty and quoted in O'Flaherty 1984:109–10.

5. At the Department of Performance Studies, Tisch School of the Arts, New York University – where I have been teaching since 1967.

3

The street is the stage

I mean our thing's for TV. We don't want to get on Meet the Press. What's that shit? We want Ed Sullivan, [the] Johnny Carson show, we want the shit where people are lookin' at it and diggin' it.

Abbie Hoffman (1969a:48)

[A constitutional republic] cannot forever withstand continual carnival on the streets of its cities and the campuses of the nation. Unless sage debate replaces the belligerent strutting now used so extensively, reason will be consumed and the death of logic will surely follow.

Vice-President Spiro Agnew, May 1969[1]

. . . old authority and truth pretend to be absolute, to have an extratemporal importance. Therefore, their representatives . . . are gloomily serious. They cannot and do not wish to laugh; they strut majestically, consider their foes the enemies of eternal truth, and threaten them with eternal punishment. They do not see themselves in the mirror of time, do not perceive their own origin, limitations, and end; they do not recognize their own ridiculous faces or the comic nature of their pretensions to eternity and immutability. And thus these personages come to the end of their role still serious, although their spectators have been laughing for a long time. . . . Time has transformed old truth and authority into a Mardi Gras dummy, a comic monster that the laughing crowd rends to pieces in the marketplace.

Mikhail Bakhtin (1984:212–13)

The role of the revolutionary is to create theatre which creates a revolutionary frame of reference. The power to define is the power to control. . . . The goal of theatre is to get as many people as possible to overcome fear by taking action. We create reality wherever we go by living our fantasies.

Jerry Rubin (1970:142–3)

What is the relation between "the authorities" and "the people" when the people occupy public streets, squares, plazas, and buildings? Do carnivals

45

encourage giddy, drunken, sexy feelings and behavior – or does the very action of taking spaces, of "liberating" them, make people giddy? Is it accidental that official displays consist of neat rectangles, countable cohorts, marching past and under the fixed gaze of the reviewing stand, while unofficial mass gatherings are vortexed, whirling, full of shifting ups and downs, multi-focused events generating tension between large-scale actions and many local dramas? And why is it that unofficial gatherings elicit, permit, or celebrate the erotic, while official displays are so often associated with the military? Can a single dramaturgy explain political demonstrations, Mardi Gras and similar kinds of carnivals, Spring Break weekends, and ritual dramas?

I'll ask these questions of six events selected for their generic range and cultural diversity:

1 The "democracy movement" centered in Beijing's Tiananmen Square from April to June 1989.
2 Breaching the Berlin Wall and other events in Eastern Europe in the fall of 1989.
3 The anti-Vietnam War demonstration in Washington in May 1970, protesting against the American bombing of Cambodia and the killing of four Kent State University students by the National Guard.
4 The Mardi Gras of New Orleans and the Gasparilla celebration of Tampa.
5 Spring Break in Daytona Beach.
6 Ramlila of Ramnagar, a thirty-one-day ritual drama of north India.

Festivals and carnivals – almost but not quite the same – are comic theatrical events: comic in desire, even if sometimes tragic in outcome. When people go into the streets *en masse*, they are celebrating life's fertile possibilities. They eat, drink, make theatre, make love, and enjoy each other's company. They put on masks and costumes, erect and wave banners, and construct effigies not merely to disguise or embellish their ordinary selves, or to flaunt the outrageous, but also to act out the multiplicity each human life is. Acting out forbidden themes is risky so people don masks and costumes. They protest, often by means of farce and parody, against what is oppressive, ridiculous, and outrageous. For one to join the many as a part(ner), is not just a sexy act, it is also a socially and politically generative activity. Festive actions playfully, blasphemously, and obscenely expose to the general eye for approval and/or ridicule the basic (and therefore bodily) facts of human life and death. Such playing challenges official culture's claims to authority, stability, sobriety, immutability, and immortality.

Sometimes street actions bring about change – as in Eastern Europe in 1989. But mostly such scenes, both celebratory and violent, end with the old order restored. Frequently, the old order sponsors a temporary relief from itself. Obeying strict calendars, and confined to designated neighborhoods, the authorities can keep track of these carnivals and prepare the police. But despite such preparations, rebellions swell to almost musical climaxes around sacralized dates – anniversaries of the deaths or funerals of heroes and martyrs or of earlier popular uprisings (as in China) or the Christmas season and the approach of the New Year (as in Eastern Europe). To allow people to assemble in the streets is always to flirt with the possibility of improvisation – that the unexpected might happen.

Revolutions in their incipient period are carnivalesque. Written on a Sorbonne wall in 1968, "The more I make love, the more I want to make revolution – the more I make revolution, the more I want to make love" (Baxandall 1969:65). This is because both revolution and carnival propose a free space to satisfy desires, especially sexual and drunken desires, a new time to enact social relations more freely. People mask and costume or act in ways that are "not me." These behaviors are almost always excessive relative to ordinary life. Sometimes people drink, fuck, loot, burn, riot, and murder; or practice rough justice on those they feel have wronged them. But sooner or later, either at a defined moment – when the church bells ring in Ash Wednesday, when school begins again after Spring Break, when a new government is firmly in power – the liminal period ends and individuals are inserted or reinserted into their (sometimes new, sometimes old but always defined) places in society. "Festivity, ceremonial form, and the transgression of social boundaries are animated with the strongest possible feeling of solidarity and community affiliation" (Bristol 1985:30).[2]

All well and good, but what about violence, dissidence, and the playing out of irreconcilable differences? René Girard argues that "the fundamental purpose of the festival is to set the stage for a sacrificial act that marks at once the climax and the termination of the festivities" (Girard 1977:119).[3] Michael Bristol (1985:33) explains:

> A substitute victim is murdered in order to ward off a more terrifying, indiscriminate violence among the members of the same community. This sacrificial murder [events such as public executions or representations such as Greek tragedy] is the partly hidden meaning of all religion and thus of all social life.

Festive sacrifice is necessary to innoculate society against "falling into interminable violence" (Girard 1977:120). Roger Caillois goes further.

In its pure form, the festival must be defined as the paroxysm of society, purifying and renewing it simultaneously. The paroxysm is not only its climax from a religious but also from an economic point of view. It is the occasion for the circulation of wealth, of the most important trading, of prestige gained through the distribution of accumulated reserves. It seems to be a summation, manifesting the glory of the collectivity, which imbues its very being.

(Caillois 1959:125–6)

The potlatches of native Americans on the Pacific coast in the late nineteenth century are clear examples of what Caillois was talking about. The public destruction of goods was both a display of wealth and an act of violent dissipation. After a great potlatch there was nothing left but to get back to amassing the resources needed to stage another. Unlike the Roman Saturnalia where a scapegoat slave was sacrificed, or the Athenian theatre of Dionysus where actors pretended to suffer and die, potlatchers gave up the real thing: the material substance of their wealth.

Caillois regarded modern European carnivals "as a sort of moribund echo of ancient festivals . . . a kind of atavism, a heritage of the times in which it was felt vitally necessary to reverse everything or commit excesses at the time of the new year" (Caillois 1959:123). As Bristol points out, in modern times state apparatus takes over from festivity the function of guaranteeing social solidarity. Rectangular and linear parades replace the more vortexed and chaotic choreography of carnivals. The state fears unregulated traffic. Over time in Europe and Europeanized America, festivals were cut to size, hemmed in by regulations, transformed into Chamber of Commerce boosterism, coopted by capitalism's appetite for profit, relatively desexualized (Miss America at least has to pretend to "innocence"), and served up as models of social order and conformity. With rare exceptions, today's festivals and carnivals are not inversions of the social order but mirrors of it. "Lords of Misrule" in the Mardi Gras or Gasparilla are rarely drawn from the lower or oppressed classes or enabled to rule (even for a day). For example, New York's Halloween parade, originating in the 1960s as a display of (mostly gay) cross-dressers, maskers, and costume buffs, meandering its noisy way through Greenwich Village's small streets, has been regularized over time, tamed and contained by police watchfulness, and rerouted on to wide main streets where it is more a parade and less an infiltration.

But unofficial culture worms or bullies its way back into public outdoor spaces. If there is a tradition (and not only in the West) of constructing grand

Plate 3.1 Guerrilla Warfare, directed by Richard Schechner. Anti-Vietnam War performers "kill a Vietcong" in the streets of New York City, October 1967. Five groups of actors performed without advance notice at twenty-two locations including Grand Central Terminal, Lincoln Center for the Performing Arts, Times Square, and the United Nations. (Photo: Diana J. Davies)

monuments specifically to present performances – arenas, stadiums, and theatres – so there is as well a long history of unofficial performances "taking place" in (seizing as well as using) locales not architecturally imagined as theatres (see Carlson 1989 and Harrison-Pepper 1990). A big part of the celebration is experiencing the transformation of work space, or traffic space, or some kind of official space into a playfield. Over the past thirty years, performance experimenters, an art branch of unofficial culture, have used outdoor spaces – courtyards, streets, walls, beaches, lakes, rooftops, plazas, and mountainsides – for a number of overlapping purposes – aesthetic, personal, ritual, and political (plates 3.1 and 3.2). And while Western dramatists from Ibsen, Strindberg, and Chekhov to Miller, Pinter, Shepard, and Mamet abandoned the public squares of Renaissance theatre for the living room, kitchen, bedroom, motel, and office, the emerging festival

Plate 3.2 Joan Jonas's *Delay Delay* performed in 1972 on a vacant lot north of the World Trade Center, Manhattan. The audience watched from the roof of a five-story loft building. (Photo: Gianfranco Gorgoni)

theatre – liminoid rather than liminal – repositioned itself in places where public life and social ritual have traditionally been acted out.[4] Doubtless, there has been a mutually fruitful exchange between art performances and symbolic public actions. By the 1960s, these actions constituted a distinct liminoid–celebratory–political–theatrical–ritual genre with its own dramaturgy, *mise-en-scène*, role enactments, audience participation, and reception. This theatre is ritual because it is efficacious, intending to produce real effects by means of symbolic causes. It is most theatrical at the cusp where the street show meets the media, where events are staged for the camera.

Many examples could be given. One I witnessed took place in Shanghai in May 1989 when millions of workers, students, and spectators flowed into Nanjing Road, Shanghai's main street and then on to the Bund, the city's riverfront avenue.[5] Looking down from an overpass all I could see, forward or back, were marchers proceeding between rows of cheering spectators lined ten or more deep on both sides of the road. Above were office workers leaning-out of windows waving handkerchiefs; construction gangs in hard hats thirty stories up unfinished skyscrapers clanging their hammers against the steel girders (in some wild simulation of the cymbals of Chinese opera) as they unfurled 50-foot banners calling for the resignation of Premier Li Peng and the retirement of Deng Xiaoping. People rushed from roadside restaurants with wet towels, cool tea, and snacks to refresh the marchers. Streets were festive, people moving hand in hand, raising their fists in exhilarated defiance or forming the "V for victory" sign with their fingers. In a drunken delirium of desire, they shouted words that even one month before could hardly be whispered: "China's present government are bums!" "Give me liberty or give me death!" "Democracy now!"

On the way back from the Bund, students from the Shanghai Theatre Academy turned off the main path of the march and approached the gates of Shanghai's TV station. One demonstrator was bound in chains, another wore a skeletal death mask, several were drenched in stage blood; all writhed in melodramatic agony: a grisly tableau of how they experienced China – a spectacle not unlike similar kinds of American guerrilla street theatre. Around the students thousands of demonstrators congealed into a mass pressing so fiercely against the TV station's walls and gate that I had the breath squashed out of me. A number of Canons, Nikons, and humbler equipment condensed from the crowd, but the students were angry and dissatisfied. They demanded a camera crew videotape them for broadcast to the nation. A man in a white shirt and pressed slacks emerged from the building. Engaging him in a hot colloquy, the students threatened – with the crowd's support – to crash the gate. The man trotted inside. A very few minutes later, to resounding cheers, out came a camera crew to begin taping the students who acted up a storm, writhing and screaming bloody murder. Now, they felt, the event was real. Shanghai and maybe all China and the whole world would see. Being seen and reported on was a morsel of the "transparency" and free press the democracy movement was so vehemently demanding.

But the Shanghai march was just a sideshow down the coast from the main arena, Beijing's Tiananmen Square.

> Tiananmen Square is no European Piazza. More than 100 acres in size, and capable of holding hundreds of thousands of people, it is the center of a city of ten million people, which is the capital of the People's Republic of China, Beijing. It is the symbol of China and Chinese government in the same way that Red Square and the Kremlin symbolize the USSR, and Washington with its white monuments the USA. . . . [In] Tiananmen Square is situated the huge Monument to the People's Heroes and the Mausoleum of Mao Zedong. On the west side of the Square is the Great Hall of the People, the meeting place for government bodies. . . . On the east side of the Square is the Museum of Chinese History, which is attached to the Museum of the Revolution. At the north end of the Square is the reviewing stand which stands over the entrance to the Forbidden City, now the Palace Museum. To the west of the Forbidden City is the Zhongnanhai compound for senior government and party personnel. . . . Running east-west . . . through the north end of the Square is [Beijing's] major thoroughfare, Changan Avenue.
>
> (Mok and Harrison 1990:xi–xii)

But until 1949 this version of Tiananmen Square did not exist. Earlier photos show a smallish open space in front of the Gate of Heavenly Peace, the southern entrance to the Forbidden City.

> Until China's last dynasty fell in 1912, it was through this gate that the main axis of the Emperor's power was believed to run, as he sat in his throne hall, facing south, the force of his presence radiating out across the courtyards and ornamental rivers of the palace compound, passing through the gate, and so to the great reaches of the countryside beyond.　(Spence 1981:17)

After the communist triumph,

> the crowded alleys in front of the gate were leveled, and a massive parade ground was created; in the center of the vast space rose the simple monument to the martyrs of the revolution. . . . During the Cultural Revolution of 1966 [to 1976] the gate, dominated now by an immense colored portrait of Chairman Mao Zedong, became a reviewing stand in front of which marched the Red Guards, a million or more strong.　(Spence 1981:17–18)

Clearly, the creation of Tiananmen Square was intended to refocus cere-

Plate 3.3 Tiananmen Square, June 1989, looking towards Mao's portrait on the Gate of Heavenly Peace. (Photo: AP/Wide World Photos)

monial – that is, theatrical – power from behind the Forbidden City's walls to the big open space, a more fitting symbol of what the new order promised. Mao, the new emperor, no longer sat on a throne behind the Gate, but was mounted in front, gazing out over the Square and from there to all of China (plate 3.3). Power was no longer to radiate from secret forbidden places but be displayed for all people to see and share. The nation itself was renamed The People's Republic of China. And what the students who came to Tiananmen Square in 1978, 1986, and 1989 demanded, more than anything, was what they called "transparency" – defined as an openness in government operations corresponding to the open square that symbolized the new China. In occupying Tiananmen Square the students were challenging the government, actualizing the students' belief that the government was not living up to its promises. There were precedents for such actions in the dramatic May 4th Movement of 1919 and the more recent democracy movements in 1978 and 1986 – all of which focused on Tiananmen Square. Joseph Esherick and Jeffrey Wasserstrom argue strongly that the 1989 democracy movement was political theatre.

First of all it was street theater: untitled, improvisational, with constantly changing casts. Though fluid in form, it nevertheless followed what Charles Tilly (1978) calls a historically established "repertoire" of collective action. This means that, even when improvising, protesters worked from familiar "scripts" which gave a common sense of how to behave during a given action, where and when to march, how to express their demands, and so forth. Some of these scripts originated in the distant past, emerging out of traditions of remonstrance and petition stretching back for millennia. More were derived (consciously or unconsciously) from the steady stream of student-led mass movements that have taken place [in China] since 1919.

(Esherick and Wasserstrom 1990:839)

The struggle in China, before it became violent, was over controlling the means and style of information. As Esherick and Wasserstrom note, state rituals, the funerals of leaders (in 1989 that of Hu Yaobang, a former General Secretary of the Communist Party who the students highly regarded), and anniversaries of earlier demonstrations or uprisings are of great importance. In 1989 the question became: would official culture or the student-led democracy movement write the script? The theatrical stakes were even higher in May because fortune laid ceremony atop ceremony. Hu Yaobang died on 15 April, close to the anniversary of the May 4th Movement; Soviet President Mikhail Gorbachev was set to arrive in Beijing on 15 May, possibly healing decades of bad relations between China and the USSR. Clearly, the leadership wanted to impress Gorbachev. The students also wanted to impress him, but with a different show. They admired the Soviet President's policies of *glasnost* and *perestroika*. If Chinese officials wanted Gorbachev to see an orderly China under their control, the students wanted him to see a powerful and seething people's movement akin to those in Eastern Europe and his own country. On 15 May about 800,000 people gathered in Tiananmen Square even as Chinese officials steered Gorbachev around Beijing pretending that this vast spectacle at the very core of power was not occurring. Instead of greeting Gorbachev in the Square, official public ceremonies were held at the Beijing airport, a nonplace historically.

Within the overall dramaturgy of the 1989 demonstrations were particular molecules of theatre related to what I saw in Shanghai. Esherick and Wasserstrom describe as "one of the best acts" that

put on by Wuer Kaixi in the May 18th dialogue with Li Peng. The costuming was important: he appeared in his hospital pajamas [on hunger strike]. So, too, was the timing: he upstaged the Premier by interrupting him at the very start.

54

And props: later in the session, he dramatically pulled out a tube inserted into his nose (for oxygen?) in order to make a point. Especially for the young people in the nationwide television audience, it was an extraordinarily powerful performance. (1990:841)

Then there was the dramatic meeting the next day, 19 May, between hunger-striking students and Communist Party Secretary Zhao Ziyang. This encounter had the quality of a tragic *perepeteia* (reversal) and *anagnorisis* (recognition). Speaking through tears, Zhao said "I came too late, I came too late . . . [but] the problems you raised will eventually be solved." And, of course, on 30 May the "Goddess of Democracy and Freedom" (plate 3.4) – a multivocal figure resembling the Statue of Liberty, a Bread & Puppet Theatre effigy, a "traditional Bodhisattva, . . . [and] the giant statues of Mao that were carried through the Square during some National Day parades of the sixties" (Esherick and Wasserstrom 1990:841). The Goddess was a big hit. Before her appearance the crowds had been sagging, but she brought many back to the Square. Earlier, on 25 May in Shanghai, a more exact replica of the Statue of Liberty had come onto the streets – thus ideas for effigies and banners, staging, all kinds of information were circulating through the movement's various parts. Students freely adapted costumes and slogans from non-Chinese sources, including "We shall overcome". Across China the democracy movement was "connected," a single organism. Serious in their demands and aspirations, the Chinese students still found plenty of time to celebrate, to dance, to enjoy the freedom of the streets (plate 3.5). At the same time, the government was getting its forces together, bringing in troops and key leaders from the far reaches of the country.

Esherick and Wasserstrom theorize that the struggle in Tiananmen Square was between official ritual and student theatre:

> there is always the chance that people will turn a ritual performance into an act of political theater. Central to the notion of ritual is the idea that only careful adherence to a traditionally prescribed format will ensure the efficacy of a performance. With any departure from a traditional script, a ritual ceases to be ritual. . . . Theatre, by nature, is more liberated from the rigid constraints of tradition, and provides autonomous space for the creativity of playwrights, directors, and actors. This gives theater a critical power never possessed by ritual. . . . Educated [Chinese] youths have repeatedly managed to transform May 4th rituals into May 4th theater. (1990:844–5, 848)

Such a distinction between theatre and ritual is too rigid (in fact, Esherick

Plate 3.4 The "Goddess of Democracy and Freedom" parading past Mao's portrait hung in front of a government building in Tiananmen Square, 30 May 1989. (Photo: AP/Wide World Photos)

Plate 3.5 Students dancing in Tiananmen Square, the Gate of Heavenly Peace in the background. Their dancing style is "cosmopolitan," not traditional Chinese. (Photo: AP/Wide World Photos)

and Wasserstrom do not always stick to it). As Victor Turner has emphasized, and as I have pointed out, the relation between ritual and theatre is
dialectical and braided; there is plenty of entertainment and social critique in
many rituals (see Turner 1969 and 1982, Schechner 1974 and 1988a).
Conversely, theatre in its very processes of training, preparation, display,
and reception is ritualized. The struggle in Tiananmen Square before the
entrance of the tanks was not between rigid ritual and rebellious theatre, but
between two groups of authors (or authorities) each of whom desired to
compose the script of China's future and each of whom drew on both
theatre and ritual. The students improvised in public, while the officials, as
always, rehearsed their options behind closed doors. The students took
Tiananmen Square, the center stage and ritual focus of Chinese history.
Official culture was literally upstaged. When Deng Xiaoping, Li Peng, and
the generals of the People's Liberation Army felt their authority slipping,
they radically shifted the basis of the confrontation from theatre and ritual to
military force. But even after the slaughter of 3–4 June, there were moments
of high theatre such as when an unarmed man, his fate since unknown, stood
his ground in front of a column of tanks (plate 3.6).

For their stage the students claimed not just any old spot, but the
symbolic and operational focus of Chinese political power. And despite the
orderliness of their demonstrations and the seriousness of their intentions,
the students acted up a carnival. Their mood of fun, comradeship, irony, and
subversion enraged and frightened China's officialdom. Students camped
out willy-nilly all over the place (plate 3.7) in patterns as different as can be
imagined from the rigid rectangles and precise lines of official gatherings
(plate 3.8). The students sang and danced, they spoke from impromptu
"soap boxes," and granted interviews to the world press. They unfurled
sarcastic, disrespectful banners including one depicting hated Premier Li
Peng as a pig-snouted Nazi officer. "Flying tigers" – students on motorbikes
– carried news to and from various parts of Beijing, linking the Square to the
city and the rest of China. Even the hunger strike, in which thousands
participated, had the feel of melodrama rather than the sanctity of one of
Gandhi's laydowns (though certainly the Mahatma knew his political theatre
– and how sanctity would play in India and Britain).

Events in Beijing from the perspective of Shanghai underline the importance of theatricalizing media. From mid-May until 8 June I was in Shanghai
directing a new Chinese play about the aftermath of the cultural revolution
at the People's Art Theatre (plate 3.9). What was happening in Beijing was of

Plate 3.6 A moment of incredible symbolism, drama, and bravery: a lone man halts a line of tanks advancing through Tiananmen Square on 5 June 1989. (Photo: AP/Wide World Photos)

great importance to me and those I was working with. During the days immediately preceding the Tiananmen Square massacre of 3–4 June, official media – TV, radio, and newspapers – kept changing tune according to whether hardliners or people sympathetic to the students were calling the shots. Once the tanks rolled in the media toed the line, but in an eerie way. The main headline of the 5 June *China Daily* (the official English language newspaper) reported the death of Ayatollah Khomeini. A lesser headline, bereft of capital letters, said, "Martial law troops are ordered to firmly 'restore order'." For several days on TV only the reporters' voices were heard, no images. Unofficial media worked very differently. At the person-to-person level, students went back and forth from Shanghai to Beijing

Plate 3.7 Thousands of exhausted but intrepid students camped out willy-nilly all across Tiananmen Square on the morning of 22 May 1989. This scene was typical in late May and early June – until the Chinese army "cleared" the Square. (Photo: AP/Wide World Photos)

Plate 3.8 The People's Liberation Army on parade in Tiananmen Square in July, 1951 for the celebration of the thirtieth anniversary of the founding of the Chinese Communist Party. Note the rectangular formations of official culture on display. (Photo: AP/Wide World Photos)

bringing news by word of mouth. Once martial law was declared at the end of May, it was rare to meet someone who "was there." People listened to the Voice of America and BBC; newspapers and magazines in Chinese and English came in from Hong Kong (for sale at the big tourist hotels or smuggled by individuals). After the massacre in Tiananmen Square, a friend rented a room at the satellite-equipped Shanghai Hilton. Even as Chinese official media were claiming that only thirty-six students had been killed in the Square, and that the students had been the aggressors, a crowd of Chinese and foreigners in the hotel room watched with terror and excitement as CNN broadcast direct shots from Beijing, routed back to Atlanta

Plate 3.9 June 1989: the Red Guard scene from Sun Huizhu's *Mingri Jiuyao Chu Shan* (*Tomorrow He'll Be Out of the Mountains*), directed by Richard Schechner and Chan Choi Lai at Shanghai's People's Art Theatre. Closed in early July, this was the last play with "democratic political content" performed in China before the crackdown. (Photo: Cao Lusheng)

and relayed by satellite to the world. The satellite link was still up, as were phone lines and faxes, when I was evacuated from Shanghai on 8 June. On 4 and 5 June rumors of civil war were brought to rehearsals. Peering at hand-drawn maps, we saw the progress of an army marching toward Beijing to overthrow Deng and Li, while 20,000 troops from Nanjing were massing just outside Shanghai in support of Deng and Li. The celebratory exaltation of May changed to fear. Access to unofficial media was sharply curtailed, especially in the countryside where most of China's 1.1 billion live. When it was certain that the government had used major force against the students, some of whom were the children of the elite, people hunkered down. Rice hoarding began; I changed my residence from the Shanghai Theatre Academy to a hotel to be out of the way of the army should it decide to move against the Academy, a focus of radicalism.

This radicalism the Chinese government called *luan*, or chaos, a word which in certain of its uses implies dissipation and drunkenness. Because of the "tigers" – and world media (more about which I shall say later) – the Chinese leadership feared the virus of luan would spread from Tiananmen Square to the rest of Beijing and China. After all, it was from the Square that official power radiated. Had the students turned inward, not attempting Chinawide and worldwide communication, the government might have waited them out. But Tiananmen Square is not an inwardly focused place: it is a consciously designed, very bright stage, visible all over China. From the government's point of view, luan acted out in Tiananmen Square could not be ignored any more than the Nixon administration could, nineteen years earlier, ignore the ever more carnivalesque anti-Vietnam War demonstrations invading Washington. Meaningful theatrical luan is a potent weapon.

From the mid-1960s, protests against the Vietnam War and in favor of what University of California activists in Berkeley called "free speech," had pitched scores of American campuses into organized theatrical chaos.[6] In the spring of 1968, students led by Mark Rudd – guerrilla theatre activist and head of the radical Students for a Democratic Society (SDS) – took over buildings at Columbia University, including the president's office. Earlier, in mid-March, Rudd and his followers had disrupted a talk by the head of the New York Selective Service System. In the back of the room, students with fife and drum, flags, toy machine guns, and noise-makers drew attention to themselves. Suddenly, someone stepped on stage and mashed a lemon-meringue pie in the colonel's face. This action, which rejected "verbalism" (an anti-intellectual tone strong in the movement of the 1960s), had catapulted Rudd to the head of Columbia's SDS. Using farce, parody, and scatology as political criticism was developed into a very high skill by Abbie Hoffman.[7] Under the name of "Free" in *Revolution for the Hell of It* (1968), Hoffman wrote:

> Theater also has some advantages. It is involving for those people that are ready for it while at the same time dismissed as nonthreatening by those that could potentially wreck the stage. It's dynamite. . . . Once committed in a street drama never turn back. Be prepared to die if it's necessary to gain your point.
> !   !   !   !   !   !   !   !   !   !   !   !   !   !   !
> Don't rely on words. Words are the absolute in horseshit. Rely on doing – go all the way every time. Move fast. If you spend too long on one play, it becomes boring to you and the audience.   (1968:27–30)

By "theatre" Hoffman clearly meant a lot more than orthodox drama or even "guerrilla theatre" as ordinarily conceived.[8] "Drama is anything you can get away with. . . . Guerrilla theater is only a transitional step in the development of total life-actors" (1968:30, 183). Or as activist Jerry Rubin put it, "Life is theatre and we are the guerrillas attacking the shrines of authority. . . . The street is the stage. You are the star of the show and everything you were once taught is up for grabs" (1970:250). It is doubtful that the activists in Tiananmen Square knew about Hoffman or Rubin's theory or practice. Nevertheless, the weeks before 3 June were in harmony with what Hoffman and Rubin thought and did.

Except that the Yippies (as the Americans called themselves) emphasized more than the Chinese the Bakhtinian/Rabelaisian mode.[9] In October 1967, a massive demonstration in Washington against the Vietnam War climaxed by an effort to "exorcize" and "levitate" the Pentagon. I was not alone in pissing on the Pentagon steps as a gesture of contempt and defiance. In the spring of 1968, Hoffman, Rubin, and others planned a "Festival of Life" for the August Democratic Party National Convention in Chicago. The Festival was conceived as both disruptive of the Convention and constructive of a new way of life. According to an ad in the spring 1968 *TDR*, *The Drama Review*, the Festival would feature "guerrilla theatre, a mock convention, and happenings." All who participated would be provided with "costumes, paint, and props." Of course, what happened in Chicago's Grant Park was a "police riot." Mayor Richard Daly's bluecoats charged into the Festival, bloodily bludgeoning demonstrators, and arresting them. Hoffman and six others were tried in 1969–70 under a 1968 federal "Anti-Riot Act."[10]

The violent, the political, the carnivalesque, and the erotic were linked again in May 1970 after the bombing of Cambodia, an escalation of the Vietnam War, triggered protests. On 4 May – an ironically appropriate date given what happened in China – the National Guard, called out to repress a protest at Kent State University in Ohio, shot four students dead. Schools everywhere went on strike, students marched, and a massive rally was called for Saturday 9 May in Washington. But despite the occasion – a protest against bombing in Cambodia and murder at home – the march on Washington quickly turned into a carnival. At dawn, Nixon, like Zhao, visited the students attempting to make peace with them. As he spoke, some students taunted him with shouts of "Fuck Nixon! Trash Nixon!" raising garbage can lids with his face embossed on them (plate 3.10). The demonstrations began with speeches reminding the activists of the contingent causes of their assembling in the nation's capital. But soon, warmed by the

Plate 3.10 In May 1970, while Nixon spoke, trying to appease student demonstrators, some in the crowd raise garbage can lids as they shouted, "Trash Nixon!"
(Photo: unattributed)

sun and more tuned in to Woodstock Nation than "verbalism," many
youths stripped in the hot sun and jumped naked into the Lincoln Memorial
Reflecting pool (plates 3.11, 3.12), smoked dope, made out, and lounged on
the capital's sumptuous lawns.[11] The frolic – with its characteristic whorling
choreography, the dispersal of orderly ranks into many intense and volatile
small groups, the show of private pleasures satisfied in public places –

Plates 3.11 and 3.12 Washington, DC, 9 May 1970. Bathers – some of them naked – frolic around and in the Reflecting Pool of the Lincoln Memorial, with the Washington Monument in the background. Even bitter protest may turn into carnival. (Photos: *The Village Voice*: Fred W. McDarrah)

subverted and mocked the neo-Roman monuments and pretensions of imperialist Washington. On that summery May Saturday many bravely but mistakenly believed that this festival was in fact what such events can never become – a rehearsal or preplay of America's political (or social or sexual) future. Washington that day felt very much like Shanghai or Beijing in 1989. And although there was no single massacre as in Tiananmen Square, the American "big chill" from the mid-1970s into the 1990s accomplished the same end. Nixon and Agnew were driven from office, as Deng Xiaoping and Li Peng might be, but social systems do not rest on one person or a dozen.

The system of communist domination of Eastern Europe and the USSR, and the cold war between that system and the north Atlantic alliance, was symbolized by the Berlin Wall. Existing for only twenty-eight years (1961–89), the 103-mile-long Wall lacked architectural grace or ornament. Like the Bastille, it not only symbolized a hated regime and physically helped preserve it, but was demolished as soon as that regime fell. While it was there, more than 5,000 people went over, under, or through it – climbing, leaping, ballooning, gliding, tunnelling, and ramming. At least another 5,000 were captured and 191 were killed trying to escape.[12] Ugly and mean, the Wall disgusted and attracted people, including Presidents John F. Kennedy and Ronald Reagan, who exploited it as a theatrical backdrop for communist-bashing speeches. Still others considered it a tourist "must."

The events leading to the destruction of the Wall – and the collapse of communism throughout Eastern Europe – are complex.[13] The system was imposed from without, sustained by military force, and failed to deliver the material goods people desired. There were many revolts and several major uprisings crushed by Soviet armies or the clear threat of Soviet intervention. When in the mid-1980s Gorbachev began restructuring the USSR, Eastern Europeans saw an opportunity, but the actual license for radical change was not issued until Gorbachev's declaration on 25 October 1989 that the USSR had no right to interfere in the internal affairs of its Eastern European neighbors. He may have been driven to this position by events. The social drama began in the summer of 1989 – shortly after the brutal crushing of the democracy movement in China – when Hungary opened its border to East Germans. Many thousands got out of the GDR at rates unequalled since the building of the Wall.

Throughout September and October, the East German government – led by one of those who authored the Wall, 77-year-old Erich Honecker –

shilly-shallied regarding the exodus. Meanwhile, the festival that always accompanies a "revolution from below" began.

> A carnival atmosphere greeted the first large convoy of jubilant East Germans to arrive today in this city [Passau, West Germany] on the Danube in south-eastern Bavaria. Hundreds of onlookers watched and cheered as five buses unloaded an estimated 700 East Germans who were welcomed with speeches, free balloons, bananas, beer and soft pretzels. . . . A similar welcome was given to East Germans arriving at five tent cities set up by the West German Red Cross in nearby towns.   (Protzman 1989b:A1, A14)

Following a Bakhtinian script, headlines in the *New York Times* proclaimed: "Exodus galls East Berlin/Nation's sovereignty seems to be mocked" (Schmemann 1989a:A14). But the climax was not yet reached – the streets of Berlin were relatively quiet and empty.

Then, as in China earlier in 1989, an important date sparked street protests. Friday 6 October was the GDR's fortieth anniversary. Ordinarily one could expect a rectangular parade of military muscle in front of and below rigidly saluting generals and commissars mounted on a viewing stand. As in China that May, globe-hopping Gorbachev was scheduled to make an appearance and, as in China, the official celebration turned sour. "Honecker faces the birthday party . . . humiliated, derided, and threatened" (Schmemann 1989b:A1). Gorbachev was seized on by both sides, soon becoming a contradictory sign. Addressing "an elite congregation gathered in the glittering Palace of the Republic . . . [he] assailed demands that Moscow dismantle the Berlin wall," while earlier many Berliners hailed him with shouts of "Gorby! Gorby!" a known code for the reforms they were demanding from Honecker's government (Schmemann 1989c:A5). On 9 October more than 50,000 demonstrated in Leipzig. On 18 October Honecker was replaced by his protégé, 52-year-old Egon Krenz – a man who had just paid a praising visit to Li Peng and Deng Xiaoping.

The East German people replied with more demonstrations. People were openly disrespectful of Krenz.

> A retired factory hand, speaking in the pungent accent and mocking vocabulary of the Berlin working class, nearly exploded with derisive laughter. . . . "From him?" he asked with a snort. "After he went to China to congratulate them for the blood they spilled? After he rigged our last election? After being the boss of State Security? The sparrows on the roof wouldn't believe him."
>   (Kamm 1989a:A16)

Ferment was spreading. On 23 October 300,000 marched in Leipzig demanding change, including the legalization of opposition parties and an independent labor movement. Smaller demonstrations took place in Berlin, Dresden, Halle, Schwerin, and Magdeburg. People grew bolder. Political debates erupted in the streets of East Berlin. Meanwhile big demonstrations were starting in Prague. Not only were East Germans challenging their leadership, the once docile press and TV were giving open coverage to the emergent debates. The demonstrations got more and more festive. On 30 October, Leipzig's "old city center was virtually taken over for three hours by people of every age and from every walk of life. . . . The center [was filled] with cheers, jeers, and chants from all sides" (Schmemann 1989d:A17). On 2 November the East German government dropped its ban on travel and thousands crossed into Czechoslovakia heading west. On 7 November the East German cabinet resigned, but the Politburo – the core of official power – held fast. By 8 November more than 50,000 East Germans a day were streaming from Czechoslovakia into West Germany where, according to law, they instantly became citizens.

On 9 November, the GDR government opened its borders. Once the announcement was made,

> a tentative trickle of East Germans testing the new regulations quickly turned into a jubilant horde, which joined at the border crossings with crowds of flag-waving, cheering West Germans. Thousands of Berliners clambered across the wall at the Brandenburg Gate, passing through the historic arch that for so long had been inaccessible to Berliners of either side. (Schmemann 1989e:A1)

The Brandenburg Gate, like Beijing's Tiananmen Square, is heavily symbolic. Erected in 1888–9 at the western end of the Unter den Linden, and soon dubbed Germany's Arc de Triomphe, the Gate celebrates the military prowess of Prussia and the unity of Germany. On 9 November, in a flash, the Berlin Wall's symbolic value was reversed. What had been avoided or surpassed became the chosen place of celebration. Because it had been such a terrifying barrier it was now where people wanted to act out how totally things had changed. People couldn't wait to climb it, sit on it, pop champagne and dance on it, and chip away souvenir chunks of it.[14] Formerly murderous East German border guards went out of their way to be friendly. The show on the Wall was a media bonanza. Dominating the front page of the 10 November *New York Times* was a four-column photograph of "East Berliners dancing atop the Berlin Wall near the Brandenburg Gate." The same picture, or others very like it, appeared on front pages around the

Plate 3.13 Germans joining hands and dancing atop the Berlin Wall in front of the Brandenburg Gate in November, 1989. (Photo: AP/Wide World Photos)

world (plate 3.13). Again and again, TV showed people clambering on to and over the Wall.

The Wall was not "interesting" everywhere along its 103-mile route. The focus was on the segment in front of the Brandenburg Gate or bifurcating Potsdamer Platz which, before the Wall, was the center of Berlin, among the busiest intersections in Europe. Just as Tiananmen Square was the necessary stage for China's democracy movement, so the Wall at these places was where Berliners focused the "unparalleled celebration that swirled through Berlin day and night."[15] "Cheers, sparkling wine, flowers and applause greeted the new arrivals. . . . At the Brandenburg Gate . . . hundreds of people chanted, 'Gate open! Gate open!' " A middle-aged East German woman broke through a police cordon to give flowers and a "vigorous kiss" to a young West German cop as "the crowd roared." "A festival air seized the entire city. West Berliners lined entry points to greet East Berliners with champagne, cheers, and hugs. Many restaurants offered the visitors free food. A television station urged West Berliners to call in with offers of theater tickets, beds, dinners, or just guided tours." The popular Hertha soccer team gave away 10,000 free tickets for its Saturday game. That giddy weekend the West German government gave every visitor from the East 100 marks of "greeting money" for spending in West Berlin's glittering shops. "In an unprecedented step for a place with the most rigid business hours in Western Europe, West Berlin banks will be open on both Saturday and Sunday for East Germans wishing to pick up cash." It was only a matter of time before the East German state collapsed into the arms of the West.

It could have ended otherwise. Craig R. Whitney reports that "there was a written order from Honecker for a Chinese solution" (1989:A27). But the Politburo overrode its aging boss. Once events are in the saddle, the speed of the reversals is breathtaking. A faltering regime in China suddenly reasserts itself; a seemingly invincible state in East Germany crumbles like dust. Hindsight discloses the "inevitability" of events. But "what if" haunts all such talk. What if the Chinese leadership had not sent in the army? What if the East Germans had? At what point does a regime lose control of its military? There are too many variables for anyone to answer these questions. What can be known is that when oppressed or angry people sense official power weakening, they take to the streets. Their carnival can last only so long – every Mardi Gras meets its Ash Wednesday. Whether or not that Wednesday will see a new order or the return of the old cannot be known in advance.

China and East Germany in 1989 or the USA in 1970 are examples of festivals where the outcome was unknown. The excitement of such social dramas – not unlike what grips whole populations during some sports matches, especially those like the soccer World Cup where teams and nations are closely identified – is rooted in the tension between known patterns of action, stunning instantaneous surprises, and a passionately desired yet uncertain outcome. At the other extreme are festivals where written dramas are enacted. Here the excitement derives from immersing oneself in a known flow of events. One of these festivals, the Ramlila of Ramnagar, India, offers an intriguing variation on the theme of the critique of ordinary reality. In most carnivals, the revolution is from below: the underdog, or the top dog disguised as underdog, rules. But in Ramlila the critique is from above. For a month Ramnagar is where Hindu gods and mythic heroes walk the earth and rule the realm.

The epic story tells of Rama's birth, his boyhood education, his exile, the kidnapping of his wife Sita (also a god), his war against the demon-king Ravana, his victory and triumphant return home to his rule as India's ideal

71

king. During Ramlila, Vibhuti Narain Singh is celebrated by hundreds of
thousands of devoted spectators as the "maharaja of Banaras," representative
of Shiva and worshipper of Rama. Never mind that the maharaja was
stripped of both princely title and kingdom shortly after Indian independence in 1947. The maharaja is the principal spectator and occasional
participant in the reenactment of Rama's life. Spectator-participants regard
Ramlila month as time out from their daily grind. When the boy actors enact
the gods, spectators regard them as divine. Inversions abound. Ramlila is a
time when rich persons dress simply and eat street food while poor persons
dress beyond their means and enjoy expensive, voluptuous sweets; when the
maharaja bows down before the boy actors, feeding them with his own
hand; when the barely literate farmer playing the demon-king Ravana is
honored by all; when slick lawyers and gruff shopkeepers, books in hand,
meekly follow the sacred text word by word. And of course the largest
inversion of them all: five Brahmin boys become gods.

For thirty-one days, Ramnagar ("Ramatown") is taken over by Ramlila.
The streets, back lanes, and courtyards become theatres. Sadhu spectators
dance themselves into delirium worshipping Rama and Sita. Crowds follow
Rama, Sita, and Lakshman into exile; they flood the streets in majestic
processions (plate 3.14). The characteristic choreography of Ramlila is a
procession from one place to another where a scene is performed on a raised
stage or within a complex environment of stages, small buildings, and
gardens. Spectators take part in the processions and then gather in front of
the stages or within the theatrical environments. Moving from one place to
another is so important that often one day's lila will stop near the end of a
scene so that shortly after the next day's lila begins, the whole crowd – actors
and spectators alike – move off to another location several kilometers away.
Great crowds take over the streets, but there is little rebelliousness. This is
not only because Ramlila is a religious festival (religious devotion can
sponsor rebellion, as Gandhi knew) but because in today's India the
Ramnagar Ramlila is an expression of official Hinduism. A few spectators
identify with Ravana, the demon outsider who they regard as heroically
resistant to accepted values and an enemy of caste oppression. (This opinion
of Ravana is more strongly felt in south India than in the north.) Also,
Ramnagar, aside from being the residence of the maharaja and the venue for
Ramlila, is today not an important town either politically or religiously.
Berlin at the Brandenburg Gate, Tiananmen Square, the Lincoln Memorial
or the Pentagon – these places reflect history, radiate power, to take them

Plate 3.14 Amidst a great and joyous crowd, the maharaja of Banaras sets out from his Fort to the battlefield of Lanka on dasahara, 1978. (Photo: Richard Schechner)

over makes a statement. Politics were more important at Ramnagar Ramlila's inception in the nineteenth century, when the performance proclaimed Hindu nationalism against both British and Mogul authorities. These and other aspects of Ramlila are discussed more fully in Chapter 5.

The New Orleans Mardi Gras is like and unlike Ramlila. Both are religious festivals, both involve masking and seething public processions, and both engender a sometimes wild celebratory ecstasy. But while the eroticism of Ramlila is redirected into the naked sadhus' furious dancing and singing and a general feeling of abandoning one's self to the gods, Mardi Gras is literally drunk and sexy. New Orleans' "fat Tuesday" revels descend from European pre-Lenten carnivals that are the basis for so much theorizing by Durkheim, Bakhtin, and Turner. By the mid-nineteenth century – at about the same time that Ramnagar Ramlila was taking its present shape – the New Orleans Mardi Gras had become what it is today – a mix of fun, sex, commercial exploitation, and hype. As in classic carnivals, inversion of social roles was the order of the day. Whites dressed as blacks and blacks as whites. And whatever New Orleans offered, there was more of it during Mardi Gras.

The holiday is charged with ludic double negatives. Socially prominent people pretend to be kings, queens, and mythic personages ruling over temporary realms as they glide above the streets on great glittery floats throwing fake jewelry to crowds of ordinaries scrambling for crummy souvenirs (and spending like crazy). These Lords and Ladies of Misrule are not poor people empowered for a day but the New Orleans bourgeois ruling class pretending to even greater power and authority. It seems that those in power cannot tolerate even a temporary mortgaging of their authority. Far from giving the poor or oppressed a chance at a day or two of free play, or permitting a charivari-like critique of established norms, Mardi Gras privileges the already privileged. The festival is a hyperbolic display of social relations in the Crescent City.

So where does this leave New Orleans' African Americans on Mardi Gras? The majority of them are very poor and *de facto* segregation is endemic. Blacks cannot attend the white Mardi Gras balls except as servants or sex chattels; nor can they ride on white floats – they walk beside the floats as *flambeaux*, carrying blazing torches as negro slaves did before Emancipation and the Civil War ended slavery in the 1860s. But there used to be a critique of official culture in the anticarnival carnival of King Zulu's parade, first organized in 1910 by a few poor and middle-class blacks. Zulu was not only a parody of the white parades, it was a parody of white racist attitudes toward blacks. On Mardi Gras day, King Zulu preceded the final, biggest, and most prestigious white parade, that of Rex, King of Carnival. While white parades had defined routes passing in front of reviewing stands loaded with notables (not unlike a military procession), the Zulus meandered through black neighborhoods or chased on the heels of Rex.

Looking at Zulu as it was in the 1940s, one can see how it functioned in the Bakhtinian sense – as popular culture playing out and mocking race relations, expressing the often violent ambivalence with which blacks performed their "place" in New Orleans society. Even the name "Zulu" – in a New Orleans not familiar with Shaka (not to mention Buthelezi) – carried a racist double message: savage, African, foreign, and dangerous; yet silly, ridiculous, and primitive. King Zulu and his court were dressed in "the traditional costume of the krewe – long black underwear that covered them to wrists and ankles, grass skirts, and woolly wigs. Faces were blackened and eyes and mouths were circled in white" (Tallant 1948:232) (plate 3.15). The blackface was an attempt to localize Zulu as a minstrel show; the makeup was what even black minstrel show performers were required to put on: a theatrical restatement of the social "blackness" or "negritude" of African Americans.

If Mardi Gras' white elite displaced their identities upwards towards royalty, myth, and godhead, whiter than white, the Zulus' identity, both royal and primitive, was blacker than black. King Zulu's court included a garishly overdressed "Big Shot of Africa" and a "royal witch doctor" with "a horned headdress and a golden ring in his nose, carrying a spiked mace." Zulu himself

> wore a gold paper crown, dangling earrings, and strings of gleaming beads about his neck. His mantle was dark blue velvet trimmed in gold and edged with white rabbit fur. He carried a jeweled scepter, with which he now and then threatened the small page boy who kept pulling at his mantle. He also wore a leopard-skin vest. (Tallant 1948:232–40)

More than a little hostility marked the shenanigans of the Zulus. At least into the mid-1960s, when I last saw Mardi Gras, the Zulus acted out the feelings of many New Orleans African Americans regarding race relations in "the city that care forgot" (a local motto). King Zulu and his court did not toss baubles, they hurled black and gold painted coconuts like cannonballs at white spectators.

The Zulus of the 1990s are very different from those of earlier days. With

Plate 3.15 King Zulu's parade as it was in 1946. In the foreground, a member of Zulu's court surrounded by spectators. In the background, a steamship float with Zulus atop it. (Photo: Willam Russell, Hogan Jazz Archive, Tulane University)

at least the appearance of improved race relations, King Zulu's parade has been made part of official Mardi Gras (though still last and still regarded by many as a parody). Zulu's floats are fancier than before, sometimes borrowed from one of the white parades; the costumes are more dignified, the exaggerated blackface less common. Tellingly, Zulu's coconuts are more often handed out than pitched – even though the Louisiana Legislature in the late 1980s exempted Zulu from liability for injuries caused by coconut throwing. Nor is the Zulu Social Aid and Pleasure Club any longer all-black. Quite the opposite, it is "now the most integrated of all Carnival organizations. The club realized that there was a significant number of white folks in town who also enjoyed mocking the elite" (Branley 1992). But saying Zulu is the "most integrated" is a way of underlining the lily-whiteness of the other krewes (several of which also exclude Italians and Jews). Most are all-male. On 19 December 1991 the New Orleans City Council passed an ordinance denying city services – including permits to parade – to organizations that discriminate on the basis of race or gender. The ordinance was to take effect in 1993. Promptly, Momus and Comus announced they would not parade in 1992 as a protest against the new law. Momus is the oldest of the extant krewes, having first entered the streets in 1857 and Comus is among the most prestigious (Branley 1992). Much brouhaha and maneuvering resulted in a modification of the ordinance. The New Orleans power structure – including many African Americans – wanted to avoid a disruption of Mardi Gras that would keep tourists away. Still it is doubtful if Momus and Comus will parade in 1993 – or ever again. Nor will they be missed for long. Other krewes, more amenable to people of color and women, promptly applied for permits to fill open parade dates. Mardi Gras can celebrate, and even cause, change.

As Zulu became less dangerous and more governable, more a part of New Orleans' official culture, it lost some of its double-edged bite – a parade that was offensive to both black and white higher-ups even as it was a very popular amusement. Many African Americans disparaged the Zulus, feeling "they satirize their own race and do nothing to uplift it, and many critical Negroes are embarrassed by their antics" (Tallant 1948:239). Nowadays, the Zulus are "whiter," more peaceful, coopted and to a degree stripped of their parodic clarity. Instead of bootlegging an anticarnival into the heart of carnival, the Zulus – with some whites in blackface participating – now more or less collaborate in an elitist masquerade.

No counter current of any kind roils Tampa's Gasparilla Festival, started in 1904 and celebrated each February. Like Mardi Gras, Gasparilla is an end of winter event designed to attract tourists, and features masking, parading, the dispensing of cheap baubles, exclusive balls, and public drunkenness. The Festival honors a fictional pirate who many believe sailed the Gulf. The "Mystic Krewe of Gasparilla" is "an all-white, all-male organization, including some of the Tampa Bay area's most wealthy and influential lawyers, doctors, and businessmen" (Kenyon 1990:A8). The city's elite – among whom in 1990 were three former mayors, the publisher of the *Tampa Tribune*, the owner of the professional football team (appropriately named the Buccaneers), and George Steinbrenner – disguised as pirates, literally blast into town aboard a cannon-booming frigate towed through a harbor teeming with everything from yachts to rowboats (plate 3.16). Dockside, Tampa's mayor surrenders the city to the masqueraders in a redundant ceremony: these "pirates" already own Tampa. The underlying narrative of Gasparilla has hardly changed since the turn of the century.

> Disguised as Latin pirates, members of the Anglo establishment invaded the city, acting out violence that was as much a part of themselves as the pirates they played. However, as soon as they landed, the violence disappeared in two ways. The social violence vanished through an apparent redistribution of wealth, and the ethnic tensions faded away as the Anglo businessmen adopted Latin disguises. Through this dramatization of the very real violence that pitted the repressive Anglo establishment against restless Latin workers, the ritual celebration of Gasparilla became a fraternal festival that attempted to bridge the social and ethnic gap that split the city. . . . The ritual of the festival tried to open a safety valve to release the ethnic and social tensions in a city where the relations between the different classes and the different ethnic groups were marked by repressive violence in which a largely Anglo elite confronted mostly Latin and particularly militant workers. From its very origin, the festival had its roots in the establishment. (d'Ans 1980:25).

African Americans do not count at all in this equation, except as passive consumers. In both New Orleans and Tampa the white elite is fearful of surrendering its authority even for a day; and too stingy to distribute any goods or services of real value. In fact, Mardi Gras and Gasparilla serve the "business community" by milking money from ordinary folks, both locals and tourists, who pay by the drink for their participation in the festivals.

An "invented tradition" not at all shy about its consumerist obsession is Daytona Beach Spring Break Weekend.[16] Occurring at the calendrical cusp

Plate 3.16 Gasparilla's pirate ship is towed through Tampa harbor. (Photo: Fotobanc)

between winter and spring, taking over the streets at the point where rectangular motels meet an undulating beach and ocean. Encouraging drinking, carousing, sex, and public display, Spring Break Weekend has the narrative shape of carnival. The Daytona Beach celebration began in 1962 after 1961 riots made the college kids *non grata* in Fort Lauderdale. Actually, Lauderdale came back during the 1980s – in 1985, 300,000 high school and college youths descended on the beach resort. But the city went sour on its rowdy if heavy-spending visitors. 750 students were arrested in 1986 and 2,000 in 1987. That finished it for Fort Lauderdale, about which students rhymed, "Come on vacation, leave on probation." The action shifted 200 miles north to Daytona Beach. By the late 1980s, more than 400,000 students swarmed into Daytona each Spring Break, a tradition that continues into the 1990s. It may not be accidental that these immense gatherings of booze-happy white youth began in the early 1960s as an "innocent" copycat of the emerging, and politically dangerous (for the ruling class) mass demonstrations among blacks. Later, African American college kids devised their own Spring Break celebration in Virginia Beach.

In 1963, 65,000 students descended on Daytona. The event was described "by a motel owner as 'a wild, drunken orgy' " (Wright 1964:5). Fearing that the influx of so many orgiastic students would destroy Daytona's reputation as a "family resort," but not wanting to lose the college business, Daytona police chief A. O. Folsom wrote to all colleges with students likely to come south, warning of arrests. His list of "forbiddens" is a reliable index of what the students were doing:

> No drinking of intoxicating beverages on streets or sidewalks; no possession of alcoholic beverages by those under 21; no starting of fires on the beach or any other public property; no obscene or indecent markings or designs on private cars; no trespassing on private property without the consent of the owner; no littering of the beach or streets with beer cans or other rubbish; no camping on the beach; no use of profane or indecent language; and no destruction of private property.   (Wright 1964:5)

Daytona businesses offered the students "a free dance every night with two bands, plus twist contests, talent contests, bathing beauty contests, limbo contests, volley ball, basketball, touch football, tug-of-war, and other athletic events" (Wright 1964:5). By the late 1980s, with Fort Lauderdale off limits, Daytona was the place to go.

Sex, booze, and sun brings them south, but the narrative action of Spring

Break is compete and consume. Competition among brands for consumer dollars, the American way, is rearticulated as an endless series of contests. Twentieth Century Fox sponsored a "best buns" contest, Budweiser a "best male body" contest, DeKuyper peach schnapps a "DeKuyper's DeBody DeLight" contest, Hawaiian Tropic a "Miss Hawaiian Tropic" contest, Playboy Ujena a "summer wear bikini" contest, Caribe suntan lotion a "wet T-Shirt" contest – to name just some. "Students race to suck down three cans of Coors from a funnel, then compete to see who can vomit the most. 'This is just the preliminaries!' shouts the hotel's master of ceremonies as one contestant loses his breakfast all over the crowd" (Lipman 1989:8). Sex, excess, violence, and competition are linked.

> A beauteous vacationing co-ed was being asked to choose between three vacationing college men. Each of the three was instructed by an announcer [Mojo Nixon] to describe his philosophy of being in Florida on Spring Break. "I came, I saw, I kicked ass," said the third man. The co-ed selected him and they were sent off on their date. The announcer asked him to come back and report "every dirty detail."   (Greene 1988:29)

All events are sponsored by brand products. As an adman told a reporter, the idea is to "blanket the hotel–bar complex" with brand images (like the B-52 "blanket bombing" of Vietnam or Iraq?). The dozens of companies competing for attention included Southern Comfort liquor, Columbia Pictures, and Rubber Ducky condoms. Miller beer offered free phone calls home, movies, and T-shirts in return for Miller cans to be recycled. Doritos handed out more than 30,000 1-ounce bags of chips.

> Dozens of banners for Caribe suntan lotion, Roffler hair products and other products are strewn from the balconies, a two-story inflatable Simpatico beer bottle sits near the pool, a giant inflatable Spuds MacKenzie [Budweiser beer mascot] watches over outdoor beer kegs, and hot balloons emblazoned with "Plymouth Sundance" [car] and "Karate Kid II" [movie] are anchored nearby.
> (Lipman 1989:B1)

> In a half-mile stretch along the beach are volleyball games sponsored by Pontiac, Diet Pepsi, Coppertone, Coors Light, and Plymouth. The skies drone with airplanes pulling ads, and the beach – on which cars are allowed – is a parade of mobile billboards.   (Lipman 1989:B7)

As one company executive told a reporter from the *Wall Street Journal*, "We're not down here for sales, we're down here for image" (Lipman 1989:B7).

This executive said college-age youths are "brand conscious but not yet brand loyal." Spring Break is the time to excite them, inebriate them with sex and alcohol, while burning brand names into their minds. The banners in Tiananmen Square in 1989 and the costumes of King Zulu and his court in the 1940s were made by participants. But in Daytona, banners, T-shirts, inflatables – whatever is on display – are made elsewhere by others. The students are there only to receive, like cattle to be branded. But do the kids listen? "The market has become so cluttered in Daytona that every last casual beach volleyball game, every raunchy hot-body contest, has a corporate sponsor" (Lipman 1989:B1). One student told Lipman, "You don't even notice it because it's everywhere you look." But the sponsors obviously think otherwise. To them it's worth the money. It doesn't even matter that the students remember which brand. The important thing is to learn that the only things worth owning are brand products. Spring Break is a capitalist carnival initiating and training young upscale Americans in their lifelong roles as consumers.

The scenography of Spring Break serves its capitalist carnival function well. The Daytona police make sure that the revels are confined to "the strip" – beachfront motels, the streets immediately adjoining them, and the beach itself. The revels are thus squeezed into a thin, easily managed strip. There are no plazas or public squares available to the Daytona Beach celebrants. The crowds are elongated, not allowed to mass in big circular groups as they did in Tiananmen Square, Washington, Leipzig, or Berlin. The shape, if not the flow, of a parade is maintained. And parades – long thin lines – are easy to police and control. Also the beach itself and the strip of airspace above – long billboards – are well suited to saturate the youths with brand name messages.

The scenography and choreography of what I call "public direct theatre" vary according to whether official culture or rebellious, even revolutionary, counterforces are on the move. Official culture likes its street displays to be orderly, arranged in longitudinal rectangles moving in one direction, and proceeding from a known beginning to a known end in time as well as space. Soldiers, big weapons, citizens, and nubile cheerleaders all moving to band music and passing below a reviewing stand is the perfect example of this celebration of official culture. Countless parades around the world conform to this type. Sometimes, as in Macy's Thanksgiving Day Parade, Pasadena's Parade of the Roses, or other civic and ethnic marches, the military do not participate. But the band music and the style of marching, as well as the sheer size of the floats and inflatables, disclose the militant narrative behind the glitz and flowers. The scheduled Mardi Gras and Gasparilla parades and the Ramlila processions are a little different. They move along fixed, known routes in a rectangular fashion. But they are looser in form and include audience interaction and participation. Here official culture smiles as it asks ordinary people to confirm the existing power structure. Religious devotion characterizes Ramlila. The dispensing of fake jewels in Mardi Gras and Gasparilla is a charade of the rich distributing their wealth. It's amazing that such empty gestures are accepted. Daytona Beach Spring Break is not a parade as such, yet its squeeze along the strip and the plethora of contests and visual advertisements give it the longitudinal shape and image overload of a parade. In addition to spatial restraints, all of the above have set time frames. Ash Wednesday is a strict master, as are the resumption of classes after Spring Break and the phases of the moon that govern Ramlila. Big parades occur on holidays such as Thanksgiving or New Year's Day or days marking important dates in the history of the state. Sometimes, as in New York's Halloween parade in its early days or in the Zulu parade before 1970, meandering and creative chaos are more obvious than timetables or close accountability regarding exactly where the event goes. Zulu's freedom, however, was restricted to African American neighborhoods; its critique of official culture had to masquerade as a self-deprecating black-on-black parody.

In "direct theatre" large public spaces are transformed into theatres where collective reflexivity is performed, and fecund and spectacular excesses displayed. Parades, mass gatherings, street theatre, sex, and partying – everything is exaggerated, ritualized, done for show. Masquerading encourages experimenting with behavior, identity slippage, and acting as if one were someone else. Rulers are either exalted as at Mardi Gras, Gasparilla, and Ramlila or challenged as in America and China or overthrown as in Eastern Europe. The difference between temporary and permanent change distinguishes carnival from revolution. In Eastern Europe, China, and America there was a critique of social, political, and economic relations "from below," from the perspective of those who do not hold power – that is, from the perspective of everyday life. There is no critique from below in Mardi Gras and Gasparilla, where the Lords of Misrule are actually the cities' elite. Ramlila is more complex. Worshipped as gods, the boys are at other times ordinary people, while the maharaja who witnesses and authorizes their sacred performance is a former king who, for the month of the festival, annually acts out his fully recollected royalty.

Official culture wants its festivals to be entertaining. Mardi Gras, Gasparilla, and Spring Break are dizzying, drunk, disorderly, and mystifying. Mystifying because they present official authorities as fairy tale royalty, buffoons, clowns, pirates, laughing dispensers of free goods, and benign corporate sponsors of drunken erotic contests. The elite, enjoying their thin disguises, entertain a submissive and grateful population. It's the old "bread and circuses" trick. Mardi Gras attracts street performers to downtown New Orleans as well as thousands of ordinary people who take to the streets in masks and costumes. Much Spring Break entertainment is provided by the students themselves as contest participants or partyers, wearing T-shirts and hats provided by big-time sponsors. Contrastingly, displays such as Macy's Thanksgiving Parade, the Pasadena Parade of the Roses, or New Delhi's Republic Day Parade keep the spectators separated from the entertainers. Police manage the onlookers and no one marches who isn't licensed. Still, people have fun. Less so for mass turnouts such as those in Moscow's Red Square marking the anniversary of the Russian Revolution. For this kind of thing, marchers and spectators alike are recruited and choreographed. For whom are these displays staged? Since the development of television, the audiences are whomever mass media can reach, including the leaders of opposing nations. But there is another audience, too, those on the reviewing stands. The arrogance of the leaders looking down from reviewing stands is matched only by their insecurity (both actual and imagined). They need reassurance of their popularity and invincibility. Each salute given and returned, each tank rolling by as part of neat and obedient phalanxes, warms the hearts of these leaders, democrats and despots alike.

When entertainment is really free, when it gets out of hand, when there is no fixed calendrical conclusion to the celebration, then the authorities get nervous. Such festivals reverberate through the population in unforeseen ways. People in Beijing and around China thrilled to the whorling choreography of the students in Tiananmen Square, just as people throughout Eastern Europe took their cues from what was happening at the Berlin Wall. At these times, official leadership is no longer the focus of attention, no longer in control of the means of producing or controlling public celebrations. The power to produce public fun passes into the hands of new leaders, often ordinary people. The single-focus reviewing stand gives way to many diverse pockets of participation and leadership. Instead of prepackaged "media opportunities," not even the leaders themselves are sure of what's happening. Still, events take a theatrical turn. Effigies appear, as do homemade banners and posters; street theatre flourishes, soap box orators draw cheering crowds. Official leaders are cut down to size. If they show up, they run the risk of being mocked or chased away as Zhou, Nixon, and members of the GDR Politburo were. Official entertainment provides scripted fun contained within ritual frames, while unofficial festivity re-writes ritual, dissolving restrictive frames. When rituals are restaged as carnivals, the activity in the streets grows more free-flowing and loose, unpredictable in its outcome, if clear in its desires: to change the basis of social relations and/or state organization. On these occasions, the efficacious function of ritual is reassigned to entertainment.

The May 1970 Washington antiwar protest and the 1989 Tiananmen Square movement were enactments of the kind of society the students wanted to come into being. In America there was the feeling that anger and revulsion at the Kent State killings and the bombing of Cambodia had turned the tide of American public opinion against the Vietnam War. And with the end of the war would come a general restructuring. In China, the relative liberalism of Deng's regime seemed to open the way to big, funda-mental changes. Many believed these festival theatres were in fact what they could not become – rehearsals of the near future. The American big chill and the dispirited Chinese I talked to in Shanghai in August 1990 (see Schechner 1991) reconfirmed this interpretation. After millenary hopes are dashed, people furl their banners, hunker down, and ride out history.

The popular street carnival–demonstration is actually a utopian mimesis whose focused, idealized, heated, magnified, and transparent clarity of consciousness dissolves once the show is over. But those involved in a festival of political desire too often deceive themselves into believing their utopian show will run forever. It is not only the tanks of Deng Xiaoping which enviously and with terrible clarity destroy the fun, but the only slightly longer process, when the revolution is successful, of postrevolution-ary jockeying for power. This decay of festival into "dirty politics," the inevitable end to spontaneous communitas, is what the Chinese students now underground or in exile have learned, a lesson most American radicals of the 1960s and 1970s never studied. The carnival, more strongly than other forms of theatre, can act out a powerful critique of the status quo, but it cannot itself be what replaces the status quo. For the modern world, this much was made clear by Robespierre: the carnival indefinitely in power is the Terror.

Ramlila, Mardi Gras, Gasparilla, and Spring Break are in many ways "classic" carnivals. As such, they exhibit little structural antipathy between ruler and ruled. What inversions occur happen in an expected way. Disruptions have the quality of riot or individual expression rather than revolution. That is not to deny underlying hatreds and social contradictions laid bare on these occasions. But there is no chance that Mardi Gras, Gasparilla, or Spring Break will suddenly transmute into a revolution on a par with the Chinese democracy movement or what happened in Germany. In Ramlila, one feels the opposite of social tension. For the month of Ramraj (King Rama's just reign), modern India's terrible disjunctions of caste, religion, and class are suspended. Although the staging of all these direct theatres is similar, their narratives are different. Those taking to the streets in a classic or modern festival know beforehand they have only too short a time to enjoy extraordinary liberties. The idea is to squeeze as much pleasure as possible from a brief time and a well-defined space. Oppositely, the pleasures of the revolutionary carnival derive from its existence as an antiofficial event, and the illusory but very strong desire to extend, into as long a time and as big a space as possible, liberties taken.

Revolutionary street actions are not predictable because there are at least two desired outcomes, one or more sought by the people taking to the streets, the other by the authorities. It is not that Ramlila, Mardi Gras, Gasparilla, Spring Break and other classic carnivals are devoid of political content, but that this content is unitary rather than dialectical. Ramlila affirms north Indian Hinduism and nationhood. Mardi Gras celebrates the absorption of New Orleans Catholicism into American capitalism. The divisions and conflicts played out in classic carnivals are ritually necessary, temporary disruptions of an underlying unity. But the 1989 events in China and Germany, and the 1970 protest in Washington, did not follow fixed scripts, even if particular details of behavior – waving banners, marches, face-offs with the military, moments of rehearsed guerrilla theatre – were predictable. Such predictable molecules of action give to direct theatre a ritual quality, the feel of a "destiny" being played out. But revolutionary street actions are rare examples of history in its molten state; things really would be different in China if Deng and Li were overthrown or in America if the Nixon presidency, and the power of those sustaining Nixon, had ended in 1970. The 1989 action in the streets of Berlin, Leipzig, Prague, and Budapest – with a climactic finale in Moscow in August 1991 – has made a difference.

When I call such events "direct theatre" I am not using the word "theatre" metaphorically. The audiences for direct theatre are several, consisting of the participants themselves, journalists, especially TV reporters, the mass spectatorship TV enjoys, and high-level decision-makers watching in their offices or bunkers. These high-level spectators are forced to participate in direct theatre for fear of missing the worldwide audience TV gets to. Either they go to where the action is – as Nixon and Zhou did – or they stage their own shows as Saddam Hussein did during the 1990–1 Gulf War. The dramaturgy is further complicated by the fact that the TV apparatus is far from neutral. The medium asks for news to be "made" not "found." And in many places, the same commercial sponsors who underwrite Spring Break feed money to TV. This means that all programs – news, as well as sports, dramas, sitcoms, talk, and game shows – are actually profit-making entertainments. TV stations are owned or controlled by various corporations with interests allied to those making high-level economic and political decisions. Nor is TV news made – as movies are – to be kept and reshown long after the events it records are over. TV news is a multilayered throwaway flow of images and words received in homes, bars, hotels, community centers, and offices. TV news combines on-the-spot action with sophisticated editing and framing procedures to make a narrativized, ritualized, short-take product (see "News, sex, and performance theory" in Schechner 1985).

The direct theatre is itself a reflexive first theatre, or raw material, for a near-universally displayed second theatre, the television newscast which includes (often improvised) responses to the first theatre. This direct theatre is reflexive insofar as it is produced for the TV cameras and designed to force a response. Events are immediate (being there), mediated (taking place on the TV screen), and responsive (reactions to what happens on the screen). Used this way, TV is hot, interactive. The millions of screens function as a collective forum (though not a free forum). Criticism of the direct theatre is provided not by aestheticians but by "pundits" who summarize and explain. Political direct theatre is different from neocarnival direct theatre such as Mardi Gras, Gasparilla, or Spring Break. These have been drained of political content, while the made-for-television (or at least highly "media aware") direct theatre is mainly political. Or, to put it in a slightly different way, the politics of Mardi Gras and Spring Break are hidden and static, conservative and supportive of the status quo. Therefore, there is no "news" coming from them except a feature story buried near the end of a telecast; or, if the celebration gets out of hand, an account of rioting answered by the police. The theme is that social order will be, must be, restored; the causes of the "disturbance" will be "looked into" so that the disruption is not repeated next year. On the other hand, the politics of the direct theatre of Eastern Europe or China is to challenge the status quo, to overthrow or change the state.

Turner treated what he called "social drama" as a more or less unconscious process – a "natural" or ahistorical way of resolving social disputes. But the political direct theatre is consciously devised. Scenarists–organizers know they are staging events in terms of a clear narrative progressing from confrontation through climax to resolution. In their stagings they knowingly, and sometimes ironically, manipulate powerful intercultural symbols such as the Chinese students' Goddess of Democracy or their show of the "V" sign. They invade places of power and/or symbolism such as Tiananmen Square, the Berlin Wall in front of the Brandenburg Gate, and the White House, Lincoln Memorial, or Pentagon. Deployments in such places force a dialectical–theatrical split into protagonists and antagonists. Political direct theatre is carnivalesque in that the struggle – at certain key moments – is an exposure of what is wrong with the way things are and an acting out of the desired hoped-for new social relations. It's war, all right, but also fun (what Turner called "spontaneous communitas"): a dreamed-of utopian "state" in both senses of the word.[17] Events are synecdochic and transparent: issues are debated, symbols paraded, agonists put square in the public eye. People – both present and viewing on TV – have to decide which side to be on.

This direct theatre is always staged as, or ends in, swirls, vortexes of activities, people in self-expressive dress or undress, moving in spirals and circles without easy to locate centers or heads. Multivocal and multifocus, a popular deconstructing of hierarchy, the enacting of small-scale dramas and guerrilla theatre events, characterize direct theatre. The eyes to which this theatre appeals are the roving multiple eyes of many cameras simultaneously ingesting images. Contrastingly, the street displays of official culture parade or line up in neat rectangles, uniformly garbed, carrying identical or coordinated posters, banners, and weapons. Everything and everyone is hierarchically subordinate to the single eye of the reviewing stand. When armed troops arrive, the intense whorling of direct theatre stops. People slip toward hiding, prepare for guerrilla war, or reform as lines with only the bravest standing against the guns (plate 3.17). If armed forces open fire, ordinary people scatter.

The direct theatre in Tiananmen Square, at the Berlin Wall, or in Washington exemplifies Brechtian theory and the practices of Augusto

Plate 3.17 Student anti-war protesters confronting armed troops at the steps of the Pentagon in October 1967. (Photo: unattributed)

Boal.[18] The direct theatre is not "about" something so much as it is made "of" something. It is actual + symbolic rather than referential/representational. Hunger-striking Chinese camped out in Tiananmen Square, Germans climbing on or chipping away at the Wall, or young Americans frolicking in the Lincoln Memorial Reflecting Pool are performing more than naked actions. But their symbolic deeds are not imitations played by named characters who exist within copyrighted fictional narratives authored by individuals. Real people – from anonymous players to Wuer Kaixi, Zhao Ziyang, the East German Politburo, Berliners, Abbie Hoffman, Mark Rudd – play their roles in public, pursuing not only Stanislavskian objectives and through lines of action, but also historical dialectics.

Television produces and reproduces this popular drama, showing over and over again specific highly theatrical bits (or bytes), what Brecht would call *gests*, creating both a *verfremdungseffekt* and a ritual effect. The layering of contending historifications begins with on-the-spot reporters interviewing participants, ordinary people as well as leaders. Many of these "spontaneous" interviews are setups. The material is then laundered by various interpretations and editings – "spin controls" (on all sides): rebel and government spokespersons, TV commentators, academic experts. Participants and viewers alike are told what's going on, how to relate to it, and what the future holds. The ultimate layers are hidden from public view, taking place in editing rooms and government or corporate headquarters. This editing process ensures that what's broadcast conforms to the policies of whoever owns/controls the TV apparatus. TV news gives the impression of – a performance of – "multivocality." But, just as aesthetic dramas project many voices (deployed as characters) originating from a single voice, the playwright's, so TV works in the opposite direction toward an identical end, knitting together many voices into a unitary broadcast fabric. The finished TV broadcast differs according to which culture's channels a person tunes into. Of course, some direct theatre doesn't need all this interpreting. Those with low impact on global politics, such as Gasparilla, Mardi Gras, Spring Break, and Ramlila remain more or less localized within their own parochial traditions.

Notes

1. Vice-President Agnew uttered these words in a speech before the Young Presidents Organization in Honolulu. In 1973 he was forced to resign as vice-president because of corruption and bribe-taking while holding office in Maryland where in the 1960s he was Baltimore County executive and governor. His Honolulu speech is quoted in Baxandall 1969:52.
2. Bristol is echoing ideas first enunciated early in the twentieth century by Arnold Van Gennep 1908 and Emile Durkheim 1915. See also Victor Turner 1967, 1969, 1974, 1977, 1982, and 1983 for his emendations to Van Gennep and Durkheim as well as his own theories regarding liminality, the ritual process, and antistructure.
3. See Chapter 7 of this book for a discussion of the relation between Girard's ideas and theatre.
4. See Turner 1977, 1982, and 1990 for distinctions between the liminal and the liminoid.
5. See Schechner 1989a and 1991.
6. The Free Speech Movement (FSM) emerged in 1964 on the Berkeley campus of the University of California. It was a radical political movement, a carnivalesque display, an alternative lifestyle, and an attack on white middle-class values. The actions of the FSM served as a model for any number of student rebellions during the 1960s and early 1970s. An insider's account is given in Jerry Rubin's

Do It! (1970). Rubin begins one of his short essays, "Revolution is theatre-in-the-streets" (132–43), this way: "You are the stage. You are the actor. Everything is for real. There is no audience." Abbie Hoffman understood very well the potential of the media linked to mass demonstrations as operators of radical action.

7. For a more detailed exposition of Hoffman's views see his: *Revolution for the Hell of It* (1968), *Woodstock Nation* (1969a), and *Steal This Book* (1971), as well as his testimony as one of the "Chicago 7" in *The Tales of Hoffman* (1970), edited by Levine *et al.*

8. The term "guerrilla theatre," adapted from "guerrilla warfare" (especially the styles practiced by Che Guevara and the Vietcong), was first enunciated in print by R. G. Davis (1966), who said he got the term from San Francisco Mime Troupe member and playwright, Peter Berg. Davis, elaborating on Brecht's ideas, said the theatre must "teach, direct toward change, be an example of change" (1966:131). He suggested that universities would be good home bases for guerrilla theatre; and that techniques drawn from *commedia dell'arte* were well suited to the hit-and-run style of guerrilla theatre. Over time, guerrilla theatre came to mean short, political theatre pieces happening suddenly in public spaces that often were felt to be "enemy territory." For more on guerrilla theatre, including scenarios and scripts, see Schechner 1969, Baxandall 1969, Lesnick 1973, and Weisman 1973.

9. "Yippie" is from the acronym for Youth International Party (YIP) founded by Rubin, Hoffman, and others. YIP never was intended as a "serious" political party but as a gadfly. Yippie is taken from "Hippie," what the "flower children" of the 1960s, inhabitants of the Haight–Ashbury section of San Francisco, were called or called themselves. Hippie was soon applied to many of the "turn on, tune in, and drop out" generation of American youth. Hippie is a diminutive of "hip," or "hep," a word from the world of jazz (or crime) first used in the 1910s by African Americans but adopted/adapted by the Beat Generation writers of the 1950s and meaning someone "in the know." All these terms connote alternative lifestyles. The 1980s adaptation, "yuppie" – a "young upwardly mobile person" – is a parody of the earlier terms, signaling the very opposite in social status.

10. The trial began with the government charging eight persons with "crossing state lines with intent to incite riot" and once in Chicago with rioting. The eight were David T. Dellinger, Rennie Davis, Tom Hayden, Abbie Hoffman, Jerry Rubin, Lee Wiener, John Froines, and Bobby Seale. Seale, bound and gagged during part of the trial, was severed from the others and tried later. The jury acquitted two defendants on all charges and all defendants on the conspiracy charge. All, including the defense lawyers, were given heavy sentences for contempt of court. I believe that all the penalties were set aside on appeal. The behavior of Judge Julius J. Hoffman was severely criticized as strongly biased against the defen-

dants. But, as Dwight MacDonald wrote in his introduction to *The Tales of Hoffman*, a selection from the trial's transcripts, "If the defendants were out to show up American bourgeois justice, as they were, Judge Hoffman aided and abetted them beyond their fondest, most alienated dreams of revolutionary glory" (Levine *et al.* 1970:xi). For another account of what happened in Chicago at the Convention, see Rubin 1970.

11. Woodstock Nation was Hoffman's term for the youth culture whose most massive manifestation was the August 1969 two-day rock festival held in Woodstock, New York. Woodstock Nation broadcast two images of itself: that of peace-loving, nonviolent, loving youth, and Rubin's hyperbolic:

> And we were motherfucking bad. We were dirty, smelly, grimy, foul, loud, dope-crazed, hell-bent and leather-jacketed. We were a public display of filth and shabbiness, living-in-the-flesh rejects of middle-class standards. . . . We were the outlaw forces of Amerika [sic] displaying ourselves flagrantly on a world stage. (1970:169)

Both images, benign and outrageous, are smack in the middle of the avant-garde–bohemian tradition.

12. The statistics and anecdotes are taken from McFadden 1989. See also Peter Clay Schmidt's 1990 video, *The Fall of the Berlin Wall*.

13. A "domino effect" swept through the world from China in May 1989, Germany in August, and then to Czechoslovakia, Romania, the USSR, Albania, Yugoslavia, and South Africa. Although extremely disparate at one level, the demands in all these places were similar at the level of wanting more representation within, or independence from central authorities.

14. Berlin Wall chunks soon found their way into the "collectibles" market. Americans sent away for "genuine" fragments of the Wall, mounted and placarded. Of course, who was to say if the chunk of concrete someone paid $50 for was really from the Wall? Do you think the distributor, faced with a shortage of Wall amidst a frenzy of money, would hesitate to "simulate" a little piece of the Wall? Would this simulation, should it have occurred, be considered forgery or theatre or both?

15. All quoted examples of celebrating are taken from accounts reported in *The New York Times* on 10, 11, and 12 November 1989.

16. See Hobsbawm and Ranger 1983 and "Restoration of behavior" in Schechner 1985.

17. See Turner 1969:94–164 for a discussion of liminality and "spontaneous communitas" – the feeling of unbounded fellowship characteristic of carnival as well as of certain religious, political, and millenarian movements at the moment of their annunciation. Some of Turner's theory is based on his opinions about the hippies.

For the hippies – as indeed for many millenarian and "enthusiastic" movements – the ecstasy of spontaneous communitas is seen as *the* end of human endeavor. . . . Spontaneous communitas has something "magical" about it. Subjectively there is in it the feeling of endless power. But this power untransformed cannot readily be applied to the organizational details of social existence. . . . Spontaneous communitas is a phase, a moment, not a permanent condition. (1969:138–40)

18. For more on Boal's "theatre of the oppressed" – a post-Brecht anti-Aristotelian theatre that directly involves the community and is designed both for consciousness-raising and direct action, see Boal 1980, 1983, 1985, 1990a, 1990b, 1990c, and 1992; and Cohen-Cruz 1990, Cohen-Cruz and Schutzman 1990, Schutzman 1990, and Taussig and Schechner 1990.

4

Waehma: space, time, identity, and theatre at New Pascua, Arizona[1]

Yaqui spaces, Yaqui identities

Pascua Pueblo (New Pascua) is southwest of Tucson in the Arizona desert, not far from the airport. Soon after turning south off Valencia Road on to Camino del Oeste, one enters the Yaqui reservation of 998 acres. The reservation was only 220 acres in 1978 when Public Law 95–375 granted "the Pascua Yaqui Tribe of Arizona the same status as all other federally recognized Indian tribes in the US" (Pascua Tribal Council 1985a). The adjoining Tohono O'odham (Papago) San Xavier reservation is 71,095 acres, the larger Sells Tohono O'odham reservation is 2,774,536 acres, while Navaho reservation is 10,847,291 acres. Organized around a central plaza defined by the eastward-facing, wide-doored, low church (plate 4.1) and the southward-facing fiesta ramada, New Pascua consists of single story free-standing homes of concrete, brick, cinder block, and/or adobe plus administrative buildings, firehouse, school, a senior citizens' center, and playground. Facing Camino del Oeste, away from the plaza, is a large bingo hall where the Yaquis, free from state laws regulating gambling, offer big jackpots in an effort to earn the dollars of gringo gamblers.

Walking the streets of New Pascua in the 1980s I felt the tribe's sense of pride and accomplishment in winning their own reservation. Their homeland has always been important to the Yaquis, as the wars fought against Spanish and Mexican encroachment testify. Although Pascua Pueblo is not in the Rio Yaqui area of northwest Mexico, the "real" homeland, it represents an achievement in its own right, a piece of turf that belongs exclusively to the tribe (figure 4.1). In their own view, the Yaquis have never been conquered. Even after the terrible genocidal diaspora of the nineteenth century – when many Yaquis were deported as peons to Yucatan while others fled into the mountains of Sonora and still others slipped across the

Plate 4.1 A Deer dancer and singer cross in front of the Yaqui Catholic church in New Pascua as seen from the east end of the plaza in November 1981. (Photo: Richard Schechner)

Note: The Pascua Pueblo Yaquis do not want Waehma photographed. They do not want their religion to be made a spectacle of. They do want their guests involved, not peering from behind lenses. At the same time, the readers need to see what Waehma looks like. All but one of the photos published here have already been published elsewhere; the exception (plate 4.1) I took on a nonceremonial occasion with permission of the Yaquis. All photos but that one are not of Pascua Pueblo. But there is a close similarity among the Yaqui communities regarding the practices of Waehma.

border into Arizona – the Yaquis were able to regather into communities and begin once again to stage their Lenten cycle drama, the *Waehma* (from the Spanish, *Cuaresma*). At the height of the dispersion, there was a hiatus of twenty or so years, from 1886 to 1906, when no Waehma was fully performed anywhere (E. Spicer 1974:313). During this time individual Yaquis carried the scenario in their heads. Thus when the Yaquis were able to restore their Easter cycle, they could consciously choose what to include, drop, or modify.

During the diaspora and until today, the Yaqui struggle to remain Yaqui expresses itself most clearly in their need to perform Waehma. Quite

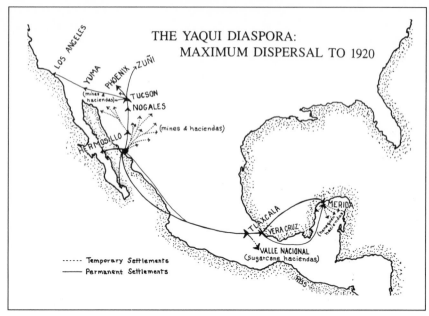

THE YAQUI DIASPORA:
MAXIMUM DISPERSAL TO 1920

----- Temporary Settlements
——— Permanent Settlements

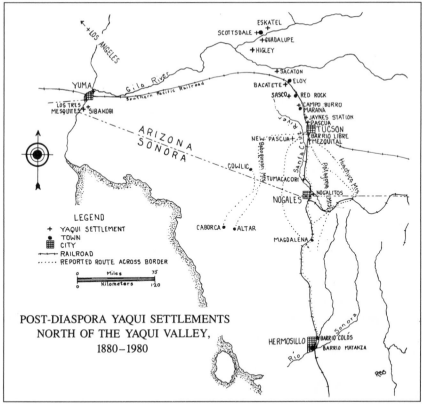

POST-DIASPORA YAQUI SETTLEMENTS
NORTH OF THE YAQUI VALLEY,
1880–1980

LEGEND
+ YAQUI SETTLEMENT
TOWN
CITY
RAILROAD
REPORTED ROUTE ACROSS BORDER

Figure 4.1 Yaqui diaspora and postdiaspora settlements north of the Rio Yaqui Valley, 1880–1980. (Maps drawn by Rosamond B. Spicer, courtesy of University of Arizona Press)

literally, the scattered body-politic of the Yaquis is unified during this season when individuals return to their communities to fulfill their ritual obligations; the inhabitants of each community know that their fellow Yaquis in all other Yaqui communities in Mexico and the USA will also be performing the same actions on the same days with the same fullness of devotion. The spatial motifs of these performances are very particular: written into the theatrical-religious geography of the performance is a model of Yaqui history and experience as modern Yaquis have restored it. Studying accounts of the Waehma in different settlements and in different years makes it clear that Waehma is performed with great consistency and attention to detail. The cycle's dynamic landscape – for Waehma is a drama of interpenetrating and interacting spaces – is so characteristic that I would say it is what makes Yaquis Yaqui.

Once settled in Arizona some Yaquis named or accepted the name of "Pascua" for two of their settlements. Pascua means Easter – and to the Yaquis Easter means Waehma. The Yaquis are masters at appropriating what has been imposed: Catholicism, Spanish and English languages, towns organized around a church and its plaza, even diaspora. Certain key words, spatial arrangements, and actions evidence how the Yaquis of Pascua Pueblo (and other Yaqui communities) negotiate the complex, dynamic, living relationships among native American, Catholic, Spanish, Mexican, and US cultures that repeatedly, and with shifting emphasis, play themselves out during Waehma. Many of the key words used in Waehma are Yaqui transliterations of Spanish, but this does not make these terms – or the actions they index – any less Yaqui than the French words absorbed into English after the Norman Conquest of the eleventh century are less English.[2]

The spatial feel of the residential area of New Pascua is that of an "ordinary" American subdivision, *sans* general purpose shopping area. But this ordinariness is deceptive. To a New Yorker, at least, the physical setting of New Pascua is both cruel and beautiful, and very unlike Tucson neighborhoods which green out the desert or obliterate it with commercial bustle. New Pascua is set down in the Sonora desert, open to the sun and wind. The pueblo's Yaquiness is mostly expressed not by its homes but by its church, its ramada, and its plaza. During the Easter season the dawn sun breaks across the rim of the hills and sends its flat, warm rays streaming on to the church's dirt floor. But this very Yaquiness is a version or transformation of what was imposed: in the early seventeenth century the Jesuits brought a religion needing church buildings, and the churches needed plazas, and the plazas needed and created eight towns along the Rio Yaqui. Whether or not the ramada – a roofed, three-sided space – was pre-Spanish or not remains an open question.

The Yaquis responded to the Jesuits' impositions by interiorizing pre-Spanish spaces: the *huya aniya, yo aniya*, and *seya wailo*, "wild" or "magic" places. During Waehma – which developed its present dramaturgy during the 150 years when the Yaquis had minimal contact with Europeans or Mexicans – the huya aniya, yo aniya, and seya wailo are manifest in public places of display; they are manifest especially in the interplay among Chapayekam, Pascolas, and Deer dancers. The actions of these beings undermines the Europeanness of the church–plaza–town. What is European occupies a middle ground between the "natural"/"supernatural" Yaqui desert–mountains–huya aniya and the individual yet shared interiority that is the ultimate free space of Yaquihood. This three-way tension between "beyond," "middle ground," and "shared interiority" is complex because its reference points shift, depending on what is taken as the middle ground. The *Loria Vo'o* (the Glory Road, a wide L-shaped path from the church to the ramada) is middle, while the headquarters of the *Kohtumbre Ya'ura* (the Customs Authority, those responsible for Waehma) on the north side of the church is beyond; the area enclosed by the *Konti Vo'o* (Way of the Cross) is middle, while the town is beyond; the town is middle, while the desert is beyond; the human world is middle, while the huya aniya is beyond. The middle spaces are locations of public ritual displaying but not resolving tensions between non-Yaqui and Yaqui ways and beliefs. Many individual Yaquis are capable of holding in their minds this whole scheme: the proof of the durability of this scenography is the completeness of the Waehma drama when it was restored after the twenty-year hiatus. Waehma is multiplex, dynamically interweaving by means of theatre this triple interaction among interior, public, and beyond – a beyond which folds back into the consciousness of each Yaqui who practices Waehma. Thus, the core subtext of Waehma – its overt text being the Passion – is working through how to be simultaneously Yaqui and Catholic. Since the seventeenth century that has been the major problem of Yaqui history.

Of course, questions of turf and identity can be stated as tensions between native–indigenous versus imported–imposed. Syncretism, or how effectively (consciously or not) Yaquis appropriated those very actions they could not avoid accepting, is central to any discourse concerning the Yaquis. Over the years, the Yaquis have claimed as their own Catholic practices both liturgical and theatrical; they have both welcomed and resisted the curiosity of anthropologists and tourists. When, during the 1981 meetings on Yaqui performance,[3] an anthropologist spoke eloquently about how "the most precious thing that human beings have developed is their cultural difference" and asked, "How can we protect this earth's treasure, this wealth of human creations?" (Wenner-Gren 1981:10), Anselmo Valencia, head of New Pascua's Kohtumbre Ya'ura, answered:

> The first impulse in answering the anthropological question of "what can we do to help" of any Yaqui is, "Leave us alone and let us do our thing and we will continue." I'm not going to say that because I myself in some way or another am leaning towards the methods of anthropology because I'm asking, I'm always asking, Why are we doing this and this? The preservation of cultures, of the Indian cultures, really belongs to the Indian.   (Wenner-Gren 1981:10)

Valencia stated that "we have rescinded the questioning [by anthropologists] because we did not understand what anthropology means. . . . And if it was explained, it was not done very well" (Wenner-Gren 1981:13).

While working in New Pascua I felt both welcomed and a bit out of place. I adjusted by accepting my position as an outsider. I watched, but very rarely asked questions. I sat in the church, ate snacks at the foodstalls, and spent many hours of good silence letting events speak in their own ways. Where I felt no resistance, I entered the ceremonies as in the Judas procession on Holy Saturday morning. In 1982, when my son Sam was almost 5 years old, a Yaqui trimmed a cottonwood switch for him and he slept Good Friday night on the church floor with the Little Angels. But he was not among their ranks on Holy Saturday. The Yaqui concern for protecting themselves even from the manifestly sympathetic attention of outsiders must be understood in spatial terms: not only *who* the Yaquis are, but *where* are they? And where does an outsider stand in relation to them?

In Pascua Pueblo the signs are literally very clear. Rules disallowing cameras and tape recorders are posted. "Again, we welcome you to our sacred religious ceremonies this year," said a flyer printed in English by the Pascua Tribal Council for the 1982 Holy Week events. "We trust you will honor our people's wishes that no photographs be taken nor otherwise engage in any act disrespectful of our religion and our cultural way of life." I witnessed an example of these determinations of Yaqui ground firsthand on Good Friday 1987. Shortly after the Crucifixion, during a midday break in the action, a station wagon backed up to the east edge of the plaza. A woman got out, and then a man. They opened the back hatch of the station wagon and began to unload a tripod and what looked like a movie camera. Near the foodstalls next to the Kohtumbre Ya'ura headquarters a few men stood drinking Pepsis. It was hot; there was little movement around town. A few *Chapayekam* (masked *Pariseom*, Yaqui for Pharisees), were slumbering next to the church. But eyes were turned on the station wagon, the film equipment. It wasn't long before Anselmo Valencia went to the station wagon. I didn't hear what he said to the woman. He looked down at the ground a lot, poked the dry dust with his boot-tip. After about two minutes the man loaded the camera and tripod back in the station wagon, and off went woman, man, camera, and car. People were watching – their attention focused on the interaction – but in a Yaqui way: indirectly, a glancing, side-striking intensity.

By contrast, the Gloria of Holy Saturday is a regular theatrical event, where large crowds sit on blankets or deck chairs munching snacks, armed with confetti to throw on the villains of the day, the Pariseom. In Old Pascua a grandstand accommodates Gloria's urgent specularity. But other key Holy Week Waehma events – Tenebrae (performed in illumination that goes from dim to totally dark), the pursuit of the *Viejito* (the little old man), the capturing of Jesus at Gethsemane, the Crucifixion, the midnight procession marking the Resurrection, the Chapayeka fiesta of Good Friday night – do not attract outsiders and are not watched as theatre even by residents of New Pascua. On two occasions – the pursuit of the Viejito and the procession to a house in the pueblo to fetch Jesus' bier – a young Pariseo was dispatched by Kohtumbre Ya'ura leaders to tell me I should not follow. If I was to watch at all, I needed to keep my distance. Besides myself, the only visible spectators of these activities were one anthropologist and a few young kids. The often funny antics of the Chapayeka fiesta attracted only a handful of people, mostly men, who stood by the foodstalls occasionally smiling or chuckling almost privately. Usually, throughout the hours of day and often through most of the night, there were a few women and some men sitting on folding chairs near the church entrance. These people could hardly be called spectators by Western standards. To an untrained outsider it might appear as if Waehma's events go by unobserved, but they are carefully taken notice of, from the side, Yaqui-style. This way of spectating establishes a key spatial–rhythmic pattern of Waehma, a pattern of individuality and interiority. People *feel* and

Plate 4.2 A crowd lines up in front of the church to watch the climactic events of the Gloria on Holy Saturday in Old Pascua, Tucson, 1937. (Photo: David J. Jones, Jr.)

know Waehma is being performed rather than see it through their eyes. The Yaquis respect the privacy of each other's ways of fulfilling their ritual obligations.

This was brought home to me clearly early on Easter morning 1982. At about midnight on Saturday night, exhausted after days and nights watching dancing, drama, processions, and more, I fell asleep. At about 4 a.m. I woke to the sound of guitars and violins. When I got to the plaza I saw in front of the open doors of the church the Matachinis, thirteen of them, dancing to the accompaniment of six musicians. A couple of dancers were literally asleep on their feet as they moved through their graceful, intricate steps. For more than sixteen hours they had been dancing more or less nonstop. I was the only spectator, and I was an accident. Feeling that my presence, if noticed, might be regarded as an intrusion, I stayed near the foodstalls, out of sight. The Matachinis danced in front of the open church door, before the Yaqui-Catholic altar. Were these dancers dancing their love for Jesus? Their vows? Their tradition? What they always did at this season? I don't know – though this last feels right: the Matachinis were doing what they always did at this season, dancing. I stood there in the cold desert predawn and wept. The Matachinis' art was accomplished; they did not let up because there were no human spectators. Truly they were making a sacrifice, an offering. This is typical of Waehma.

Not all New Pascuans are so fervent in their devotion. Throughout Holy Week 1987, even during the Crucifixion and Gloria, the playground near the plaza was busy with kids who apparently did not care at all about Waehma's momentous events. Nor did anyone fetch them or ask them to stop playing. Among new Pascua's adult population, too, many seem not to participate. Perhaps these people were participating inwardly, or maybe they just didn't care.

But for those who do attend, participation is valued over any kind of passive or even scholarly spectating. In 1982, Valencia made fun of my notebook, one of a set I've carried for twenty-five plus years – a writer's rather than an anthropologist's journal. In 1985, he asked me not to bring it into the plaza so I wrote notes in my camper. In 1987, I left my notebook in Tucson, carrying instead a mini tape recorder. When I wanted to make notes I went to my car and spoke quietly to my machine. Yet here I am, writing and publishing. Am I entitled to express my construction of Yaqui events? Does anyone, even the Yaquis themselves, "own" Yaqui history, religion, art, or ideology? The methods of performance theory, of any analytic discourse, do not please Waehma's current authors, many of whom see such discourses as intrusive attempts to capture, dissect, and export Waehma. Not all Yaquis feel this way. Felipe Molina has collaborated with Larry Evers in bringing to the attention of English speakers Yaqui poetry, folklore, songs, and dances.[4]

However they feel about non-Yaqui views of the Yaquis, many Yaqui leaders, Valencia and Molina among them, want to tell the Yaqui story to the outside world. "Something about the Pascua Yaqui Indians," distributed in New Pascua during Holy Week, says:

Yaqui Indians are notable on three counts: (1) they are the last North American Indians to be regarded by white men as a serious military threat; (2) they are among the most widely scattered of North American Indian groups; and (3) they have retained their own ethnic distinctness almost everywhere they are to be found in Mexico or in the US. (Pascua Tribal Council 1985a:2)

These three qualities constitute a narrative: because the Yaquis are so strong in resisting white men they have been singled out and brutally attacked, oppressed, and scattered. But the Yaquis have prevailed over diaspora by *performing their identity* as Yaquis.

This is exactly what Waehma does. The straight-line military formations of the Kohtumbre Ya'ura, the bunched informal processions of the church group, the intense stamping of the Deer dancer, the back-and-forth slightly bent movements of the Pascolas, and the rectangular steps of the Matachinis each incorporates specific aspects of Yaqui history and cultural identity. On Holy Saturday, the battle for the church is also a battle of dance styles. At the climax of the drama all the groups are *moving*: the Pariseom's straight lines are transformed first into curves and then into a frantic helter-skelter charge toward the church. In order to repulse this attack, the Matachinis and the Deer dance, the Pascolas throw leaves and confetti, the Little Angels, armed with cottonwood switches and aided by their godparents, beat the Chapayekam and Soldiers of Rome. The great numbers of spectators present on Holy Saturday – most of them non-Yaquis, many of them throwing confetti on the Pariseom – are participating witnesses to the Yaquis' perseverence; they are even the Yaquis' allies on this day of the Yaquis' renewed triumph not only over the enemies of Jesus but over all those who would exterminate them. As Valencia said:

We consider our people very Yaqui because they did not let the Deer dance, the early dances, die away. At a certain time of the year, whether the enemy was around or not, they'd get together and at least three songs were danced – and then you started running away. And . . . they would withdraw to the mountains at least for one day. First they'd make masks and swords and everything, and then perform at least one day. In many cases, in the later wars, the early 1900s, while they were performing these religious things they were surrounded and many, many people lost their lives in that way. But they were performing their Yaqui duties. We are not going to tell it as a once-upon-a-time religious ceremony. (Wenner-Gren 1981:8)

Waehma's seven interacting spatial spheres of action

The tightest, most intense space is the Loria Vo'o (Glory Road), a path as wide as the wide church door running eastward from the church then turning northward to the fiesta ramada (figure 4.2). On Holy Saturday morning Chapayekam sweep the Loria Vo'o clean, outlining it in ashes and cottonwood sprigs. The Chapayekam are responsible for keeping the Loria Vo'o swept, clean, and clearly marked. Of the multiple roles the Chapayekam play during Waehma, caretaker is but one. The Loria Vo'o is strictly patrolled so that unauthorized persons – non-Yaqui and Yaqui alike – do not enter or cross it. The same path under different names is marked on Palm Sunday (*Tako Vo'o*, Palm Road) and Easter (*Aleluyapo Vo'o*, Hallelujah Road). The western terminus of the Loria Vo'o is the altar at the rear of the church and the northern terminus is the altar inside the ramada – this ramada altar opens to where the Deer and Pascolas dance. Since this dance space "is imagined to be the huya ania, the forest world of the Deer and other wild life . . . [and] the Pascolas . . . trailing with them memories of the Surem, those little people who preceded the Yaquis and who may still be seen and heard in remote caves and secret places in the mountains and desert" (Painter 1986:409–10), the Loria Vo'o (in any of its names) both separates and unites the Catholicized world of the church with the Yaqui worlds of desert and myth. The Loria Vo'o is a theatre of war, the focused avenue of struggle between church forces and the Pariseom, as well as the link between the Roman church Yaqui-style and the huya aniya contained within the eastern half of the ramada, a Spanish-type structure. In the western half of the ramada women cook food for the performers of Waehma. The eastern half of the ramada is split in half again. The far east quarter is where the Deer and Pascolas dance, while the mid-east quarter is

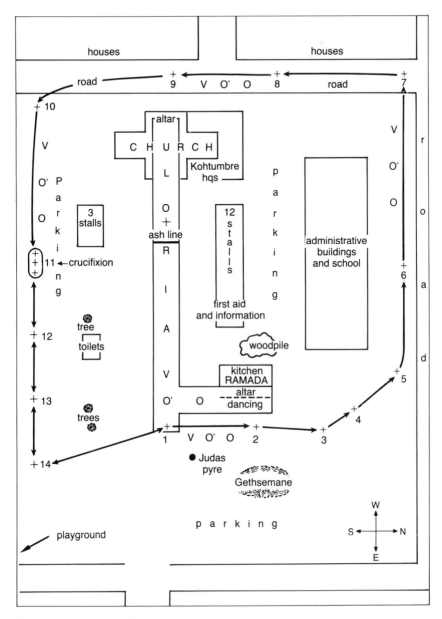

Figure 4.2 Plaza area of Pascua Pueblo as it was in 1985 showing the Loria Vo'o, the Konti Vo'o, church, ramada, foodstalls, Judas pyre, Gethsemane, and surrounding town roads and buildings.

where the altar is. Thus, one small building, its parts open to each other, focuses the meeting of three interpenetrating realms and actions: the community's daily need for food, the religious devotion of those who maintain the altar, sing, and recite prayers, and the huya aniya danced into presence by the Deer and Pascolas.

The *second* spatial sphere of Waehma is a more or less neutral ground beyond the Loria Vo'o but before the Konti Vo'o, the Way of the Cross. In this neutral or resting space are the arms of the church building containing pews, storage areas, and open spaces; the *Kohtumbre Waaria* (Kohtumbre barracks or headquarters) set up against the church's north wall; the ramada kitchen; snack and toystalls mostly on the north side of the plaza; an information and first-aid center; public toilets; and parking spaces. In 1982 the foodstalls of Pascua Pueblo were temporary wooden structures; but by 1985 they had been erected in cinder block. The stalls are open for business during Holy Week and during other big fiestas. The neutral ground is both a buffer between two powerful performance spaces, the Loria Vo'o and Konti Vo'o, and also a kind of offstage "green room." In the barracks the Pariseom rest, sometimes gathered around a fire. Near the barracks' entrance Chapayeka spears are stuck neatly in the sandy soil, the masks resting on the spears like helmets on rifles; at the foodstalls Chapayekam might be seen not wearing their masks, drinking Cokes; women chat robustly as they prepare what seem to be an endless supply of tortillas, roasting them on the top of steel drums full of hot mesquite coals. This neutral space is equivalent to the pregnant "waiting time" that is a prime source of Waehma's effectiveness.

During the first five weeks of Lent nothing much seems to be happening. Even on Holy Thursday afternoon or Good Friday after the Crucifixion when the Arizona sun heats up the dusty plaza, there is no visible theatrical action. But hard to detect microrhythms are models of Waehma's overall rhythm: energy is gathered in, time is slowly bunching up, performers return to the pueblo to take up their roles, events occur with accelerating frequency – the density and heat of Waehma increasing week by week, then day by day. Some of the energy is discharged in the many processions that punctuate Waehma, but most of it is saved for the dramatic rituals of Holy Week: Tenebrae, Gethsemane, the Crucifixion, and especially the Gloria. Easter Sunday is a day of gentle after-shocks, with its Pascola sermon, Alleluia, final procession, and Maestro (Yaqui–Catholic priest) sermon. Two Chapayekam whose masks were not burned wear them on Easter Sunday on top of their heads facing backwards, the way Pascolas sometimes wear their masks. Waehma reverberates again on 3 May, the feast of the Holy Cross, when the Kohtumbre Ya'ura marches in formation for the last time (until next year).

From a narrative point of view, the appearance of the Kohtumbre Ya'ura in formation on 3 May is out of place. After all, it was defeated and transformed on Holy Saturday. But theatrically and socially there are reasons for its appearance at Holy Cross. Such powerful presences as the Kohtumbre Ya'ura are not so easily sent away. The weeks from Holy Saturday–Easter Sunday through Holy Cross are a liminal time, a period of transition – there is an overlapping of feeling and tone as the dark season of Lent gives over to the lighter half-year, as the Kohtumbre Ya'ura yields to its successor, the Matachin society. Something similar may be said concerning the "early" appearance of the Matachinis, Deer, and Pascolas on Palm Sunday. By Palm Sunday, the Kohtumbre Ya'ura is present in full strength, wholly in charge. Yet Jerusalem is celebrating Jesus' entry into the city. The story demands a fiesta and a fiesta needs the Matachinis, Deer, and Pascolas. Furthermore, the relatively small fiesta of Palm Sunday prefigures the year's biggest celebration on Holy Saturday. On Palm Sunday people are permitted to see beyond the terrifying events of the week coming up; they can glimpse the ultimate triumph of the church forces. The dancing is a preview both of the fiesta of Holy Saturday and the taking of authority by the Matachin society. These ideas are performed, they are part of the theatre of Waehma. And although to some "theatre" might suggest falseness and hypocrisy, the Jesuits felt, and the Yaquis apparently concurred, that theatrical narrative could be a vehicle of truth. The Yaquis may not have had narrative theatre before the Jesuits arrived, but surely they had a theatre of dance and song which they used as a vehicle for truth. Waehma effectively combines these two kinds of theatre.

The *third* spatial sphere is actually a narrow band of space, the Konti Vo'o, the Way of the Cross. The Konti Vo'o holds the inner drama in and keeps the ordinary life of the pueblo out. The Konti Vo'o is the border between the highly charged theatrical–mythic–religious interior spaces of Waehma and the more diffuse spaces of the village and beyond. The many processions around the Konti Vo'o reinforce this boundary even as they prefigure the Crucifixion, after which all the crosses are knocked over as if such a great event obliterates the distinction between inner and outer, divine and human, Yaqui and non-Yaqui. Most of the processions move counter-clockwise around fourteen stations but some go "backwards" or split into two groups, one group moving clockwise and the other counter-clockwise. During the processions, the warring factions somewhat coalesce, though the Soldiers of Rome and their Chapayekam allies keep to the outside ambivalently guarding/harassing the church groups.

The Konti Vo'o is a powerful, fluid public stage displaying all the key figures of the drama: Soldiers of Rome, Chapayekam, Kabayum, Jesus, Marys, Little Angels, Maestros, and keening women. Few pueblo residents observe these processions. In fact, except for the Gloria and the fiestas of Palm Sunday and Easter eves, the Waehma is not a theatre that attracts spectators, even though its actions retain most of the specularity characteristic of their European predecessors. But while processions in Spain or Italy are traditionally thronged by thousands of spectators, the Yaqui way is to observe by means of glancing, avoiding intense frontal gazing. In fact, one might say that the staging of Waehma retains many conventions from Europe, but the ways of spectating and participating in these events is very native American. Most of the European-style spectators for the Gloria are outsiders. And although the fiestas attract many Yaquis who obviously enjoy the dancing of the Deer, Pascolas, Coyotes, and Matachinis, they look on in the Yaqui way: again those who press in hardest, most anxious "to see it all" are usually outsiders.

From 1982 to 1987 the Konti Vo'o of Pascua Pueblo expanded, moving out laterally from its position close to the rear of the foodstalls to a more generous band enclosing the school and administrative buildings to the north and a parking area to the south. Waehma literally advances into the town as the Konti Vo'o weaves its way from the first cross where it intersects the Loria Vo'o near the ramada to where it sets out into the pueblo from crosses 4 to 9 (to the north and west of the church). The Crucifixion, at cross 11, occurs behind some foodstalls near to a parking lot and the public toilets – a Golgotha, a liminal space between the town and the plaza. These penetrations into town space are not deep; the Konti Vo'o sticks close to the boundaries of the plaza. Crosses 7, 8, and 9, behind the church, are set in the middle of a paved street. For processions traffic is halted, and when the procession is over, these crosses (mounted on wooden stands) are temporarily stored on the sidewalk or in the front yards of nearby houses. It is different for *limosnas* (food- and fund-raising expeditions) or when the Kohtumbre Ya'ura marches into the pueblo to fetch the bier of Jesus. These excursions go wherever necessary. This respiratory rhythm of space is also true of time – Waehma breathes, sometimes expanding to cover all available space, filling time with startling and dramatic events. And sometimes there are extended periods of quiet, an inhalation of space and time back to the church, the barracks, the ramada.

Beyond the Konti Vo'o is the *fourth* sphere of space, the town of Pascua Pueblo. Processions, limosnas, and a number of individual activities begin in the area of the Loria Vo'o and extend into the town. People from the town come to the plaza to participate in or observe Waehma events. But ordinary town life goes on too, although in 1987 the bingo parlor was closed during Holy Week. But however "ordinary" Pascua Pueblo appears, it is a Yaqui settlement and as such very different from the *fifth* sphere, the non-Yaqui world of highways, the airport, and Tucson. From this perspective, New Pascua and the other Yaqui communities of Arizona, lying on a north–south axis from Guadalupe near Phoenix back to the Yaqui homeland of the eight villages along the Rio Yaqui in Sonora, Mexico, are small islands in an alien sea. Yaquis regard this non-Yaqui world suspiciously, with good reason.

But the Yaquis regard the Anglo and Mexican world, the fifth sphere, as itself an archipelago strewn across the *sixth* sphere, the desert, bush, and mountains so beloved by the Yaquis. And this sixth sphere is transformable into a *seventh*, the huya aniya (including the yo aniya, and the seya wailo). From the church door one can see the mountain rim and feel the desert: this positioning is no accident. The huya aniya is always imminent, and the boundaries marking off the seven spheres of space from each other are porous (figure 4.3). They are especially porous at decisive, ritually powerful times such as Waehma. Then the nonhuman worlds surrounding the pueblo penetrate to the very heart of the settlement. Thus, when the Pascolas arrive, or when the Deer dances, or even (I say) when the Chapayekam appear, Yaquis are reminded that they were not always people of the town, that once they were people of the desert and mountains. Here Yaqui history and myth agree that the Surem (whatever their physical stature), ancestors to the Yaquis, moved freely through the huya aniya, the untamed land. It was the Jesuits, arriving in 1617 and staying until 1767, who imposed town, plaza, and church.

"Civilizing" the Yaquis; taming the Chapayekam

The huya aniya, yo aniya, and seya wailo, being mythic and primeval, can't be measured on fixed quantitative scales. The Chapayeka masks, called *sewa* (flower), the Pascolas, and the Deer dancer derive their power from places where the Surem lived.[5]

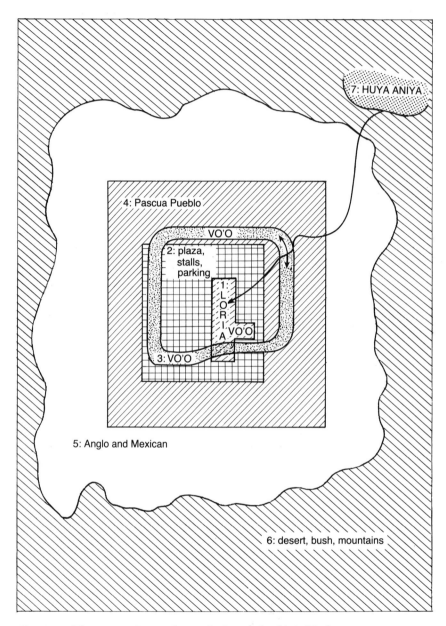

Figure 4.3 The seven spheres of space in Pascua Pueblo's Waehma.

Long ago there were Surem – tiny people who lived peacefully in the
Wilderness World (Huya Ania).   (Molina and Kaczkurkin 1980:1).

Before the Talking Tree, the Surem were little people about 3 feet tall.[6] They
were the ancestors of the Yaquis. . . . They did not know anything then. They
were wild. They didn't know heaven or hell or God or Jesus or Mary. We
inherited everything from the yo ania.   (Painter 1986:4).

Wild, peaceful, ignorant, without God or Jesus, Mary, hell, or heaven – yet
perfectly happy: from such a place and state of being the Yaqui "inherited
everything." The 1987 mimeo handout explaining Waehma to outsiders
encapsulates the ambivalence: "The Yaqui Indians lived in the fertile river
valley of the Rio Yaqui in Sonora, Mexico, for centuries before *Jesuit priests
brought Catholicism and civilization to them* in 1617 [my italics]" (Pascua
Tribal Council 1987:1).

The quintessential Yaqui task is to keep open a road between the everyday
world and the huya aniya, the modern and the originary, the Catholic and
the Yaqui, the "civilized" and the idyllic wild. Nowhere is this struggle to
use, but not be submerged in, European ways more clearly acted out than in
the drama of the Chapayekam (plate 4.3). While this drama is part of the
overall Waehma scheme, it also exists in itself as a paradigm of the Yaqui
situation. The Pascolas and Deer appear, and then intervene in the drama,
but they are not changed by it. Only the Chapayekam, and that special
Chapayeka, Judas (both as scapegoat and Viejito, the little old man who on
Holy Thursday represents Jesus), "imitate" the life, death, and rebirth of
Jesus.

In the recent Yaqui view the "pre-Catholic, pre-civilization" worlds are
not distant primeval truths encoded in myths and songs, but contingent,
actual energy sources.[7] The Deer and Pascolas come from the yo aniya – the
place of enchantment and magic – and the Chapayekam from the huya aniya,
the wild place of untamed beings. As a Yaqui told Painter:

The yo ania is encanto. Invisible things. . . . That is the way it happened to
those Deer dancers. They go to some place and see themselves about the Deers.
Underground, invisible Deers. They learn to dance that way. The Pascolas, the
same thing. [The Matachinis?] No, not the Matachinis. [The Chapayekas . . .?]
No, just the two things, the Deer and the Pascola.   (Painter 1986:26).

The Matachinis are clearly from Europe, the Deer and Pascolas from the yo

Plate 4.3 Chapayekam playing near the church of Old Pascua in 1937. (Photo: David J. Jones, Jr.)

aniya. But what evidence is there that the Chapayekam are from the huya aniya?

The first Chapayeka appears from under the church altar on the first Friday of Lent.

[It] is obviously out of place in the church. It looks around as though in puzzlement, but it is not easy to know what it thinks, for it says nothing and seems to be expressing uncertainty by knocking two painted sticks together tentatively. Moreover no facial expression is visible. The being wears a helmet of hide painted black, green, red, and white with two large loosely flapping ears and a slender pointed nose. It ignores the services in front of the altar where hymns and prayers preparatory for going around the Way of the Cross are in progress among the assembled townspeople. The Chapayeka goes up to the prayer leader and insolently cocks its head to look at him better, shuffles among the kneeling people, but when the name of the Blessed Virgin is mentioned begins to shiver and shake and then appears to wipe filth from its thighs with one of its sticks. In the midst of the solemn devotions, the Chapayeka suddenly shakes deer hoof rattles on a belt around his waist, momentarily drowning out the sacred chant. Turning his back on the altar, he trots among the people and out the door of the church.

(Edward Spicer 1980:76)

This Chapayeka is the first of many to join the Soldiers of Rome in the hunt for Jesus. Each Chapayeka is a Judas – and so, like the sorcerer's apprentices, Judases multiply until there are thirty or forty of them. At the end all but two of the Judases will go up in flames together, that is, the Chapayeka masks will be burned. Two will be saved: one to be worn by next year's effigy Judas, the other in case a member of the Chapayeka society dies during the year.[8]

As the church group proceeds around the Konti Vo'o the Kohtumbre Ya'ura assembles outside its headquarters. A flute plays three descending notes in a minor scale, a drum answers, and the Kohtumbre Ya'ura begins to march in formation around the cross set up near the entrance to the church. Music, marching, and formation forecast the attack the Kohtumbre Ya'ura will make on the church nearly six weeks later at Gloria. By then it will number many more.

The people say many things about the first Chapayeka who is representative of the whole bunch. He is Judas; he is born under the altar; he is an evil spirit; coming from the altar means he comes from Christ; he says many prayers and asks God's help in order to do this bad work of hunting Jesus (Painter 1986:372–3). The Chapayekam represent contradictory meanings; they are an overloaded sign. To understand them thoroughly one must separate the men from the masks from the works they perform.

Chapayeka masks are sewam, flowers: powerful, good, the blood of Jesus, a bridge between the huya aniya to the human world.

> We call it [the masks] flower because what we do here is not really done in an evil spirit, but represents evil . . . and the Chapayekas, when they do their penance, they earn grace by wearing their mask. And that is why it is called sewa. (Painter 1986:212–13)

What is this "penance" other than the whole collection of tasks the Chapayekam have vowed to do – acting in the drama, going about town reminding people that the ceremonies are about to begin, doing heavy work like gathering firewood or keeping the Loria Vo'o clean? At the end of that long road of obligations, after Gloria, the men in the masks will be reaggregated into the Yaqui community: escorted, fed, comforted, and congratulated by their godparents. While they are being reborn (in the Waehma Christ is not resurrected as a man, but reborn as a baby), their masks – the visible sign of Chapayekadom – are ablaze on the Judas pyre.

The men performing as Chapayekam undertake "the most arduous of any duty" (Painter 1986:209) – being a Chapayeka is not only tough labor, it is hard theatrical and spiritual work. Putting on the mask means putting on the character of a Chapayeka. Each masker holds a rosary crucifix in his mouth to remind him of his holy purpose and to defend him against the "evil he wears on his head" (Painter 1986:221), the murder his mask must commit. The mask is felt to be animate and powerful.

> if he does not perform his vows with good heart, if he breaks any of the special taboos surrounding the mask, . . . and especially if he allows contamination of the mask by an outsider, he risks retaliation by the mask. This animistic attribute of the mask is unique to this one item of regalia, and it is so recognized by informants. It is said variously that the mask may stick to his head when he tries to remove it to throw on the Judas pyre at The Gloria; or he may wear the face of the mask after death; or he may be condemned and return as a ghost to be heard in the village; or the mask and his rattle belt and weapons may be heard going around the Way of the Cross during the night. These beliefs are current and well documented, and it is clear that they concern only the Chapayeka mask.
> (Painter 1986:221)

Those playing Chapayekam "have commented on the difficulty of having to 'act in two ways,' that is, keeping the mind on Jesus in His service, and at the same time performing derisive acts as enemies of Jesus" (Painter 1986:224).

Holding the crucifix between the front teeth performs another function – it prevents Chapayekam from speaking. The nonhuman nature of the Chapayekam is emphasized by their inability to speak. They communicate by jumping and shaking their deer-hoof rattle belts, stamping their cocoon ankle rattles, clicking their swords together, cocking their heads, and performing other actions in pantomime. They perform farcical skits; they use their daggers and swords as props such as telescopes, canes, even drinking bottles; they parody the Maestro, dance groups, and individuals. They howl like coyotes or crawl stealthily on their bellies. And they march with heavy treads or dance with light steps. The tap-tap-tapping of their wooden daggers against their wooden swords is a leitmotif of Waehma. It is heard every time they march. The Crucifixion itself – the hammering of imaginary nails with a wooden hammer into a large cross laid out at station 11 of the Konti Vo'o – echoes, gathers, and recapitulates this sound of wood-on-wood.

Over the duration of Waehma a great and accumulating tension develops between the Chapayeka mask-role and the man-performer inside the mask. He is enacting a role, fulfilling a vow, wearing a mask that is extremely powerful in its own right: the mask pulls the man inside along with it. He made it, but it rules him. His ordinary humanity is temporarily drained from him, the mask rendering him vulnerable, his only protection being his prayers, the crucifix between his teeth, and the encouragement of his fellow performers. The mask leads its wearer down an arduous, tricky path out from the good of the huya aniya into the bad of opposing the church group and hunting Jesus and back again to a new level of good as a Yaqui-Catholic member of the community. When the masks burn the men are temporarily freed from danger. But the next year, in the weeks before Lent, in secret, they will once again build the masks that will constrain and endanger them even while serving as redemptive instruments of renewal. The generative powers of the masks are not destroyed by the flames of the Judas pyre. On the contrary, the sacrificial burning guarantees the birth of a new generation of Chapayekam.

But who are these Chapayekam – bulls, goats, sheep, dogs, rabbits, bears, birds, raccoons, an insect with bulging eyes, Moors, a man in a top hat with a black face smoking a big cigar, another with Dracula teeth, and always the mask of an old man, the Viejito?[9] Some specific faces change over the years, but all masks conform to an underlying unity: the helmet style covering the whole head down to the neck, the big jug ears, the thin pointy nose. Perhaps, as Edward Spicer suggests, the masks are linked to Hopi and Zuni Kachinas (1980:61–2), which would relate them to peoples living north of the Yaquis. Yaquis say the Chapayekam come from the north or from overseas. Wherever they are from, the Chapayekam are "not from around here," they represent the Other, the non-Yaqui, the outsider, the exotic, strange, dangerous, weird, hilarious. The Chapayekam are disoriented – they have come from "somewhere else," they are "out of place" in the pueblo, they must be tamed and educated in their evil/holy purpose.

There is much concrete theatrical evidence of the Chapayekam's "wildness." On Palm Sunday when the palms are put through the rear of their belts, they buck like wild horses being broken – jumping up and down, kicking their legs backwards. During Tenebrae they howl like coyotes. In several scenes they lie on the ground or crawl. Frequently they act not unintelligent but dumb, as if in need of educating, or childlike, as if they need to grow up. When a new object is presented to them – as on Holy Thursday 1987 when one of them stole my Australian flat-brimmed squatter's hat as I was sleeping under a palo verde tree at the far end of the plaza awaiting the Viejito performance – they examine it as if its function is unknown. Two Chapayekam played with my hat to determine what it was, how to use it, and finally, once it was clear that it was a hat, where to wear it. Finally, an unmasked Pariseo came over to me and told me that I could "ransom" my hat back for a "buck or two" which I gladly did. When the Chapayekam are thoroughly acculturated – as they are by Good Friday night when they celebrate their fiesta – they behave like typical "bad" Yaquis: drinking, dancing American-style cheek-to-cheek, playing Mexican music, getting into fights. Other details could be added, leading to the general conclusion that the Chapayekam begin as wild or "natural" (as opposed to "civilized" in the Yaqui sense) beings from outside the town and end as Yaquis. Chapayekam, however, are more than wild beings in the process of acculturation. They are also clowns; scouts and irregular soldiers increasingly on a definite mission; animals; humanoids; and fantasy figures expressing the creativity of the individual Yaqui men who conceive, construct, and paint the masks during the weeks before Lent.

The Chapayekam are like the Namahage of Ota in Japan, or Halloween maskers in Euro-America: comic and sinister, from here and from someplace else simultaneously.[10] Originating in "the north," "overseas," "the mountains," "the dead," this type of figure manifests itself actively in the human world on a definite and predictable yearly schedule. None of these masks really belongs to the world they temporarily inhabit and disrupt. The Chapayekam are more complex than the Namahage or Halloween masked characters because Chapayekam develop, grow, change and ultimately are defeated and destroyed, while the men inside the masks are liberated, revealed as loved relations and trusted neighbors: a fact everyone knows but, according to theatrical and religious convention, agrees to ignore. This "willing suspension of disbelief" is no trivial thing: it is a key to the worlds of subjunctivity and "as if," to what Artaud (1958) called the "theatre and its double." Chapayekam act within a double negative field of possibilities. They are not the men under the mask and they are not the mask itself acting autonomously (as Namahage are presumed to be). Neither one nor the other, they are the interaction between the two.[11]

Waehma's core drama is transformative: the wandering, enticement, enlistment, taming, training, war, and defeat of the Chapayekam. Once the Chapayekam are defeated, the men performing the masks are liberated and transformed, they are redeemed, their vows fulfilled as they are joyously welcomed back into the Yaqui community. This transformation of wandering wild ones – the "original Yaquis" from a Yaqui-Catholic perspective – into obedient members of the community casts its own shadow. Murdering Jesus and giving up the right to be a Chapayeka whenever one pleases (or whenever the old tradition demands) is necessary if one is to be a Catholic – that's the cruel heart of the "civilization" brought by the Jesuits. Not only must the Christian story be enacted, but the rules governing the use of the Chapayeka masks must come under the authority of the new civilization. One of the climaxes of the Christian story Yaqui-style is the destruction of the wild Chapayeka masks. The scene at the end of the Gloria is paradigmatic of the underlying tensions of Waehma. Just before the men rush into the church to be redeemed, the masks are thrown on the pyre – this decisive action flies off in two directions to two fates with two meanings represented by two contrasting theatrical actions. The core drama is a model of the ambivalent yet triumphant course of Yaqui history as the Yaquis conceive and enact it.

The men in the masks are converted to Yaqui-Catholicism by means of playing their roles as Chapayekam. As it is for the Chapayekam so it is for all of the Kohtumbre Ya'ura and, in fact, everyone participating in Waehma. The focus is on the Chapayekam because they enact the *whole drama*: beginning as ignorant strangers, animals, wild ones, they learn first to be Yaquis and then to be Yaqui-Catholics. As wild ones from the huya aniya they enter the town and are enlisted by the Kohtumbre Ya'ura; as liminal beings, both part of and apart from the main Yaqui community, they pursue and murder Jesus; and as Yaqui-Catholics they discard their masks and renew their faith as they kneel before the altar at the Gloria. Of course, at all phases of this three-part development or transformational process, the Chapayekam are Yaquis – their underlying action is their devotion to the vows they have taken to perform in Waehma. But within this large frame, they play several roles, undergo a basic and necessary transformation. It may be that the Chapayekam are most essentially Yaqui during the main body of the drama, especially during Holy Week *before* the Gloria. During this time they know of Catholicism, but resist it; they are able to manipulate its symbols, yet because they have not been absorbed into a Roman Catholic world, they are able to play with these symbols, simultaneously honoring and mocking them. This is shown very clearly in the pursuit of the Viejito of Thursday afternoon and the Chapayeka fiesta of Friday night.

Through Waehma the Yaquis act out *both their acceptance of Catholicism (and certain European ways) and their resistance to this very same Catholicism and the European ways*. This fits the New Pascua Yaquis' own ambivalent view of themselves as "the last North American Indians to be regarded by white men as a serious military threat . . . [as people who] have retained their own ethnic distinctness" and people who also say that "Jesuit priests brought Catholicism and civilization to them."

Finally, the wild Chapayekam are tamed, defeated, and destroyed, while the men who wore the masks are saved and brought fully into the Yaqui community. At the crucial sacrificial moment of the Gloria, after the assault on the church has failed, as Jesus and his allies demonstrate their power, a real conceptual and physical distance opens between Yaqui men and Chapayeka masks. The men rush full steam into the church, after throwing their masks with equivalent urgency onto the Judas pyre. But the burning does not settle the matter once and for all. Two masks are saved, as seeds for the coming year, when once again during Lent the whole Waehma will be reenacted.

The Gloria's back door

During Waehma, the domain of the good shrinks. Some of the good is invisible – the rosary crucifix behind the mask, the feelings in the hearts of the men performing as Chapayekam and Soldiers of Rome, while visibly, day by day, the church group is squeezed back to the church itself. On Palm Sunday the Deer, Pascolas, and Matachinis perform – an Indian summer, for the events of Holy Week show how dominant the powers of evil are. Tenebrae is literally a dark service, punctuated by the howls of coyotes and the sounds of whipping. The whipping is repeated in full daylight on Thursday afternoon when the Chapayekam pursue the Viejito around the Konti Vo'o. And what is this representation of Jesus as an old Chapayeka, a Judas? It plays like mockery but feels full of deep sorrow. On Thursday night Gethsemane falls to the Soldiers of Rome, Jesus is taken prisoner, the church is theirs. Throughout the long night the only sounds are the shaking of deer-hoof belts, the clicking of swords and daggers, and the piercing keening of church women. Friday noon is Crucifixion time followed by the uprooting of all the crosses in the pueblo. Spatial spheres collapse inwards, chaos is loose amidst the desert heat, desolation, and dust. The midnight procession marking Jesus' resurrection is also full of confusion as the men's group and the women's group go in opposite directions and the Chapayekam engage in a mock battle of exploding firecrackers in the street behind the church. (In 1987 the moment was further blurred when the church bell suddenly began to peal. I was told that exactly at midnight someone in the pueblo died and the bell tolled his passing.) The Chapayeka fiesta late Friday night celebrating their victory over the church is not very celebratory. Relatively few people watch, the farce scenes unfold desultorily: somehow the Chapayekam know that even if the battle is won, the war is lost.

On Saturday morning the scene changes dramatically. The Loria Vo'o is clearly marked out. An ash line about 50 feet from the church door marks the boundary separating the domain of the Pariseom from the forces of the church. The church has gained impressive new allies – Deer dancer, Matachinis, Pascolas, and hundreds of spectators who have brought or bought bags of confetti representing sewam, the flowers, the blood of Jesus, that will defeat the Pariseom. There are many vivid descriptions of the Gloria, when the Soldiers of Rome and Chapayekam three times assault the church and each time are forced backwards by the combined powers of the Little Angels (some of whom beat the Chapayekam mercilessly with cotton-wood switches), the dancing of the Deer and Matachinis, and the sewam thrown on them by the church group, Pascolas, and spectators. The battle ends with the church victorious, the Pariseom kneeling in thanksgiving at the church altar, the Chapayeka masks and Judas effigy in flames, and the whole crowd ready for the year's biggest fiesta.

But what does the Kohtumbre Ya'ura want on Saturday morning? Jesus has already been resurrected. Why fight a battle after the war is lost? When I asked Rosamond Spicer that question she conjectured that, after the Resurrection, the subject of the drama shifts from what's going to happen to Jesus to who is going to control the Yaqui town. And for this phase of the drama numerous outsiders – Anglos, nonbelieving Yaquis, Papagos and other Indians, tourists, students, anthropologists – crowd into Pascua Pueblo. Of the original seven spheres of space only two remain: the spectators' space collapses desert, Tucson, Konti Vo'o, and foodstalls into one space pressing in on the Loria Vo'o, which itself absorbs the huya aniya because of the powerful presence in the drama of Deer and Pascolas oppos-

ing the Chapayekam. The outer secular world gathers to watch the Yaqui
sacred world play out an ultimate struggle. Finally, in a riot of transformation and antistructure the secular collapses into the sacred, the Kohtumbre
Ya'ura surrenders its authority (almost), the masks burn, the town returns
into the hands of the Yaqui-Catholics, the fiesta opens its arms to all, Yaqui
and non-Yaqui alike, as the victorious dancers and others spend more than
the next twelve hours performing and celebrating.

There is a back door to it all: on Saturday morning, before the final battle,
the Chapayekam carry the effigy of Judas – by far Waehma's biggest figure –
from their barracks. Judas is a Chapayeka, his mask one of two not burned
the previous year. His procession is both a parody of the church processions
and a genuine procession on its own. Again, ambivalence is the word. An old
paintcan-censer filled with foul-smelling, smokily burning dirty rags spreads
its stink; Chapayekam play jolly Mexican-style music bootlegged from their
fiesta of the night before as off they go traveling clockwise (the "wrong"
direction) around the Konti Vo'o, Judas himself facing backwards. Soon,
however, the procession is joined by women, many of whom are pushing
strollers or carrying infants, a Maestro, a few men, and kids. This procession
moves in a bunch, as the church processions do, not in the strict, linear,
military movements of the Soldiers of Rome. The Chapayekam treat Judas
as the church women have treated the Marys or Jesus: they bunch around
him, jostling against each other to get close to him. Judas wears a crown of
cottonwood, like Jesus.

This is the most "open" of all the processions of Waehma. In 1987, far
from being sent away by anxious Pariseom, I and my by then 9-year-old
son were invited in. A member of UCLA Professor Allegra Fuller Snyder's
class, in from Los Angeles to observe Waehma in several of the Yaqui
communities in and around Tucson, was asked to be one of the men carrying
Judas (and this was not the first year one of Snyder's students was so
selected).[12] The procession was joyous as it meandered the wrong way
around the Konti Vo'o. There was a kind of subversive delight that I was not
alone in feeling. From the perspective of Judas, which can be construed as
the perspective of all the Chapayekam, Waehma runs backwards, upside
down, left-handed. The wrong is right, the church silly, the disciplined
formations of the Soldiers of Rome compulsive. What counts is having a
good time, being with one's friends, soaking up the sun, welcoming the
new season. But isn't this what Easter is really all about? By Saturday
morning the drama is over, there is no suspense, all that's left is the exciting

theatrical display of the Gloria, and the celebratory good time of the fiesta.

When the procession completed its circuit, a liminal time opened. Everyone knew that the Gloria was soon to begin. That was the big show of the morning. But up at the far end of the plaza, near the ramada, about 150 persons gathered around as Judas was installed on his pyre, busily being prepared by Chapayekam. Judas was attached to an upright pole, not a cross, but his arms were outstretched forming a cross. The Chapayekam, still wearing their masks, began a vigorous circle dance with upraised knees, almost a parody of Plains Indians' war dancing. The Viejito of Thursday afternoon was the drummer – still further identifying Judas with Jesus.

Then many people – mostly women, but some men too – approached Judas with offerings. In 1985 there was a toy tractor, a teddy bear, a rubber snake, a stuffed blue elephant. In 1987 there were various toys and the bunny rabbit substituted for the Nazarene on Friday night. Also on the Judas pyre were props from the Chapayeka fiesta, the paintcan-censer from the Judas procession, and two plastic garbage bags filled with trash. Most of the offerings stacked up against Judas were things associated with children. A large number of people approached Judas one by one and tied scarfs around his arms or legs. Both my son and I offered something to Judas and were not discouraged from doing so.

I asked about all this. A woman told me, "Say a boy dies by falling off a tractor – then a toy tractor is given to Judas." Another said, "A child dies, we give his favorite toy." "Someone gets sick and recovers – we tie a scarf on Judas to remember that." Judas is where some Yaquis bring bad things that happen to children – either events suffered and overcome like sickness, or events with a bad outcome like the death of a child. The fire that burns Judas burns out the bad (plate 4.4). Scholars are mute concerning these actions: I have found only Painter's brief reference.[13] It may be that this Judas ceremony is new or that so much attention is focused on the other end of the Loria Vo'o that observers have not noticed it. Clearly it was not only the Chapayekam but many ordinary Yaquis, especially women, who appealed to Judas with respect. Judas had become a backdoor saint, a popular scapegoat–protector. During the times I watched in 1985 and again in 1987, maybe fifty or sixty people came up to Judas to make offerings to him or to tie scarfs on him. The Chapayekam continued their slow circle dance with lifted knees until there were no more people approaching Judas. Then several Chapayekam "combed" Judas's hair with their wooden daggers, stroked his face, shoulders, and arms. Finally, the Viejito bade Judas

Plate 4.4 Helmet masks and Judas go up in flames. Note the ribbons signifying vows tied on to Judas's arm. This photo, probably taken in 1969 or 1970, does not show dolls and toys being "sacrificed," as I saw in Pascua Pueblo in the 1980s. (Photo: Western Ways)

farewell; pretending to weep, he wiped his eyes with a handkerchief. This farewell was both farcical and moving. One Chapayeka version of Judas/ Jesus mourning another.

There are European analogies to the Yaqui Judas ceremony. Whether or not these are prototypes I have no way of knowing. In a general sense, one thinks of the burning of heretics, the European belief in the purificatory powers of fire. The Catholics transformed Judas into St Jude because "the ancient cult of Judas continued . . . and couldn't be eradicated. The fictitious St Jude became very popular in the Middle Ages" (Walker 1983:483). "St Jude enjoys great popularity as a powerful intercessor for those in desperate straits" (Attwater 1965:203). More specifically, in Madrid during the 1600s "Holy Saturday was celebrated by burning the Judas figures which hung in all of the barrios of the cities" (Alvarado 1974:81). Gallop reports that:

> The custom of burning a straw effigy of Judas Iscariot on Easter Eve, which used to be observed in parts of Germany, is common throughout Portugal, even though the traitor is often clad in the blue overalls of a mechanic and hung from telegraph wires. At Monchique this ceremony is performed with great gravity in the presence of the parish priest. The effigy is stuffed with rockets and fireworks which, on exploding, release a black cat previously sewn up inside. The ashes of the German Judas were afterwards kept and planted in the fields on May 1st to preserve the wheat from blight and mildew.
>
> (Gallop 1936:115–16)

Time, space, and narratives gathered, folded, extended

The very last words on the 1987 handout describing Waehma for outsiders are:

> Time as space measurement is not [an] essential part of our activities, although we set an hour of the day or night for certain events, we do not keep a strict schedule. Yaqui time is two hours before or after any given event, the activities are not for the purpose of attracting the attention of spectators or tourists. These activities are dedicated to our Lord, in gratitude of spiritual and corporal benefits received. Yaqui Lenten activities are to be viewed with respect as they are the cultural religion of the Yaqui Indians. Visitors are welcomed – donations are gratefully accepted. (Pascua Tribal Council 1987:7)

Much could be said about the system of ambivalences expressed by this statement. Visitors and their dollars are wanted, but on the Yaquis' own terms. The authors are trying throughout the seven-page handout to explain not only what Waehma is, but what and how the Yaquis think about themselves. There is a fine line between offering friendship, explaining to outsiders how to behave, outlining cultural differences, and appearing hostile. Most scholarly and popular accounts of Waehma focus on the actions, the events, on "what's happening." What the Yaqui handout hints at is another, more Yaqui, system that would foreground the waiting, the undoing, the gathering of energies. Time is not a point to be approached, met, and sailed away from. Yaqui time is fluid, bending to events, almost Einsteinian.

From a European perspective, the Yaquis "got" Waehma from the Jesuits. But from an orthodox Yaqui perspective, Jesus lived among the Yaquis sometime between 901 and 1414, long before the Europeans arrived – even though the Pascua Tribal Council 1987 information sheet stated that "Jesuit priests brought Catholicism and civilization to them [the Yaquis] in 1617."[14] The question is not about linear objective "truth" as Euro-American scholarship might write it, but of how the Yaquis construct their own history. They construct it ambivalently, with conflicting myths and attitudes. Waehma is all Yaqui and it is imported; it expresses both Yaqui and European values without hiding the tensions between them. Waehma's beliefs, narratives, staging, costumes, masks, and characters cannot be traced to single-point origins.

The question of Waehma's sources is further complicated because of the many interactions and similarities between the Yaquis and other native groups. Helmet masks similar to those of the Chapayekam are found among the Hopis and Zunis. The Pascola and Deer songs, masks, and dancing – felt by many Yaquis to essentialize their culture – are like what is found among the Huichol and other peoples of northwest Mexico. It's not clear who got what from whom. Almost certainly, marching in straight-line military formations, and the hierarchical military organization of the Pariseom, is derived from European models. But during the 150 years when Europeans were absent, the Yaquis assimilated these military ways as thoroughly as they did Catholic ritual.

The functions of Waehma are similarly multiple. Of course, a religious view of the world is enacted – a story which the Yaquis say they perform not only for their own benefit but on behalf of all the world's peoples. That is one reason they welcome guests to Waehma. But Waehma also serves some distinctly homegrown political purposes. Their village is called Pascua Pueblo, literally "Eastertown." Their tribal emblem, seen on flags, buildings, and official documents, is a Deer dancer. Those who organize and lead Waehma have status within the community. Waehma "positions" the Yaquis in relation to non-Yaquis even as it serves as a vehicle for the exercise of authority within the tribe.

Waehma's recurrent large-scale movement pattern expresses the Yaquis' ambivalence toward the religion and customs imposed on them by the Jesuits and other outsiders. This pattern is of encirclement, then concentration in a small area, followed by a violent yet celebratory flinging out. One sees this pattern in the many processions and marches around the Konti Vo'o; in the Chapayekam's stealthy entry into the church on Tenebrae followed by the rush to get to where the men are being whipped in the plaza outside the church door; in the encirclement and capture of Jesus from Gethsemane; in the elegiacally slow Crucifixion procession around the Konti Vo'o on Good Friday followed by the breakneck overturning of all the crosses in the village by the Chapayekam; in the assault on the church on Holy Saturday; in the wild, multifocused fiesta of Holy Saturday afternoon and night. Still, for all this, the experience of Waehma – at least my experience of it – is not of a fragmented or interiorally conflicted event, but of a performance of magnitude and unity, reflecting the collective wisdom and deep-felt practice of the Yaqui. This sense of wholeness is connected to the ways Yaquis watch and participate in Waehma and their ways of manipulating time and energy.

Waehma's underlying rhythm is of long hours, or even days, when time is gathered in, what an outsider might experience as waiting, punctuated by short bursts of intense activity. To regard Waehma as mostly the presentation of intense actions is to Westernize Yaqui ritual theatre, to aestheticize it in the direction of an Aristotelian action–climax–resolution pattern. In terms of Yaqui aesthetics, what's going on is the gathering up and spending of a long time – six weeks – during which many people's whole devotional and physical energies are required. The long rhythm of Waehma steadily and thoroughly absorbs all activity into itself. Some of Waehma's energies are saved up to be spent in short intense bursts; other accumulating energies are played out in longer, quieter rhythms. The Yaquis' ability to coordinate the short and long rhythms gives Waehma its powerful, inclusive formality. Western-style theatre can be "watched," handled from the outside, literally grasped. The time of spectating is always longer than the time of performing. The spectators' consciousness can contain the performance. Even those Western theatre directors who have experimented with extended performances in space and time, like Robert Wilson and Peter Brook, rarely create anything longer than twelve hours.[15] But Waehma's big span of six weeks, its smaller span of one week (Palm Sunday to Easter), and the short bursts of intense activity that comprise individual scenes, enclose and contain participants, especially those who live in the village. When a short intense scene is concluded, the drama is not "over," one simply reenters the Waehma flow of time. Sooner or later one is led into another intense event.

Waehma can be thought of as a river – now flowing slowly, folding back on itself, now rushing along wildly – carrying along in its uneven yet extremely powerful current many different kinds of events. During Waehma sins are taken away, confirmations occur, vows are made: a series of observances and rituals that are not strictly part of the Passion. The Passion of Jesus is just one of three major narratives of Waehma, the other two being: "how the Yaquis came to be Catholics ('civilized')," and "who controls the community?" These narratives are folded into each other and worked through simultaneously. The answer to the question of the third story – "who controls the community?" – is that authority is shared, the year is divided between the Matachin society and all it represents – church, summer, Eurocentric ideas – and the Kohtumbre Ya'ura and what it represents – a much more ambivalent attitude toward all things European, a darker vision of experience, a fierce Yaqui warlike pride.

The most often repeated group action of Waehma is circling the Konti Vo'o. The church group moves as civilians do, in a devotional bunch (plate 4.5), while the Kohtumbre Ya'ura marches in straight-line military formations. As the weeks pass, more participants are drawn into these processions around the extended rectangle that is the Konti Vo'o. The processions climax, but do not end, with the Crucifixion. During the Gloria the straight line dominates, or almost does, until it is broken by the force of sewa. A deep sense of these rhythms can be gained only over time because Waehma grows by accumulation. Holy Week, from Wednesday evening on, appears to be one climactic action after another. But in Pascua Pueblo itself one experiences the full slowness of time as events precipitate and evaporate even as their frequency accelerates during Holy Week. If one is not impatient the waiting is meditative, the multiple meanings and grandeur of it all settle in. It is as if the quiescent periods release one's attention from any bondage to action. Or as if the future is literally felt approaching, drawn in "ahead of time," as members of the Kohtumbre Ya'ura doze, Little Angels play quietly on the floor of the church, a few people gather near a foodstall, hawks circle

Plate 4.5 On Easter Sunday, after the climactic events of Waehma are over, the Church Society brings Jesus into the church. The Resurrection is accomplished, good has triumphed over evil, the ceremonial year turns. (Photo: Tom Ives)

overhead, the sun makes its way across the sky as day gives over to the desert night that cools down quickly into cold when the hours pass midnight. Offstage, the women prepare food, or Jesus' bier, or they tidy up the altars, or execute any of the many other nonpublic activities that support Waehma from within.

The Yaquis do not like to explain. They prefer to let events speak for themselves. That becomes clearer the longer one waits, the more one considers what Valencia meant when he said that the Yaquis have "rescinded" the rights of anthropologists. My son Sam said, "I watch what they are doing and let that answer my questions," to which my wife, performance scholar Carol Martin, replied: "What I love about it is its unspokenness."

Notes

1. I observed many of the ceremonies at New Pascua from Palm Sunday to Easter in 1982, 1985, and 1987. In this article I will not describe the whole cycle of Waehma as such – three excellent accounts are given by R. Spicer 1939, Painter 1971, and E. Spicer 1980. I will concentrate on "problems" or "aspects" of the ceremony, especially the organization of space, the underlying narratives, and the multivocal roles of the Chapayekam.
2. Even the Yaquis' own name for themselves is not easy to pin down. "Hiaquis" is what the Spaniards of the early seventeenth century thought the Yoeme called the Rio Yaqui. But, as E. Spicer reminds us, "the Yaquis' own name for themselves came very slowly into use. In . . . the early 1600s a variant of the Yaqui word *yoeme* (pl. *yoemem*) appeared. . . . The first publication to use Yoeme in the title as the tribal name . . . uses Yaqui in the text" (1983:262). And today's New Pascuans say that "The Pascua Yaqui Indians of Arizona are descendants of the ancient Toltecs. . . . After some thousand years of living in the valleys and mountains of this area [Yaqui and Mayo rivers], these Indians came to call themselves Yaquis" (Pascua Tribal Council 1985a).
3. The November 1981 Wenner-Gren sponsored meeting focused on Yaqui Deer and Pascola dancing. It was one of three conferences concerning theatre and ritual convened by Victor Turner and me. The other two were held in New York in 1982. See *By Means of Performance* (Schechner and Appel 1990) for writings arising from these meetings, including a dialogue among Anselmo Valencia, his wife Heather Valencia, and Rosamond Spicer.
4. Molina is coauthor, with Larry Evers, of *Yaqui Deer Songs: Maso Bwikam* (1987). The book is accompanied by a tape of Deer songs. He is also author, with Mini Kaczkurkin, of the one-page "A Yaqui folklore map" (1980). Molina has been governor of Yoem Pueblo, an Arizona Yaqui settlement near Marana. Molina is active as a Deer singer and as a Coyote singer. In 1987 he was leading and training a group of Yaqui boys in Coyote dancing. I saw them perform at Old Pascua during the Holy Saturday fiesta. At one of their Coyote dances, the boys and Molina invited my then 9-year-old son Samuel to dance with them.
5. "The music . . . of the Deer Dancer and the Pascolas . . . is their [Surem] kind of music. Often in the huya aniya around the towns you hear a water drum or a drum and whistle or violin and harp" (E. Spicer 1980:172).

6. The Talking Tree is one key to Yaqui religion. The Tree predicted the future of the Yaqui in a language only the young girl Yomumuli could understand.

> Up to this time there had been no war and no fighting. Now the Surem would have to face the rest of the world. The tree predicted monsters that would ride steel rails, and big birds that would drop eggs to kill everyone around. The Surem who wished to remain pure would have to leave. Those who wanted to stay in the world would have to change. . . . Those who stayed became Yoemen, or Yaquis. Yaqui people still see Surem, usually out of the corners of their eyes.   (Molina and Kaczkurkin 1980)

This is the way Yaquis watch Waehma, "out of the corners of their eyes." Edward Spicer says the myth of the Talking Tree "undoubtedly developed in some post-Jesuit phase . . . [providing] sanction for the conception of the dual universe" of Christian and pre-Christian Yaquis (1980:172). One might say that this division continues in every Yaqui singly and in their Waehma collectively: what is visible is mostly Christian; what is invisible is mostly Yaqui.

7. By "recent" I mean from 1935 to the present as expressed in Waehma, quoted in Painter 1986, and recorded and interpreted by the Spicers in their many writings.

8. I don't recall where I heard/read about the second mask, the one saved for a deceased Chapayeka. Nor do I know how the mask would be used – if it would be buried with the Chapayeka or used in some other way.

9. All these masks I saw during my three Holy Weeks in New Pascua. Others have seen other kinds of masks – the repertory is large and although there are conventions governing the structure of the masks, the personae represented are an open category. Only the Viejito is required.

10. Namahage are ogres, strangers, maybe gods or ancestors, represented by big masks and bulky straw costumes, who descend from the mountains just after New Year for a brief sortie through villages on the Ota Peninsula of Japan. Namahage tease and scare "women and children" into behaving properly and demand snacks and saki from the householders. To be visited by the Namahage is good luck; to seize a straw from a Namahage's costume is particularly beneficial. In each town where the Namahage descend, a young men's association is responsible for animating the figures and maintaining the masks and costumes which are refurbished yearly. "The Namahage must be obeyed, yet one cannot predict what they will do or say. The anxiety and fear generated by their unpredictability is shared by all. . . . Yet all find pleasure in the visits" (Yamamoto 1978:13).

11. For a discussion of the negative capability of performing, see Schechner 1985:3–150.

12. I don't know if by coincidence or design, but the student invited to carry Judas was one year an African American and another an Oriental. If by design, then

the Yaquis might have been signaling that they wanted to include non-Yaquis who were like Yaquis in relation to mainstream white Anglo culture. African Americans and Orientals are people whose "position" or "place" is analogous to the Yaquis' own.

13. Painter notes only that "on him [Judas] are pinned some of the toys with which the Chapayekas have been playing and perhaps other old toys or ornaments" (1986:473). Spicer doesn't mention the practice at all. What I saw was a fully developed set of ritual actions loaded with meaning and deserving of more study.

14. Donald Barr sets out the opposing Yaqui and European view of things and then concludes,

> Thus the difference between Europe and Yaquis was not over belief versus nonbelief in the basic facts about Jesus' life, or over the acceptance of saints, the acceptance of the Christian calendar, etc. Rather, it was in the Yaquis' insistence that these elements originated in their own country prior to the European arrival, and Europe's insistence that the elements derived from a European-led spiritual conquest of the Yaquis.
>
> (In Spicer and Crumrine, in press)

15. Wilson specializes in long performances sometimes extending over big distances. His 1973 *Life and Times of Joseph Stalin* was staged in a theatre, took twelve hours to perform, from 7 p.m. to 7 a.m., while his 1972 *KA MOUNTAIN AND GUARDenia TERRACE* took a week to perform and ranged over an Iranian mountain. Brook's 1985 *The Mahabharata* was performed both in three sections on three different nights and as one nine-hour performance sometimes beginning in the afternoon and sometimes extending overnight. The Ramlila of Ramnagar in north India is a thirty-one-day cycle (see Chapter 5 and Schechner 1985:151–212).

5

Striding through the cosmos: movement, belief, politics, and place in the Ramlila of Ramnagar

I will now proclaim the manly powers of Vishnu
Who measured out earth's broad expanses,
Propped up the highest place of meeting:
Three steps he paced, the widely striding!

For [this], his manly power is Vishnu praised.
Like a dread beast he wanders where he will,
Haunting the mountains: in his three wide paces
All worlds and beings dwell. . . .

The marks of his three steps are filled with honey;
Unfailing they rejoice each in its own way.

Rig-Veda 1, 154 (Zaehner 1966:4–5)

One of Varanasi's greatest events – a performance of magnitude, a pilgrimage, a display of the maharaja of Banaras's splendor – the Ramlila of Ramnagar takes place not in the city itself, but across the Ganga, on the "east" bank, a few miles upriver. The Ganga swerves northward at Varanasi so that its southern bank is actually to the east. In Varanasi the sun rises over the river. And when crossing the Ganga from north to south one is moving from west to east. This conflation of directions is of great importance. Kashi, the Luminous City, arose at the place where pilgrims crossing the river and returning would move in all four cardinal directions. Directionality, defined spaces, and movement have been decisive qualities of Vishnu from the earliest accounts of his acts.[1] Vishnu means "expander," who by striding through space establishes his lawful authority. Following in his steps is, the Veda tells us, to step in honey. Rama, Vishnu's seventh incarnation, is known for his "goings" or "journeying" (the *yana* of *Ramayana*).[2] The core subtext of Valmiki's *Ramayana*, Tulsidas's *Ramcharitmanas*, and the

131

Ramlila is the expansion of Rama worship. Even Ravana, in death, is absorbed into Rama.

This worship is the orderliness Vishnu–Rama brings (back) to a troubled world. Measurement is a paradigm of order and proportion, while movement toward the sacred is pilgrimage. Both of these the Ramnagar Ramlila has plenty of. Ramlilas everywhere, but especially Ramnagar's, are celebratory performances tracing the footsteps of Vishnu. The town of Ramnagar contains in one scene or another all the worlds: divine, human, animal, and demonic. Sometimes Ramnagar is India and Lanka; sometimes it is the kingdoms of Kosala and Videha, homes of Rama and Sita. During the closing days of Ramlila, Ramnagar is Ayodhya, Rama's capital city. The shifts in locale and scale occur organically during the course of the thirty-one-day theatrical narrative. The various locations are not represented by ordinary theatre sets but by permanent sites that are part of Ramnagar's townscape. When not in use they are still called by their Ramlila names. Some sites are physical structures or walled-in enclosures, others are open fields, ponds, or known locations with no special quality to them except that during Ramlila they are part of the story. One is the intersection of Ramnagar's two main streets where, at the end of their exile, Rama and Lakshman are reunited with their brothers Bharat and Shatrughna. Others, like the great pool of the Durga temple that serves as the *kshir sagar* (ocean of milk) where Vishnu sleeps before incarnating himself as Rama, preexist Ramlila by several centuries. Besides the fixed sites, and just as important, are the roads and pathways connecting focal points. Thus Ramlila's movement map is a complicated web consisting of nodal sites and linking pathways. Many Ramlila environments were constructed, and the connecting routes laid out, some 150 years ago when Ramnagar Ramlila took its present shape.

In all the versions of the Rama story throughout India and south Asia journeying, wandering, pilgrimage, and marching – movements large and small, secular, religious, adventurous, and military – are decisive. Virtually every Indian knows the Rama story; many believe it to be historical fact. In Hindi-speaking north India especially, Rama is king of kings. There is something deeply Indo-European about the *Ramayana*: the Aryans who probably brought the story with them into the subcontinent were nomadic; in other areas of Asia and Europe where they went the Aryans brought similar stories of perilous journeys, adventurous expeditions, and wars fought to recover stolen wives.[3] Movement over great distances in the

Ramayana is made necessary by a war that expresses lust, religion, and politics; a war involving the whole cosmos, from the gods of heaven and demons of the underworld to the human and animal inhabitants of middle earth. The divine–human heroes admire and collaborate with monkeys and bears (who the authors of the *Ramayana* might have thought of as less-developed humans: an early example of the radically hierarchical structuring still characteristic of Indian society).

Moving from site to site is characteristic of Ramnagar Ramlila. It is the dramaturgical, processual, and ritual way of demonstrating how Vishnu–Rama rids the world of Ravana. Rama prepares India for its golden age, the *Ramraj* (kingdom of Rama), by "widely striding" – first by going into exile, then by pursuing Ravana south through the spine of India and across the sea to Lanka, and finally by returning to Ayodhya in a triumphal recapitulatory procession. Even at the very end of Ramlila, after his coronation, durbar, and public sermon, Rama continues to move – mounting the royal elephants for the journey from Ayodhya to the palace of the maharaja of Banaras (a ceremonial visit that takes place in no other Ramlila but Ramnagar's). Throughout Ramlila, Rama "takes steps" in both senses of the word: he acts, he moves. And thousands of spectators follow in his footsteps. He meets Sita by traveling from Ayodhya to Janakpur. He puts the action of ridding the world of Ravana in play by surrendering his claim to the throne and voluntarily going into exile. He pursues Ravana to Lanka. He displays his authority over Kosala and all of India by riding his royal elephant through the streets of Ramnagar–Ayodhya.

But any summation of the narrative is bare bones. What those attending Ramlila experience is a rich mix of texts: literary, dramatic, choreographic, ritual, religious, popular, musical, spatial, and temporal. The choreographic, spatial, and temporal texts concern me here. The crowds who attend Ramlila join Rama on his journeys through the mythopoetic space of epic India. As they follow, they identify with Rama: Ramlila is not a theatre of make believe but of hyperreality. Rama's movements are reinforced by the corresponding movements of spectators and the maharaja of Banaras. Even getting to and going from the Ramlila grounds constitutes an important dimension of the performance.

Word texts and narrative structures

Ramlila incorporates several texts, both literary and performative. The Sanskrit *Ramayana* (attributed to Valmiki), never uttered but always present, is the fiber of Rama's story. But what the crowds at Ramnagar Ramlila gather to hear is the chanting of Tulsidas's *Ramcharitmanas*, composed in the sixteenth century, and the recitation of poetic dramatic dialogues called *samvads*, texts stitched together in the nineteenth century by scholars under the patronage of the maharaja of Banaras and revised in the 1920s. The *Manas*, sung by twelve ramayanis, household priests of the maharaja, is as familiar to Hindi speakers of north India as the King James Bible is to English speakers. The ramayanis always sit close to the maharaja, making him the principal auditor of the *Manas*. The samvads render the *Manas* into almost contemporary vernacular Hindi. Throughout the performance, the chanting of the ramayanis alternates with characters reciting the samvads. The samvads are not spoken in a naturalistic style as in modern Indian theatre, but shouted out sing-song, slowly, so that the assembled thousands catch every word. When Rama speaks, the crowd roars back *"Bol! Raja Ramcandra ki jai!"* – "Speak! Victory to King Rama!" At emotional or highly dramatic moments people break into *kirtans*, songs whose only text is *Jai sitaram!* – Victory to Sita and Rama! People cheer, dance, sing, and worship, animating the Ramlila with the rich energies of north Indian Hindu practice.

But Ramlila is more than the proclamation of texts, the display of spectacle, and energetic audience participation. It is the carefully crafted enactment of a narrative transmitting information and values concerning sacred history and geography (closely linked by means of a complex Indian pilgrimage system), social hierarchy, ethics, and the personalities of gods, heroes, and demons. Ramlila plays out Rama's story starting with his birth and that of his brothers Bharat, Lakshman, and Shatrughna; his education and early adventures; his winning of Sita by breaking Shiva's bow (symbolically asserting Rama's dominion over Shiva). Then, just before Rama is to be crowned king, Kaikeyi – the youngest of Dasaratha's three queens – insists that the old king grant her two wishes he had promised her. "What do you want?" "That my son Bharat be king and that Rama be sent to the forest for 14 years!" Forced to grant these wishes (a promise is a promise), Dasaratha keels over, dead of grief. But Rama feels no anger towards his stepmother or half brother. All is part of the cosmic plan, Vishnu's great lila (sport, play, theatre, see chapter 2). Accompanying Rama into exile are Sita and Lakshman.

At Chitrakut Rama establishes a royal residence in exile. Bharat visits him and begs him to return to Ayodhya. Rama refuses and moves further into the forest, south to Panchavati. At Panchavati Shurpanakha, sister of Ravana, seeing Rama and Lakshman, is struck by their beauty. She assumes the form of a comely woman but first Rama and then Lakshman reject her. Lakshman ridicules Shurpanakha and cuts off her nose and ears (a bloody but comic scene in the Ramlila). Assuming her demonic shape, hurt, humiliated, and enraged, Shurpanakha flees across the sea to Ravana's kingdom in Lanka. Her brother dispatches an army of demons to avenge her. Rama and Lakshman promptly slaughter them. Then, using a golden deer as a decoy, Ravana lures Rama and Lakshman from Sita, kidnaps her, and carries her to Lanka. The divine brothers gather an army of monkeys and bears – including Rama's beloved devotee, the monkey god Hanuman. They pursue Ravana the length of India and across the narrow straits to Lanka. Meanwhile, Sita, refusing Ravana's advances, is imprisoned in a garden of ashoka trees where she calmly awaits her liberation. After many preparations and adventures – including Hanuman's foray into Lanka where he meets Sita, is captured, and, when Ravana sets fire to his tail, grows to gigantic size and burns down the demon-king's capital city – Rama's army invades Lanka. A great war ensues. Ravana's demon hordes are annihilated. Finally, Rama meets Ravana in single combat and slays him. Sita is rescued, her chastity proved in a fire ordeal. Then Rama's party load on to Ravana's magic flying chariot, the *pushpaka*, and make their triumphant journey back to Ayodhya, roughly retracing their outgoing path. Wherever they go joyous crowds greet them. As they approach Ayodhya, Bharat and Shatrughna rush to meet them and the four brothers are reunited in the famous "Bharat Milap" (reunion with Bharat). Rama is crowned king in Ayodhya, marking the start of Ramraj, the golden age of his rule.

The three big movements of the epic – birth to marriage, exile to war, triumphant return and Ramraj – are divided into five main action groups in the Ramnagar Ramlila:

1 A prelude where Brahma implores Vishnu to take on human form and rescue the world which is being terrorized by Ravana.
2 The birth, education, and initiation of Rama, culminating in his winning and marrying Sita.

3 The fourteen years of exile during which Rama acquires political, ethical, and spiritual knowledge as well as martial prowess by means of ordeals, meetings with sages, and war. The thirteen years of exile before Sita's kidnapping take six Ramlila days while the fourteenth year, the war against Ravana, takes eleven days, more than one-third of the entire performance.

4 The coronation of Rama, his teachings, and the start of Ramraj.

5 A postlude, the *kot vidai* (farewell), performed only at Ramnagar.

At the kot vidai the maharaja and his family welcome the swarups to the Fort and feed them in a ceremony witnessed by a huge audience of dignitaries and commoners. The next day, in private, the maharaja pays the performers for their services. These two actions – honoring the gods, paying the actors – bring the story of Rama into a field controlled by the maharaja. It frames the mythos within the political-economic realities of modern India. But not quite; the noumenon of Rama is not so easily paid off.

The narrative structure of Ramlila can be imagined as a looped, sometimes even backwards-moving, set of events. Rama is a god; he can overcome all difficulties; he is conscious of his divinity and power. So there will be no dramatic conflict unless Rama agrees to play the part of a man. It is his lila (literally his sport, his drama) to do so. In this way, the action of human emotions and demonic energy is included; in fact, these give the story its kick. If Queen Kaikeyi's envy and ambition had not forced King Dasaratha to stop Rama's coronation and exile him, there would be no drama, just a straight line from Rama's birth, education, and marriage to his golden rule as king. He would not encounter Ravana, leaving unfulfilled Vishnu's promise to Brahma. The heart of Ramlila is what happens to Rama during his exile: the kidnapping of Sita, the march southward through India, the meeting with Hanuman, the war against Ravana and his demon hordes, the liberation of Sita, and their triumphant return home. In Ramnagar, the movement from one theatrical environment to another gives specific performative actuality to this complex narrative structure. The enacted Ramlila makes plausible and theatrically exciting Vishnu's incarnation as Rama, giving flesh, emotion, conflict, words, songs, and sights – drama – to Rama's earthly acts as student, son, brother, warrior, husband, protector of brahmins, wandering ascetic, priest, and teacher: all the roles possible for a devout Hindu upper-caste male. It brings into full view a marvelous cast of characters from the arrogant, magnificent Ravana to the humble, simple, loyal, and strong

Hanuman, from the scheming hunchback Manthara to the blissful Sita, from witty Angad, son of the slain monkey-king Bali, to Marica the wily magician . . . and dozens more sages, demons, commoners, saints, and beasts. The twenty-eight-day loop in the narration that is Rama's exile, day 9 through 28 of the Ramnagar Ramlila, is when most of the adventures take place, the theatrical core of Ramlila's *yana* or journey.

The theatrical environments

Ramnagar Ramlila is played out in a unified sacred space with nine main stations – Ayodhya, Janakpur, Chitrakut, Panchavati, Rameswaram, Lanka, Bharat Milap, Rambag, the Fort – linked by major roads, paths, and ponds. The overall pattern of movement among these stations is a gyre. The opening days' action rotates slowly around a tight axis from Rambag to Ayodhya to Janakpur and back to Ayodhya. But when Rama's exile begins, the action opens eastward from Ayodhya and then south from Chitrakut to Panchavati to Lanka. The celebrations following Rama's victory over Ravana open the gyre to its widest extent. The experience of spectators during those final days is one of ecstatic spinning through the multiple time/spaces of Lanka–Ayodhya–Rambag–Ramnagar–India.

The theatrical environments, deployed over about fifteen square miles, were defined in the early to mid-nineteenth century by religious and ritual specialists, scholars, poets, and theatre practitioners, assembled and guided by the maharajas of Banaras. The first maharaja of the present royal family, Balwant Singh, who ruled from 1740 to 1770, constructed the Fort in Ramnagar. Other maharajas have added to it so that by now it is a conglomeration of buildings and courtyards, by far the largest structure in Ramnagar. The Ramnagar Ramlila took much of its present form under the guidance of Maharaja Iswhari Prasad Narain Singh who ruled from 1835 to 1889. The present maharaja, Vibhuti Narain Singh, ascended to the throne in 1935. Of course, since Indian Independence in 1947, there is no "kingdom" in the actual political sense over which this maharaja reigns. His very identity as a king is dependent to a large degree on his patronage of and participation in the Ramlila. Vibhuti, like his predecessors, takes a great and personal interest in the Ramlila. He is active in its every aspect from the selection of boys to perform the *swarups* (Rama, his brothers, and Sita) to the careful supervision of the samvads to deciding what the spatial arrangements are to be.

Ramlila (literally "Rama's playing" or "sport") is performed in Ramnagar ("Ramatown"). All Ramlilas are a kind of environmental theatre, but none is the equal of Ramnagar's in scope or theatrical detail. A scale map of Ramnagar Ramlila as it was in 1978 (figure 5.1) shows five main fixed theatrical environments: Rambag, Ayodhya–Fort, Janakpur, Panchavati, and Lanka. The scale map discloses a somewhat different spatial organization from that seen in a map serving as a program in 1946 (Figure 5.2). The discrepancies signal either changes over the thirty-two-year gap between maps (a development I doubt) or the difference between the Ramlila space as it is and as its authors imagine it to be. The 1946 program-map conflates the distances separating Ayodhya, Janakpur, and Rambag; it pushes Panchavati to the east away from Ayodhya and closer to Lanka. It gives the overall impression of action taking place on a northwest to southeast diagonal axis, from central India to Rameswaram to Lanka. This configuration neatly fits the directionality of the narrative, making the Ramlila space an accurate model of the *Ramcharitmanas*. The 1978 scale map shows less of a correspondence between narrative and space. Chitrakut and Rambag are in the northeast, Janakpur in the northwest, Ayodhya, the Fort, and Panchavati in the west, the Bharat Milap in the center, and Lanka far to the southeast. These centers of action are linked by a dense network of roads and paths. Journeying from place to place is a hallmark of Ramlila. Often an episode will stop before the scene being performed is completed. The next day people assemble to witness the final minutes of the scene. Then all, performers and spectators alike, move to a new setting some kilometers away to begin a new scene. Orthodox staging and dramaturgy would finish a scene in place as well as cluster settings. But Ramlila undercuts ordinary dramaturgy and disperses settings in order to require frequent long moves. The pilgrimage and exile themes are integral to the performance, not only narratively but also physically.

The theatrical environment with the most scenes is in and around Rambag ("Rama's garden"), a 515 feet by 340 feet walled-in pleasure garden built in the mid-nineteenth century for Ramlila. Rambag contains several buildings, including at its center a small, exquisitely carved marble gazebo where Rama enunciates his teachings on day 30, Ramlila's next to final episode. In Rambag there is also a large building used as a shop for making effigies and props, a rehearsal hall, and from days 9 to 19 living quarters for the swarups. Ramlila opens near Rambag's front gate with Ravana acquiring the powers that he immediately abuses. But from atop a Rambag tower Vishnu answers

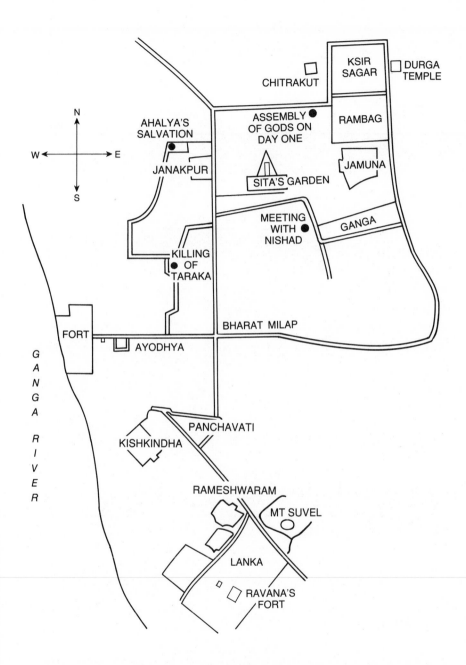

Figure 5.1 A scale map of Ramnagar Ramlila as it was in 1978, showing all the principal theatrical environments. (Drawing by Richard Schechner from a Ramnagar surveyor's map)

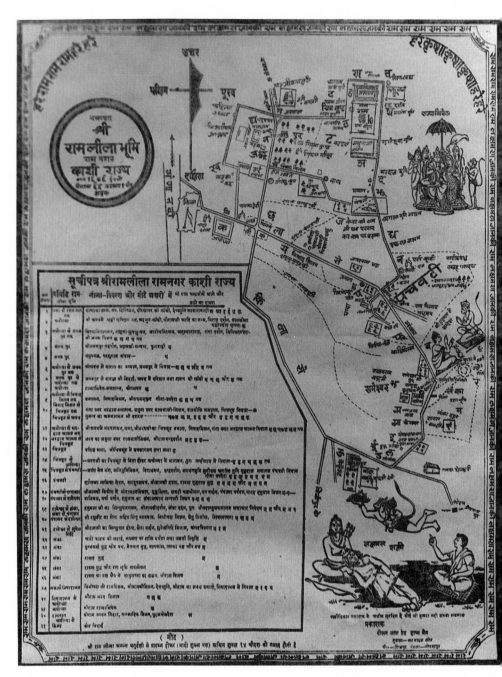

Figure 5.2 The program-map of the 1946 Ramnagar Ramlila. This way of presenting Ramlila underlines the processional and environmental theatre qualities of the celebration. (Map courtesy of Vibhuti Narain Singh, maharaja of Banaras)

the gods' prayers: "For your sake I will take on the form of a human. I will rid the earth of its burden."

That night the scene shifts to the 550 feet square pool fronting an old Durga temple just north of Rambag. Floating in the middle of the kshir sagar, the endless ocean of milk, reclining on Shesha, the 1,000-headed serpent, his dutiful wife Sita stroking his legs, Rama awaits his birth. Rama begins his exile on day 9 by traveling nearly 5 kilometers from Ayodhya through city streets and alleys into the jungle-like environments near Rambag. After spending their first night in exile in a hermitage, Rama, Sita, and Lakshman accept the humble hospitality of the tribal chief Guha who, weeping, offers them bulbs, roots, and fruits, his only food. On day 11 they cross the Jamuna and Ganga rivers signified by two small lakes south of Rambag. On day 12 Bharat leaves Ayodhya for Chitrakut, placed close to Rambag, where Rama takes up residence.

The Rambag site may have been selected because of the large Durga temple pool, and to draw strength from the female power associated with the temple. The temple dates from around 1700, more than 100 years before Ramnagar Ramlila began. How Rambag anchors the sense of Ramlila's symmetrical spatial harmony is demonstrated by an anecdote told me by the Maharaja's younger brother, C. P. N. Narain Singh:

> Some years back, but during my lifetime, the wall of Rambag collapsed so the first day's lila [set in Lanka] could not be enacted there. Everything was transferred to Retinbag near to Lanka where there also was a tank and a garden – but in miniature scale. For 10 or 12 years the Ramlila began in Retinbag – during that time only the real Lanka was used as Lanka. When Rambag was repaired a controversy arose. Some people said, Why not utilize Retinbag? There is a logical justification for continuing there, why bring it back? But other people argued, The Ramlila should start just outside Rambag. The middle of the cycle, the days at Chitrakut are also at Rambag, and the end of Ramlila is inside Rambag. The cycle begins outside of Rambag in chaos and ends inside Rambag with perfect harmony. So to many people it was less important to have the real Lanka than to experience this rhythmic harmony. So the first lila was brought back from Retinbag.

Chitrakut is situated slightly northwest of Rambag and as two photographs taken some fifty years apart show, there has been virtually no change in this environment (plates 5.1 and 5.2). Chitrakut is near the front of Rambag, close to the pool that is the kshir sagar: Rama is still close to Ayodhya, its people, and its concerns. When on day 13 Bharat arrives at

Chitrakut to ask Rama to return to Ayodhya and the throne, he is accompanied by hundreds of "Ayodhyans" – spectators who have journeyed with him from the center of Ramnagar. Rama not only rejects Bharat's pleas, he decides to move further into the forest to live as a hermit. Thus on day 14 Rama and his party leave for Panchavati deep in the Dandaka forest. The beginning of the three-mile, two-day journey from Chitrakut to Panchavati takes Rama around the Durga pool where, in front of the temple, they meet Indra "the god of atmospheric phenomena, wielding the thunderbolt and conquering darkness" (Tulasi Das 1971:512). In 1978, appropriately, a fierce tempest struck at the moment of Indra's appearance. After a pause of about an hour while performers and spectators alike took what cover they could, all resumed the trek to Panchavati.

Giving in to the weather is very much part of Ramlila. Nearly every year, several episodes have to be squeezed into days not assigned to them because the weather forces cancellations or sudden endings of a night's performance. Generally, the weather improves as the cycle progresses. By the closing days of Ramlila, the hot, humid rainy season has given way to glorious sunny days and clear, brisk, cool nights. It is as if even the weather celebrates Rama's triumph.

The environments of Ayodhya–Fort – the palaces of Ramlila's two main kings, Rama and the maharaja – are located where Ramnagar meets the Ganga river. Ayodhya is a simple 370 feet by 285 feet rectangular courtyard with a raised stage at the south end (plate 5.3) – a version of the large interior courtyards characteristic of the maharaja's huge and complex Fort (plate 5.4). Possibly Ayodhya is modest so as not to upstage its neighbor. Ayodhya is the stage for Ramlila's start and finish: Rama's birth, childhood, and early manhood (days 2 and 3); the events after Rama and Sita marry, leading to Rama's exile (days 7, 8, and 9); Bharat's placing of Rama's sandals on the throne before retiring to Nandigram for the duration of Rama's exile (day 14); and Rama's coronation, teaching, and farewell (days 29, 30, 31). But of these final events, only the coronation takes place wholly in Ayodhya – the other lilas begin there and then move to Rambag or the Fort. By Ramlila's end Rama is king of the whole world, and all of Ramnagar is his Ayodhya.

The environments of Panchavati and Kishkindha are intentionally small-scale and rustic with few permanent structures, only a small shrine atop a hill, a raised platform or two. Here in the deep forest the tone of Rama's adventures changes drastically. No longer is he concerned with the court at Ayodhya. The forest is full of reclusive sages, dangerous demons, and

Plate 5.1 Rama's palace in exile at Chitrakut as it appeared in the 1920s. (Photo: courtesy of Vibhuti Narain Singh, maharaja of Banaras)

Plate 5.2 The same environment in 1978. (Photo: Richard Schechner)

animals; a place where magic, deceit, and violence abound. Shurpanakha takes the form of a beautiful woman. Ravana's ally, the demon-magician Maricha (whose mother, Taraka, the boy Rama killed on Ramlila day 3), transforms himself into the golden deer Sita insists Rama hunt. As Rama's arrow pierces the deer, from its mouth comes a replica of Rama's voice crying for help. As Lakshman rushes to his brother, Ravana, disguised as a beggar-priest, kidnaps Sita. Violence begets violence. Ravana dismembers Jatayu, the brave vulture who tries to rescue Sita; in dire need of allies, Rama treacherously kills the monkey-king Bali to gain the aid of Bali's brother, Sugriva, whose minister is Hanuman. The only unalloyed positive happening in these places is the meeting with Hanuman.

Interestingly, Panchavati and Kishkindha are, as it were, the backyard of Ayodhya. The Panchavati–Kishkindha environments cannot be seen from Ayodhya, but a glance at the 1978 map shows how close they are to each other. This may be theatrical expediency, or it may indicate an association between Rama's capital and the crisis that precipitates his war against Ravana. On day 16 at Panchavati an intriguing conflation or vortex occurs – as if Ravana's seizing of Sita, which precipitates the demon-king's downfall and paves the way for Rama's kingship, sucks in the whole story. Thus midway in Ramlila's temporal scheme, at a place where Rama's low point (Panchavati) and high point (Ayodhya) converge, the full narrative is experienced in a flash.

Lanka is Ramlila at its biggest (plate 5.5), a vast rectangular field about 900 feet by 600 feet – larger than Rambag and the Durga temple-pool combined. Although distances covered during some of the lilas – journeys of three miles or more – are much larger than Lanka, no single Ramlila "stage" is. Lanka's vast open space is Ravana's kingdom, Ramlila's ultimate battlefield. From Rama's headquarters on Suvel Hill to Ravana's fort is 650 feet; from the ashoka garden, where Sita calmly sits accepting her captivity, to the battlefield halfway between Suvel Hill and Ravana's fort is 340 feet. Ravana's earthen fort is 120 feet by 95 feet, his meeting hall considerably smaller. On dasahara day when Ravana is killed and cremated Lanka is packed with 75,000 people. On other days, 10,000 to 30,000 assemble. These enthusiastic crowds – like those at sports matches – give scope to the epic battles bringing down Meghnad, Kumbhakarna, and finally Ravana. Expectedly, the biggest *mela* (fair, hubbub) of Ramlila assembles on Lanka's fringes where food, tea and soft drinks, toys, games, dyes, and herbs are all for sale. Ravana's fort is at Lanka's southern extreme. From here emerge the demon-king's

Plate 5.3 Ayodhya, the capital of Rama's kingdom, as it was in 1976. The scene is early in the Ramlila when Rama's father King Dasaratha was still alive. The action is taking place on the ground level, under the umbrellas. At other times, action takes place on the upper level. (Photo: Richard Schechner)

Plate 5.4 One of the interior courtyards of the Fort, the palace of the maharaja of Banaras, as the 1976 dasahara procession begins. (Photo: Richard Schechner)

staunchest allies, his son Meghnad and his nephew Kumbhakarna, 30-foot effigies cunningly built of bamboo and papier-mâché. In battle Rama systematically dismembers Kumbhakarna – first his nose comes off, then his head, and finally his trunk snaps in two. Stagehands working the demon can be seen high up in the structure.

The bigness of Lanka is a strong way to show how great a victory Rama's is. The assembly of so many beings of all kinds signifies the universality of Rama's triumph. Standing in Lanka, one is swallowed by its physical and metaphysical immensity. Yet for ordinary people especially, Rama is god in human form, human-sized. Often framed by small-scale temple architecture, or in his modest camp on Suvel Mountain, Rama radiates intensity, not size. His adversaries are beings who have distorted the shape of the world, making it monstrous like themselves. Ravana, although played by a human actor – except on dasahara night when his gigantic effigy (corpse? true self?) sits atop his fort awaiting cremation – governs a world of giants (plate 5.6).

But the final battle itself is underplayed – to emphasize its religious rather than military significance. On day 26 of Ramnagar Ramlila, after the two adversaries have drawn their war chariots up to the battleground, and exchanged a few volleys of arrows, the man playing Ravana takes off his ten-headed mask and walks over to Rama. He salutes Rama by folding his hands, bows before him, and respectfully touches his feet. Then he turns and walks off into the huge dasahara crowd. After dark Rama shoots an arrow into Ravana's giant effigy which all day has stood on Ravana's fort. Five hot-air balloons are released from behind the effigy – their tiny yellow flames remain visible for a long time in the night sky. These balloons signify Ravana's spirit rising into Rama's mouth. Then the effigy is set ablaze. In *Ramcharitmanas* the final combat is bloodier but the outcome no different.[4]

The very bigness of the demons embodies their evil. Studying old drawings and photographs, some from the 1920s, one from about 1830, makes it clear that in recent years the battles fought in Lanka are not on as grand a scale as they used to be (plate 5.7). The number of elephants and giant effigies is fewer, due to reduced budgets, if not changing tastes. In the early 1980s a small road was built across Lanka. A major highway is planned close by. "Think what that would mean," the maharaja said. "During some of the most delicate scenes – Rama's grieving for wounded Lakshman, Sita's lament as she sits in the ashoka garden – we would hear the roar of trucks, smell the benzene." Intensive lobbying has stalled the highway, but for how long? Pressures are building for further development. "Why should so much land

Plate 5.5 Lanka on dasahara, 1978. In the background, the effigy of Ravana's upper body sits atop his fort. Crowds of up to 75,000 pack Lanka on the days of big battles and especially on dasahara. (Photo: Richard Schechner)

Plate 5.6 Ravana as an arrogant, horrendous effigy awaiting cremation in 1978. Already defeated in battle, Ravana's cremation signals his final surrender to Rama and his release from his demonic self. (Photo: Richard Schechner)

just lie unused most of the year," a man told me as he cast his eyes across Lanka's expanse, "when we poor farmers have nothing on which to grow our crops?"

It is not only in Lanka that large-scale figures appear from time to time.

THE FUTURE OF RITUAL

On day 3 the demon Taraka is slain on the road to Janakpur; Surpanakha shows herself in both her human and demon forms on day 16; later that same day the big vulture Jatayu battles with Ravana; and on day 19 at Rameswaram the giantess Surasa blocks Hanuman's way to Lanka. The scene of Hanuman overcoming Surasa is a favorite of Ramlila-goers. Surasa is 35 feet high, a magnificent structure, her earrings the size of a child. Surasa, sent by the gods to test Hanuman, rises out of the sea. "Stop!" she shouts, "I am going to eat you!" Hanuman replies, "When I have finished Rama's business and reported to him about Sita, then I will enter your mouth. But let me pass now." Surasa will not. According to the *Ramcharitmanas*, each time Hanuman expands himself to get by her, she enlarges her mouth – first to a width of 8 miles, then 128, and finally 800 miles. Then, tricking her, Hanuman takes on a minute form, flies into her mouth, and comes out again, bowing his head and bidding her farewell. Surasa agrees that Hanuman has passed the test. In Ramlila this scene is played by replacing the adult Hanuman with a boy dressed in an identical costume. Little Hanuman climbs bamboo ladders tied end-to-end all the way to the giantess's mouth. Her mouth opens, revealing wide, neat rows of teeth, a red paper tongue, and the head and shoulders of the man operating the contraption. The boy climbs in, the mouth clamps shut, and big Hanuman appears at the bottom to receive Surasa's blessing.

If the forest is wild and dangerous and Lanka monstrous, Janakpur is placid domesticity. This spacious environment, larger than Rambag, is used early in the cycle (days 3 to 7). Janakpur straddles one of Ramnagar's main roads. To the east is Sita's pleasure garden, 450 feet by 300 feet. In 1978 colorful birds were tethered to tree branches while a real deer grazed the grass next to one of papier-mâché (by 1988 the live deer was gone). A small, white Parvati temple completes the bucolic scene. On the west side of the road is King Janak's palace compound, 200 feet by 325 feet. Sita's garden is "naturalistic," while Janak's compound is pure theatrical convenience (plate 5.8). The main structure is a moderate-sized temple where Sita sits. Three platforms of different heights fill out the environment. One is for Rama and Lakshman and their teacher, the sage Vishvamitra. Another is Janak's royal residence where the wedding of Rama and Sita takes place.[5] The third is for the *dhanushyajna*, the contest among princes testing who can lift Shiva's bow and win Sita's hand. No one can budge the bow except Rama who not only lifts it, but snaps it in three with a flick of his boy's wrist. The dhanushyajna is very decorous, unlike the deceitful, rough, and murderous

Plate 5.7 Lanka on dasahara c. 1830. Note the number and size of the demons, the fireworks, the height of the walls of Ravana's fort, and the number of elephants bearing VIP spectators. (The engraving is from James Prinsep, *Banaras Illustrated*, printed in Calcutta in 1830. Courtesy of Vibhuti Narain Singh, maharaja of Banaras)

kidnapping of Sita. But driving both scenes is the assumption that Sita is a thing to be won and taken.

Why is Ramnagar Ramlila so big?

Why organize the cycle at Ramnagar on such a vast scale? All other Ramlilas are more modest in both space and time. Mansa Ram, founder of the current royal line in the early eighteenth century, rose from the humble position of tax collector. His lineage gained respectability when he arranged his son Balwant Singh's coronation in 1740 as maharaja of Banaras. Balwant ruled until his death in 1770. Mansa Ram's descendants faced the difficult task of establishing their line in a new place. Balwant built the Fort in Ramnagar, establishing there his royal residence. But why would the maharaja of Banaras put his palace on the "bad side" of the Ganga some few kilometers downriver from Banaras?[6] The maharaja wished to establish firmly his power, and his tax-collecting abilities, not only in Hindu Banaras but in the Muslim countryside. He erected the appropriately named Fort as an outpost and barrier between the Nawabs (Muslim rulers) of Avadh and his own Banaras. Later maharajas confirmed and displayed the exalted position of their family by patronizing, developing, and participating in a Ramlila on the grand scale. As Induja Awasthi writes, because "Ramnagar was predominantly a Muslim population, the Maharaja, in the 19th century, in a bid to restore lost glory to the Hindus and to win them over, might have decided to accord state recognition to the Ramlila" (n.d.:2). To this end, the maharajas of the Singh line, wanting to keep hold of the people of Banaras by regularly bringing thousands of them over to the Muslim side of the river, devised a powerful reason for many Hindus to cross the river to Ramnagar where they were dramatically reminded of the maharaja's splendor, power, and devotion.

This motive is forcefully demonstrated on dasahara, also known as *vijaya-dasami* (victorious tenth) which, hardly by accident, is also Durga *puja* (temple service) day. On this tenth day of the month of Ashwina (falling in September or October), Ravana is killed by Rama, Durga – a militant form of the goddess – is celebrated, and the maharaja displays his weapons and royal–military authority with spectacular clarity. On dasahara the narration of Ramlila is interrupted as the maharaja plays out his own story – one he shares with other Indian kings. The festivities begin when the maharaja celebrates a special "weapons puja" (*hathiyar puja*) in one of the large

Plate 5.8 One of the plainly theatrical platforms within the Janakpur environment as it appeared in the winter of 1981. On one such platform the contest to lift Shiva's bow is staged. On another, Rama and Lakshman sit awaiting Rama's turn to see if he can lift the great bow. The only "real" part of King Janak's compound is the temple where Sita sits awaiting the outcome of the contest. (Photo: Richard Schechner)

courtyards of the Fort where a panoply of swords, daggers, guns, and other martial implements (mostly from the late nineteenth and early twentieth centuries) is displayed. I was not allowed to photograph this display, signaling that in some way it was a very special manifestation (I could photograph almost every other aspect of Ramlila). After the weapons puja the maharaja leads Ramnagar Ramlila's largest and most opulent procession – even the elephants have their heads painted and their bodies adorned with silver and silks (plate 5.9). The maharaja and his party, great kettle drums booming, issue from the Fort and march down the main street of Ramnagar out to Lanka. The maharaja leads the procession of elephants through cheering crowds on to the battleground across the very spot where later in the day Rama will vanquish Ravana. Abruptly they turn and leave

Lanka the way they came – having stayed less than ten minutes, never stopping.

What is the meaning of this strange procession that for the only time in the Ramlila violates the performing space? Usually the maharaja remains firmly anchored at the back of the spectators, marking the far end of the "auditorium." The weapons puja is what's left of a very warlike traditional display of kingly might that used to occupy maharajas on dasahara when they marched their armies to the borders of their domain, proclaimed the territory as theirs, confronted their opposing number across the border, and went home. Thus they showed their ability to make war. And they identified themselves with the Vedic horse-sacrifice (*asvamedha yajna*) which Dasaratha himself performs in the *Ramayana* and *Ramcharitmanas*. In this procession the maharaja of Ramnagar stakes out his territory, proclaiming in effect that the Ramlila is his. His bold overriding of the performing space clearly shows who's king of the place.

William Sax digs out the traditional roots of this action.

Rama's military campaign is a kind of *diqvijaya*, a "conquest of the directions." The term is from Sanskrit *dik*, "direction," plus *vijaya*, meaning "conquest" or "victory." . . . The *diqvijaya* begins with a fire sacrifice, then the king proceeds in a clockwise direction, travelling east, south, north, and west, conquering his enemies or receiving their submission (much as in the *asvamedha yajna*) until he has conquered or co-opted potential rivals in all directions. He then returns to his point of origin, now transformed into the capital city and center of the earth. The earliest and most famous account is probably the *Diqvijaya* book of the *Mahabharata*, where four of the five Pandava brothers conquer the world simultaneously. . . . After conquering the world by means of a *diqvijaya*, ancient Indian kings performed ritual journeys in which they displayed their royal power and commemorated the military campaigns that established their rule. Other annual, royal progresses – the *vijaya-yatra* which had as their objective "the renewal and reconstitution of cosmos, society, and kingdom" [Inden 1978:26, 59–60] – occurred annually, after the rainy season. . . . Vijayadasami implies several victories: of Rama over Ravana, of the devotee over his own sins and shortcomings, and of the goddess Durga over the demon Mahisasura in the Durga Puja. According to north Indian tradition, the five Pandava brothers, heroes of the *Mahabharata* war, took up their previously hidden weapons on this day (at the end of their exile [as Rama approaches the end of his]). . . . Vijayadasami is thus an appropriate day for weapon-worship. . . . Several old-timers in Ramnagar told me that before the British came, the Maharaja would make a procession to the very

Plate 5.9 The maharaja's fully dressed elephant and driver on dasahara 1978 awaiting their royal passenger. (Photo: Carolyn and Martin Karcher)

border of his kingdom that day, in effect challenging his enemies to give battle
if they dared.   (1989:15–16)

The maharaja confirmed this, saying that the dasahara procession was once
an actual display of military might: the reigning maharaja, accompanied by
his armed soldiers, would go to the borders of his domain, near Mirzapur,
some thirty miles east of Ramnagar. In this way, on the day of the final battle
between Rama and Ravana, the maharaja publicly marks out, or used to
mark out, the extent of his kingdom – as with Vishnu's "expanding,"
Vamana's striding (see p. 174), Rama's goings.

Whatever its extrinsic and symbolic purposes, the bigness of Ramnagar
Ramlila is consistent with its own internal logic. The intent of Ramlila's
authors was a performance that would not be a reduction or parody of the
Ramcharitmanas but a popular reproduction of it as sacred theatre. They
integrated temple ritual, pilgrimage, poetry, and drama. The kernel of
Ramlila has remained constant for more than 150 years even as diminishing
financial resources, especially during the past fifty years, roughly since
World War II and Indian independence, have meant a scaling back of the
numbers of elephants and effigies. The overall size of Ramlila and its
attraction as a devotional and pilgrimage center is intact. And compared to
Ramnagar's, other Ramlilas are small-scale. Some are famous for this or that
scene, such as Varanasi's Nati Imli Bharat Milap which the maharaja and half
a million onlookers attend, or Delhi's display of fireworks as Ravana's effigy
explodes on dasahara. But only Ramnagar combines specularity and devotion – the recitation of the *Ramcharitmanas*, the focused silence of the *arati*
worship concluding each lila episode, the many scenes of intense religious
fervor, pilgrimage both within individual lilas and as a characteristic of the
Ramlila taken as a whole. At Ramnagar the sometimes contradictory combination of magnificence and asceticism so typical of Hindu tradition is
accented. The ascetic tendencies of the story are played out within the frame
of a big-scale theatrical production. When Rama, Sita, and Lakshman enter
the forest they go as ascetics, their arms and legs neatly streaked with
sandalwood paste representing the ashes renouncers are covered with. But
they continue to wear their fancy royal–godly crowns. The maharaja says
the crowns ensure the stability of the icon for devoted spectators. Thus the
metamessage of the Ramnagar Ramlila even during the forest scenes is of
splendid royal and divine presence. The hundreds of sadhus at Ramlila,
many smeared in ashes and nearly naked, demonstrate devotion and renun-
ciation (*tapasya*). Tapasya is also the choice of many spectators walking

barefoot long distances in dust and mud, submitting to rain and other hardships, neglecting their businesses and family life for a month.

Transforming Ramnagar into a theatre, maintaining environments of scale, singing the *Ramcharitmanas*, assembling scholars, poets, and sadhus to compose the samvads, and carefully rehearsing the swarups so that the samvads are recited with clarity and feeling – all of these make Ramnagar Ramlila unique. By providing food and lodging for sadhus, the maharaja guarantees that these holy men from distant places flock to the Ramlila – further authenticating it. One could interpret the provision of food and lodging cynically, as one sadhu told Sax:

> Just understand this one thing – we come for bread. As long as the bread lasts, we'll stay. Do you see that field there? – it's filled with sadhus. But if the Maharaja were to stop feeding them bread, they'd all run.   (Sax 1982:40)

Or one could argue that it is the *dharma* (duty) of kings to feed holy beggars. In any event, the ambivalences and multiplicities of Ramlila are everywhere visible. Ramlila is not reducible to single meanings or experiences. Rather, it is an extensive cycle of events offering performers and spectators what they are looking for – ranging from devotion to bread, from excitement to meditation, from drama to pilgrimage. Ramlila is felt to be in everyone's interest but for many different reasons.

What haunts Ramnagar Ramlila is India's national dream of Ramraj, the divine rule of Rama in a golden age where the whole nation is united and strong. This vision demands size. To simulate all India – merging the mythic past with the political present – needs a big field of play. Mohandas Gandhi saw this – he used imagery drawn from Rama's story (if not Ramlila itself) to construct the mythos underlying the Indian struggle for independence from Moghul and British rule. Rama's story concerns the emergent sovereignty of an heroic Hindu solar king. This mythos, so much a part of the Ramlila, combines religious devotion with nationalist fervor. Each night, rowing back across the Ganga after the lila, those on my boat, led by boatman Ram Das (whose name means "servant of Rama"), sang the following hymn (in Hindi):

> King Rama, leader of the Raghu dynasty,
> Born from Shankara's [Shiva's] drum,
> Born from the waves of the Ganga,
> Husband of pure Sita.

Born from the mouth of the wise.
Hail to Sita's Rama,
And to Hanuman, who carries our burdens
And grants us favors.

Hail to Mother Ganga!

This is like Gandhi's rallying song, sung to the same tune:

King Rama, leader of the Raghu dynasty,
Husband of pure Sita:
May we worship this Sita–Rama.

He is known as Ishwara or Allah.
May this God bestow good sense on everyone.

Gandhi desired a modern Ramraj that would end Hindu–Muslim hatred and bloodshed. But it is not Gandhi's vision that Ramlila projects. Ramlila's politics are chauvinist; Allah is not accorded a place equal to Sita–Rama's. At Ramlila Muslims are present as fireworks technicians, craftsmen, and elephant drivers – all traditional north Indian Muslim work. If they attend as spectators (as I presume some must), they keep a low profile.

Within India's religious-theatrical tradition there is the strongest warrant for the production of a big-scale, highly skilled performance representing the widest possible range of emotions, relating sacred and royal stories, and depicting interactions among gods, humans, and demons. The first and most important Sanskrit sacred and practical text on performance is Bharata's *Natyasastra* (*NS*) (second century BCE–second century CE), which begins by narrating the origins, qualities, and functions of drama. *NS* tells how in ancient days the "people became addicted to sensual pleasures, were under the sway of desire and greed, became affected with jealousy and anger and found their happiness mixed with sorrow" (I, 7–12).[7] The gods wanted an art that would "belong to all the color-groups" (everyone, regardless of caste). Brahma then instructed Bharata in the "fifth Veda" which was drama.[8] As defined by the *NS*, drama consists of:

> representation of the way things are in the three worlds [of gods, humans, and demons]. There is [reference to] duty, sometimes to games, sometimes to money, sometimes to peace; and sometimes laughter is found in it, sometimes fighting, sometimes love-making, and sometimes killing.   (I, 107)

> [Drama] gives diversion to kings, and firmness [of mind] to persons afflicted

with sorrow, and [hints of acquiring] money to those who are for earning it, and it brings composure to persons agitated in mind. (I, 110)

The drama as I have devised it, is a mimicry of actions and conducts of people, which is rich in various emotions, and which depicts different situations. This will relate to actions of men good, bad, and indifferent, and will give courage, amusement, and happiness as well as counsel to them all. (I, 111–12)

A mimicry of the exploits of gods, demons, kings as well as house-holders in this world, is called drama. And when human nature with its joys and sorrows, is depicted by means of representation through gestures and the like it is called drama. (I, 121)

The occasion for the first theatrical production was Indra's Banner Festival depicting the defeat of demons by the gods with "altercations and tumult and mutual cutting off and piercing [of limbs or bodies]" (I, 55–8). This could be a description of Ramlila's battle scenes.

NS is a text of more than 800 pages detailing every aspect of theatrical and dance production. It establishes theatrical performance as a recognized kind of celebratory worship. Thus early in the Indian tradition, theatre is accorded a definite place equal to religious worship – there is no antipathy between the two as there is in Christianity or Islam. Ramnagar Ramlila does not follow the *NS* in details of production (as some Indian classic dance forms claim to do), but shows its kinship to the *NS* by being a large-scale, didactic, and devotional performance, designed for an audience consisting of all castes and classes.

How much have the Ramlila environments changed over time?

The Lanka environment has suffered encroachment – is this a trend? Are there other changes taking place? After studying writings, drawings, lithographs, and photographs, as well as interviewing plenty of people, the evidence shows the Ramlila is surprisingly stable in terms of its physical staging. But we know next to nothing in detail about the Ramnagar Ramlila's first century – from about 1820 to 1920. We do know that the samvads recited today were assembled in the 1920s. But from the 1920s onward there are photographs showing the physical environments and aspects of the mise-en-scene – these appear to be more or less the same over the past seventy years except that, as previously noted, the numbers of effigies and elephants have declined. This deterioration is confirmed by long-time spectators.

This is the view of a farmer who has attended for fifty-five years:

> The difference is that the maharaja's glory was far greater 30 years ago. He came with 100 horses, 30 or 35 elephants, bullock carts – so much finery that all the people in this field [of Lanka] could not carry it all. But there's no difference in the lila itself. Absolutely none. Everything is done exactly as it is written in the [Ramcharit]manas.

Spectators are forgiving concerning sumptuousness as long as what they consider the essence of Ramlila – its conformity to the essence of Tulsidas – is intact.

Ramlila is changing because India has radically changed over the past 150 years. Value systems are different, the authority of the maharajas has been reduced if not entirely eliminated, and the population has more than quintupled since 1850. Spatially speaking, Ramlila has shrunk relative to its surrounding areas. Processions that in the nineteenth century would actually have moved from city to jungle, from settled area to wilderness, today are entirely encompassed by houses, farms, factories, or other evidence of human habitation. Bharadvaj's ashram or Guha's village – both supposedly deep in the forest and probably once actually so – are today enclaves wedged into well-farmed areas. What is unchanged is the feeling of movement through various landscapes, the sense of adventure, exile, and danger followed by a triumphant return home. The Ramlila narrative is so strong and deeply believed, and in Ramnagar it is written in the theatrical environments, the paths connecting them, the acting, even the weather. Ramlila regulars warmly testify to their experience of being inside Rama's world. As Hess notes in her article:

> In tonight's Lila [day 3] the sage Vis[h]vamitra takes Ram[a] and Laks[h]man on a foray to kill demons in the woods. The use of the world as a stage set goes beyond anything the West might call "verisimilitude." We move from the main street to narrow lanes, a troop of horsemen in front, the Maharaja with his elephants behind, the golden gods in the middle gliding along at shoulder level [borne by devotees] – the swarups' feet never touch the ground [except when necessary for the drama]. Shopkeepers and laborers stop to watch the gods go by, saluting them with joined palms. The setting becomes steadily more rural. Roads change from pavement to cobblestone to dirt, houses from plaster to brick to mud, on varying levels, with glittering algae-covered ponds, fields of leafy vegetables and corn, moist greenness everywhere. People are at the doorways, in the yards, on the roofs. If Ram[a] really did go to the forest with

Visvamitra, would it not have been through lanes like this, past houses, from town to village, while the local people stopped to watch? The sky is brilliant salmon and mauve in the luminous moments before sunset. (Hess 1983:176–7)

Flow: pilgrimage, procession, and participation

Vishnu expanding creates the cosmos; Vamana's striding recuperates the three worlds; Rama's goings signify India. For several hours each day during a full month Ramnagar is transformed into mythopoetic epic India. The extended space and time of Ramlila puts one inside the action. In Ramnagar, Ramlila is everywhere – in the lilas themselves, in the mela (the temporary assembly of foodsellers, game hawkers, and merchants who gather near whatever Ramlila ground is in use), in the environments not active today but yesterday or tomorrow, in the small shrines where people sing kirtans, in the dominating presence of the Fort which signifies the maharaja who sponsors the Ramlila. Ramlila's efficacity is heightened by the way time is experienced. One does not "go to" Ramlila as to a theatre. Attending the Ramlila on a regular basis throughout a whole month is a different kind of operation. The mind and body are full of Ramlila; there is no respite from it. Yet, for the *nemis* (devoted spectators), who are regular Ramlila-goers, this total immersion is not exhausting but invigorating. Of course, as the wide variations from lila to lila in crowd size show, relatively few attend all the lilas. But a sizeable number of people see ten or more.

To go to Ramlila as a nemi takes the whole day. Preparations begin with an early morning bath (in the sacred Ganga, if possible) with memories of last night's lila still fresh in mind. Routine activities must be completed by noon. Coming from Varanasi means leaving for Ramnagar between 2 and 3 p.m. – the lila begins at 5. You can cross the Ganga by bus at the northern end of Varanasi, or from the more southerly ghats in one of a fleet of small rowboats, or push aboard the always over-crowded public ferry. Once in Ramnagar you easily fall into the stream of pedestrians, bicycles, cycle and scooter rickshaws, and motorcycles. The festive atmosphere takes over. There are snacks and tea and familiar faces. You look forward to the day's story, the next adventures of characters you already know well. The performance usually consists of two parts, one before *sandhya puja* (evening prayers) and one after. The sandhya puja break starts at about 6 p.m. and lasts an hour or more. Some people pray, many more snack and socialize. The lila usually ends by 10 p.m., though some run later and Rama's coronation is an all-night affair. After the lila most people go directly home. A few stop to sing kirtans or listen to others doing so; or buy some *pan* or tea at one of the stalls near the ghat. This mix of devotion, meditation, celebration, and socializing is typical pilgrimage behavior in India – a happy "time out" from ordinary life – part religious obligation, part vacation. If you cross the Ganga by rowboat at night (the ferry no longer runs at this hour) you sing hymns, scoop some holy river water on to your face, reflect on the lila's events. By the time you retire for the night it is midnight or after – the next day's lila is not far off. If you are a nemi, Ramlila swallows you for a month.

Many "private practices" of pilgrimage and devotion blend in with the "official" Ramlila – so much so that it is not easy always to distinguish one type of performance from the other. Rameshwaram, a town on the coast of India facing Lanka, is one of India's most important pilgrimage centers. Here Rama – before building the bridge to Lanka over which his army crosses – established a lingam (the phallic post arising from a symbolic vagina–womb signifying the Hindu god Shiva and his consort the goddess Parvati). Commemorating this, near Ramlila's Rameshwaram, is a small Shiva temple and pool. On day 19, before the regular lila episode, a group of men gather at the temple. They celebrate Rama's preparations for crossing into Lanka with his army of monkeys and bears. Often some of the men get high on *bhanj* (a kind of marijuana). When the lila begins Rama and Lakshman worship the Shiva lingam in the temple. Very few spectators can see inside the small temple. But the crowd is satisfied just knowing that the ceremony is being performed. Over the years, the gathering of men before the lila and the nearly private puja (temple service) inside the temple have been knitted into the more fully public and spectacular portions of the Ramlila. Other even more private gestures and practices have found their way into Ramlila. A Banaras businessman makes *malas* (flower wreaths) for the swarups. The man who played Hanuman for many years, but grew too old for the physically demanding role, attends to the swarups offstage, bringing them yogurt and sweets, washing them, seeing to their ordinary needs. When a man can no longer carry Rama on one shoulder and Lakshman on the other, he is no longer fit to play Hanuman. Until his death in the early 1980s, the "150-year-old sadhu," was for decades a Ramlila star. For many years an old *vyas* (a Ramlila stage director), no longer able to coach the actors, was given the task of shouting "keep quiet! pay attention!" before every utterance of Rama. In the late 1970s and early 1980s a corpulent and aggressive police sergeant was both feared and admired by the big crowds he threatened and assailed with his stout stick. The roads to and from lila places are dotted with small shrines where a few people gather to sing kirtans. These people and events contribute much to Ramlila's effect. Over time these kinds of events change, but their overall effect of thickening and enriching the Ramlila experience remains. New events and persons emerge as others die or fade away.

Ramlila incorporates pilgrimage into its mise-en-scene. S. M. Bhardwaj notes,

> The number of Hindu sanctuaries in India is so large and the practice of pilgrimage so ubiquitous that the whole of India can be regarded as a vast sacred space organized into a system of pilgrimage centers and their fields.
>
> (Bhardwaj 1973:7)

Ramlila is a model of India as a "vast sacred space." Through the agency of the Ramlila environments spectators can visit the same powerful *tirth-sthans* or pilgrimage sites that Rama passes through in his epic journeys from Ayodhya to Janakpur to Chitrakut to Panchavati to Rameshwaram to Lanka and back to Ayodhya. The crowds cross the real Ganga river to watch Rama and Sita cross the pond that becomes the Ganga in Ramlila. Furthermore, Ramnagar Ramlila is itself a tirth-sthan. People from all over India come to Banaras during Ramlila season to bathe in the Ganga, visit the Vishwanath temple and other holy sites, and experience Ramlila. In 1978, a man who for two years had been carrying his mother in a basket around India visiting holy places arrived at Ramlila (plate 5.10). Their itinerary was very full: they could spare but one morning touring the maharaja's Fort and one night at Ramlila before setting out toward another pilgrimage site.

According to the report Sax gave me in 1979 of his survey of spectators at the Ramlila Ramnagar in 1978, 80 per cent of them consider Ramlila a pilgrimage center.

> *Sadhu*: This is certainly a *tirth*. It is the biggest Ramlila in all of India. Everywhere that Ram[a] went on his wanderings is now regarded as a *tirth-sthan*: Ayodhya, Janakpur, Chitrakut . . . all of them.
>
> *Sax*: But Rama didn't come to Ramnagar on those wanderings.
>
> *Sadhu*: Look over there – do you see all those people reading the *Ramayana* [*Ramcharitmanas*]? If you experience the entire Ramlila with them from start

Plate 5.10 Ramlila is a pilgrimage center. Here a dutiful son is carrying his mother to various important pilgrimage centers in India. Two nights at Ramnagar Ramlila is one of the stops on their 1978 itinerary. (Photo: Richard Schechner)

to finish, walk, read the *Ramayana* and enjoy the lila with them, you have a total pilgrimage experience. Those people *do* go to Ayodhya, Chitrakut, and so on.

Another sadhu: It's true. Completely true. That temple over there is Rameshwaram temple and none other.

Sadhu: I've been to the four *dhams* [primary pilgrimage places], Ayodhya, Chitrakut, Mathura-Brindavan . . . lakhs [hundreds of thousands] of pilgrimage places. I've seen thousands of lilas also, but among all those pilgrimage places and lilas, I tell you that there was not one place where I got as much peace of mind as here at the Ramnagar Ramlila. And there is no place as holy as Kashi [another name for Varanasi or Banaras]. (Sax 1979)

Even allowing for the respondents' self-congratulatory tone, most people feel that the Ramlila environments are sacred and that following the performers from place to place transforms spectators into participant-pilgrims. There is no question that during Ramlila many people empathize with Rama, Sita, and other figures.

Paradigmatic of Ramlila is literally following in Rama's footsteps. By means of these daily minipilgrimages, spectators participate directly and emotionally in Ramlila. They are the admiring citizens of Ayodhya and Janakpur lining the roads or peering from windows, doorways, or rooftops celebrating the meeting and marriage of Rama and Sita; or the heartbroken citizens of Ayodhya weeping as they follow the royal couple into exile. Or hundreds of religious pilgrims joining Bharat as he circumambulates Chitrakut. They follow Rama, Sita, and Lakshman through the forests where the swarups meet gods, demons, monkeys, and *rishis* (saints and sages). They rush angrily in pursuit of Ravana after he kidnaps Sita; they accompany Rama's army of monkeys and bears when they cross from India into Lanka. When Lakshman is wounded in battle, Rama sends Hanuman to the Himalayas to fetch the only herb that can save him. Some spectators remain close to grief-stricken Rama who laments: "Oh, if I had known I would lose my brother in the forest, I wouldn't have obeyed my father. Wealth, son, wife, home, family come and go repeatedly in this world, but a true brother cannot be found!" Others scamper along with faithful Hanuman who takes one hour and covers four miles of "real" time, one night and thousands of miles of story time. After Rama defeats Ravana, and Sita passes her fire ordeal (proving her sexual fidelity to Rama) she takes her place on a huge 20-foot-high wagon next to Rama and Lakshman. Dozens of male spectators tug on the two ropes moving the four-wheeled pushpaka (Ravana's flying chariot) out of Lanka and down the long road toward Ayodhya. After a few hundred yards the wagon stops at Bharadwaj's ashram where Rama and his party will spend the night. When the next night the journey home continues, thousands of joyful spectators join in; others line the streets, wave from windows, or salute the heroes from rooftops. The Bharat Milap – the reunion of Rama and Lakshman with Bharat and Shatrughna – occurs where Ramnagar's two main streets intersect (plate 5.11). Increasingly, over several hours before the Milap, two crowds – one coming from Ayodhya, one from Bharadwaj's ashram – fuse into one.

Many spectators go barefoot at Ramlila because "you don't wear shoes in a temple, and the entire Ram Lila ground sanctified by God's presence, is

Plate 5.11 The square stage – like a boxing ring – set up at the intersection of Ramnagar's two main streets. Here takes place the Bharat Milap – Rama's reunion with Bharat, signalling the end of Rama's exile. Barely discernible outside the parameter of the square stage are the several elephants of the maharaja's party come to witness this joyous scene as it was performed in 1978. Thousands of other spectators stand at street level or peer down from roofs and balconies. (Photo: Richard Schechner)

like a temple" (Hess 1983:174). On some nights the spectators' devotion is sorely tested as they walk five miles or more through thunderstorms and mud. This "going along" with the performance is built into the mise-en-scene. If movement itself were not so important, the Ramlila could easily be structured in a more theatrically conventional way to reduce or eliminate spectator movement. But the creators of Ramlila intended it to be a kind of processional-pilgrimage. Spectators move through various terrains – city, village, farm field, forest. Most of the way is level, but around Panchavati there are a few low hills. When the crowd is settled at an environment watching a scene, male and female spectators are generally separated from each other. But during the processions or moves from one location to another, everyone mixes.

166

Plate 5.12 Lakshman, Rama, and Sita frozen in place, illuminated by bright flares, during the *arati* temple ceremony that closes each day's lila. (This photo was taken in 1978 by Richard Schechner)

Stasis: darshan, arati, and jhanki

Some people attend only a few of the thirty-one lilas or they come just for the mela. Crowds swell and dwindle not only from lila to lila but during each lila. Attendance on any given night is greatest for *arati*, each lila's closing ceremony when the swarups are honored with the waving of a camphor-flame lamp and a shower of flowers as they are illuminated by flares (plate 5.12). During arati it is felt to be particularly beneficial to take *darshan* of the swarups – that is, to get a good clear look at the five boys aged 8 to 14 (or so) who are the gods Rama, Sita, Lakshman, Bharat, and Shatrughna. Darshan means "vision" or "seeing." Hindus believe that the sight of a god, a temple icon, a holy person, or a holy site conveys benefit. During arati it is important that the swarups pose perfectly still. This is because the swarups are also *murtis* (literally, a material image), the word most commonly used for temple icons. Some temple murtis are extremely powerful like the orange-red Hanuman enshrined at Sankat Mochan Mandir in Varanasi or black Lord Jagannath of Puri's Krishna temple. Throughout India one finds sacred stones, figures, and lingams worn smooth where thousands of hands have stroked them. At sites both nationally renowned and local, people make offerings of incense, sweets, flowers, money, and various other things.

During the dramatic portions of Ramlila, the swarups speak and move, enacting the very events that constitute their godhead. At arati they attain the focused stillness of murtis. Some Ramlila gods – Brahma, Shiva, Indra, Hanuman – however convincingly enacted, are recognized as theatrical representations. During the sandhya puja break Hanuman may take off his mask and chat with spectators. But the five swarups are different. Even with their crowns off (signifying that they are not at these times divine), the swarups attract the devoted attention of many who bring them garlands of flowers or touch their feet reverently. During the long night of Rama's coronation, thousands touch and squeeze their feet black and blue in a traditional gesture of reverence and respect. The proximate presence of gods acting out mythic events on sacred grounds climaxes at arati. People surge forward for darshan, many having come miles just for the benefit of this moment. They will not tolerate having their view blocked. The swarups fix themselves in distinct poses – Rama smiles slightly, Lakshman alertly guards his brother, Sita is tranquilly resplendent in her bejeweled sari and orna-ments. Bharat and Shatrughna, when not there as part of the drama, some-times appear out of costume dressed in clean starched clothes.

Ramnagar Ramlila also offers a kind of "unofficial darshan" as spectators take long looks at the sadhus, Rama–Sita's devotees, and the maharaja, Shiva's representative. The sadhus are keenly appreciated both as holy persons and lively individuals who disregard many commonly accepted north Indian social values. Some wear only loincloths, many are smeared with ashes; vigorously dancing and singing they tease each other and the public as they celebrate Rama–Sita. They are very highly regarded and felt to be holy; some, like the "150-year-old sadhu" are believed to possess "powers." In terms of presentation of self, the maharaja is the opposite of the sadhus, a model of formal dress, decorum, circumspection, and quiet devotion. The maharaja displays himself for the public to admire as he witnesses nearly all the lila episodes. Riding atop his royal elephant or in his horse-drawn carriage or seated in the back seat of his 1928 Cadillac, his presence helps keep order. When the maharaja appears or departs, he is greeted as the representative of Shiva with shouts of *"Hara, Hara, Mahadev!"* (Shiva, Shiva, Great God!) – the counterpart to the rolling wave of voices responding to Rama's speeches with, "Bol! Raja Ramachandra ki jai!"

The darshans of Ramlila are effective because they are *jhanki*, literally a "glimpse." Jhanki is a word some Indian theatre workers use to disparage shows emphasizing spectacle over content. But jhanki is much appreciated by ordinary Indians. In Ramlila the tableaux, the frozen iconic moments are jhanki: Vishnu reclining on the serpent Sesha afloat on the kshir sagar; Sita borne into her garden on her silver palanquin; Rama standing gloriously triumphant after breaking Shiva's bow. Each lila's concluding arati is jhanki. For many Ramlila spectators jhanki distills from the flow of the action a crystalline glimpse of a cosmic, eternal divinity.

A double transformation of space

At Ramnagar a simultaneous double transformation of place – from city to theatre and from theatre to mythic geography – occurs. And just as there was a Troy and a Trojan War whose story was reshaped into the *Iliad*, so there may have been historical events underlying the *Ramayana*. According to H. D. Sankalia (1973) these events probably took place in north central India, from today's Ayodhya on the river Sarayu, south to Allahabad (Prayag), west to Chitrakut, and southwest to what was a forested area north of the river Narmada. But as Sanskritization spread, the *Ramayana* spread southward and its geographical field expanded.

> The gradual spread, first of the *Mahabharata* and then of the *Ramayana* into the Deccan, Karnataka, and Tamil Nadu, shows the slow absorption by society, high and low, of certain ethical values. . . . Simultaneously places all over India came to be associated with episodes in the *Ramayana*.
>
> (Sankalia 1973:55)

As the *Ramayana* stories carried by priests, storytellers and other kinds of performers spread south and east, they were identified with local deities and sacred spaces. Indian cultures do not erase their pasts, instead, they remember and reuse. Thus over centuries the subcontinent has become a vast palimpsest of pre-Hindu, Hindu, Buddhist, Muslim, and Western elements. Certainly in Ramlila the Hindu is dominant, but other cultures can also be clearly seen. Specific sites of sacred rivers, crossings, and hilltops are pre-Hindu; the basic narrative, celebratory devotional mood, and pilgrimage pattern is Hindu; the maharaja's elaborate pageantry and the theatrical style of performing owe much to the Moghuls; the petromax lanterns (kerosene under pressure) illuminating most Ramlila scenes, the maharaja's brass marching band, his horse-and-carriage, and his Cadillac are from Europe or America. These are just a few examples from many of Ramlila's multicultural practices.

The geography modeled by Ramlila captures ancient references to rivers and river junctions, hilltops, forests, cities, temples, caves, trees, wells, and paths. Every Indian knows the story of the *Ramayana* which has been retold in countless local variations in many Indian languages. Rama's adventures are the subject not only of Ramlila but of many other media ranging from classic dance and drama to folk theatre, modern dramas, movies, and television. In the *Ramcharitmanas* Rama rules over a great nation larger than modern India but roughly coextensive with it. One might say that Rama's geopoetic domain stretches from Mount Kailash in the Himalayas to Janakpur in Nepal, from Ayodhya and Prayag (Allahabad) on the Gangetic plain across the Ganga, Jamnuna, and Godavari rivers to the Dandaka forest of central India; from the Deccan plateau of peninsular India to Rameshwaram and on to Lanka. Rama's presence as sovereign of this domain is renewed each year by the thousands of Ramlilas performed all across north India. Each of these marks out by means of theatrical environments and definite movements a concrete model of the Indian subcontinent. The Ramlila ground conflates the historical events underlying the *Ramayana*, the mythic field of Rama's journey, realm, and rule, the modern Indian nation, and the theatrical representation of Rama's story.

Seen this way, Ramlila moves between two poles: Ayodhya = home = Rama = Ramnagar = the maharaja's Fort = rightful authority versus Lanka = away = beyond the city = Ravana = tyranny. Between the just order of Ayodhya and the unjust order of Lanka is a disorderly yet adventurous no man's land of mountains, rivers, and jungles populated by India's folk villains and heroes – demons and rishis, tribals, monkeys, and bears. In Ramlila there are lands to be visited (Janakpur), explored (Guha's place to Chitrakut) feared (Panchavati), got through (Kishkindha to Rameshwaram), and conquered (Lanka). Remarkably, this mythopoetic, dramatically active map of India has remained more or less constant from the time of the Valmiki *Ramayana* (fourth century BC–second century AD). It continues to shape the thought, beliefs, and pilgrimage patterns of dozens of millions of Indian Hindus.

Ramnagar's unique concluding scenes

During the final episodes of Ramlila, Rama's world merges with the maharaja's in a way unique to Ramnagar. Even before Rama enters Ayodhya to be crowned, a collapse of time and space occurs. From lila 27, the day after Rama's victory over Ravana, and the start of his journey back from Lanka to Ayodhya, Ramnagar first becomes Rama's kingdom and then his capital city. The scale of the action again changes, this time back to human size. In Lanka the scale was grotesquely over-sized, demonic. After Rama's victory, Lanka is forgotten as Ramnagar prepares to celebrate Rama's victory, coronation, and reign. Townspeople royal and common decorate their homes inside and out; the Fort is festooned with colored lights.

In the *Manas*, during his triumphant return from Lanka, Rama recapitulates the events of the drama:

> "Sita," said Raghubir [Rama], "look at the battle-field; that is where Lakshman slew Indrajit and those huge demons lying on the field were slain by Hanuman and Angad; and here was killed Kumbhakarna and Ravana, the two brothers who discomfited gods and sages. Here I had the bridge built and set up the image of Shiva, abode of bliss." . . . Where the Lord of grace had encamped or rested in the forest, he pointed out every place to Janaki [Sita] and told her the name of each.
>
> Swiftly the car travelled on to the most beautiful forest of Dandaka, where dwelt Agastya and many other high sages; and Rama visited the homes of them all. After receiving the blessings of all the seers, the Lord of the world came to Chitrakut, there he gladdened the hermits, and the car sped swiftly on. Next, Rama pointed out to Janaki the Jamuna. . . . then they beheld the holy Ganga. . . . "Next," he said, "behold Prayag . . . and now behold the city of Ayodhya."   (Tulasi Das 1971:429)

The Rama of Ramlila describes and remembers everything, but theatrically the journey home is abbreviated. There are no crossings of rivers, no visits with hermits in Dandaka. The pushpaka rests the night of lila 26 near a tree sacred to residents of Ramnagar (but not mentioned in the *Manas*) and the night of lila 27 at Bharadvaj's ashram. By the Bharat Milap on the night of lila 28 Ramnagar has become Ayodhya – Rama and the maharaja share a capital. On day 29 the maharaja, a visiting head of state, sits on a white cloth in Ayodhya (Rama's fort) as Rama accepts his crown so long deferred. After the coronation, the comrades from the Lanka war bid farewell to the swarups. This scene mixes joy with deeply felt sadness: everyone knows that Ramlila is coming to an end – that a long year must pass before again "the

171

gods walk the earth for a month." The young monkey Angad, nephew of Sugriva, stumbles slowly down the steps after tearfully saying goodbye to the swarups. Guha reluctantly leaves only after being invited to visit Ayodhya often. The darshan that follows the farewell is Ramlila's longest, lasting until dawn. First the maharaja, next the royal family, and finally ordinary people each bid farewell to the swarups. At dawn, preceded by his military guard who split the surging crowd in two, the maharaja returns for arati.

That evening, Ramlila's thirtieth, Rama's party and the maharaja's join in a single procession through the streets of Ramnagar to the gazebo at the center of Rambag where Rama delivers his teachings. At the head of the procession go Rama and Lakshman with Hanuman sitting behind them holding a royal umbrella. Then come Bharat and Shatrughna with an umbrella held by the Ayodhyan chief minister, Sumantra. Behind them comes the maharaja with one of his men holding the umbrella, and after him his royal family. A large population lines the streets: children jumping up and down in excitement, old and young joining palms and bowing, then rising and cheering. Need we fix these as residents of ancient Ayodhya, or persons celebrating their gods and their kings, or subjects of a medieval Hindu prince, or people of a modern Indian town enjoying a theatrical spectacle?

The next and final day's events, kot vidai (farewell), further dissolve the boundaries between Rama's world and the maharaja's. Although a portion of the *Ramcharitmanas* remains to be chanted, the events of the thirty-first day of the cycle are outside the Rama story and unique to Ramnagar. Late in the afternoon (or at night, as in 1978 when an eclipse of the moon on Ramlila's second day skewed the whole schedule), riding two magnificent elephants, the five swarups arrive at the Fort.[9] The maharaja, barefoot, dressed simply, a devotee of Rama, greets the swarups. Then they are seated on a low platform while the maharaja washes their feet, applies *tilak* (a sandalwood paste mark) to their foreheads, and garlands them. He performs arati as if he were a temple priest and they gods (as a brahmin he is entitled to perform the ceremony). Then the swarups are served a sumptuous meal. The ramayanis – the twelve brahmins led by the maharaja's head priest who, for ten days before Ramlila begins and continuing throughout the cycle, chant the entire *Ramcharitmanas* – recite the final portions of Tulsidas's epic. As the swarups eat, the maharaja is handed a one-rupee coin by an attendant. The maharaja passes this coin to a vyas (one of two priests who are the stage directors of Ramlila) who gives it to Hanuman who gives it to Rama; and the next one to Lakshman, and so on until each of the five swarups is paid.[10] Next the ramayanis and the other principal performers each get one rupee from the maharaja via the vyas.[11]

I believe this public paying of the performers is an assertion at the end of Ramlila of the "real" order of things, showing who's king in Ramnagar. However, a nemi who has attended Ramlila for many years, disagrees. "It is the *dharma* [duty] of a king to give *dakshina* [an honorarium] to brahmins." As with so much in Ramlila, the two interpretations do not cancel each other out. After the swarups have eaten – it takes them more than an hour – the maharaja again performs arati. Then each of the swarups takes off his garland and puts it on the maharaja. This gesture is repeated with each member of the royal family, as at temple the devout give and receive *prasad* (blessed offerings). Then the royal family retires into the interior of the Fort as elephants arrive to take the swarups back to Ayodhya where they give darshan to commoners.

The kot vidai is trivalent: the maharaja pays his performers even as he and his family welcome visiting royalty whom they also worship as gods. All three events take place simultaneously, accomplished by the same set of gestures performed within the confines of a palace that is also a theatre set. Witnessing the scene are the citizens of Ayodhya–Ramnagar–Varanasi. Meanings radiate outward through three frames – that of Ramnagar where Vibhuti Narain Singh is "honorary king" (his real powers having ended with Indian independence in 1947), that of the mythic narrative where Rama and the others are legendary figures, and that of the cosmic-religious system of Hinduism where gods are incarnate. The largest event cosmically is contained within a mythic event which in turn is contained within the social order of Ramnagar. Because of Ramlila, the maharaja retains much of his mystique; because of the maharaja, the Ramlila is special. Indians call such confounding situations "maya–lila," the interpenetration of multiple realities and illusions (see chapter 2). It is neither possible nor desirable to discover which is more "real" or "basic," maharaja or Ramlila. As with Vishnu–Vamana's three steps, the little encompasses the limitless.

Rama's movements, Sita's stillness

Rama is always on the move. Dynamically he fills space as Vishnu–Vamana does. Sita, by contrast, is stillness personified. She sits in her Janakpur garden, on her throne in Chitrakut, and for ten long days under the ashoka tree where Ravana holds her prisoner (plate 5.13). Many women and some men attend Sita, often touching her feet. Even as the action surges on the great Lanka battlefield, Sita sits for hours away from it all. There is nothing for her to say, nothing for her to do. Then, in lila 27, the day after Rama's victory, Sita proves that she has been sexually faithful during her captivity when, in her most active scene, she steps through a circle of fire. For most of Ramlila, Sita is passive, the object of males' desires, the victim of their tricks, the prize of their contests and wars. Yet she is celebrated as Sitaram, the coequal amalgamated deity. She is always present for the arati ceremony at the end of each night's lila.

Sita's almost absolute stillness counterbalances Rama's extreme activity. Wherever he journeys, she is "home," the place where he stops or returns to. His actions are completed by her stillness; his moves to the periphery are answered by her presence at the center. Where she is, he must go to. Much could be said from a Western feminist perspective concerning Sita's "position" in Ramlila. She is a model of the orthodox Hindu construction of "wife."

Dilations of time and space

If the bigness of Ramnagar Ramlila can be understood in terms of the *Natyasastra*'s call for a total theatre meeting the needs of all *varnas* (castes) and as an expression of the need of the maharajas of Banaras to define their authority and territory, it can also be experienced as an embodiment of Vishnu, "the widely striding." In his fifth avatar, that of the Brahmin dwarf Vamana, Vishnu restores balance to a world destabilized by the rule of Bali, a king of such just and ascetic habits that Brahma grants him sovereignty not only over earth but also over heaven. Coming before Bali, Vamana praises the king's generosity and asks for a boon. Bali, respectful of Vamana's priestly caste and flattered by his praises, tells the dwarf to name his favor. "I want for my domain as much space as I can cover in three steps." The king laughs, granting the little man's bizarre request. But growing to enormous size, Vamana with his first step spans the earth, with the second, heaven. Having covered all in two steps there is no need for him to venture a third. Vamana's power is his trickster's ability to shift scale at will, to span with his two steps the whole cosmos. Participating in Ramnagar Ramlila is stepping inside Vishnu's body, which has been dilated sufficiently to include the performance, a "lila" – literally a performance of deep play.[12]

Plate 5.13 Sita – played by a boy as are all the swarups – sits on a simple chair covered by a plain white cloth in the ashoka garden at the edge of Lanka. In 1978, a young girl is one of the many people, mostly women and girls, who stayed near Sita during her days of imprisonment in Ravana's kingdom. (Photo: Carolyn and Martin Karcher)

In the Indian traditions there are plenty of warrants for large-scale environmental theatre. Richard Lannoy calls these performances "synaesthetic," emphasizing their "total sensory awareness, a high level of audience participation, . . . [the] combination of several art forms: music, dance, poetry, costume, ritual, etc., and emotional religiosity (*bhakti*, or devotion; *lila*, ritual play)" (1971:191). Lannoy traces this kind of theatre to cave sanctuaries such as Ajanta; and he connects the practice of performing in the caves to that of retreating to the forest or mountain caves for meditation and tapasya.

> The structure and ornamentation of the caves were deliberately designed to induce total participation during ritual circumambulation. The acoustics of one Ajanta *vihara* or assembly hall (Cave VI), are such that any sound long continues to echo round the walls. The whole structure seems to have been tuned like a drum. (1971:43)

> The caves of Ajanta offer the sole remaining opportunity to visualize the way a combination of colour and form was originally fused in a wrap-around synaesthesia. . . . There is no *recession* – all *advance* toward the eye, looming from a strange undifferentiated source to wrap around the viewer. (1971:46)

Ramnagar Ramlila works similarly. Although not a cave, Ramlila's environments and actions taken as a whole surround, enclose, and incorporate the spectators. The length of the cycle, the processions and circumambulations integral to the mise-en-scene, the mix of individual devotion and small group rituals with the presentation of formal texts and splendid displays accumulate into a total experience that reverberates for an entire month. The performance comes from everywhere, is everywhere. The experience of Ramlila is not limited to the enacted lilas but includes getting to and from the Ramlila, taking part in the moves from site to site, and what happens during the sandhya puja break. Although not a retreat into the forest, Ramlila offers both in its month-long duration and in its narrative a model of such retreats. For those who attend on a daily basis, and there are thousands who do, ordinary life is put aside for a month, a dilation of time and space occurs, one enters a different world, that of Vishnu the expander. In the Indian aesthetic-religious performance tradition, *rasa* – the juice, taste, flavor, and savoring of emotional involvement – is such an experience.[13] It is also *bhakti*, whose popular meaning suggests transforming sexual desire into an ecstatic physical union with the divine, an absorption by and participation in the noumenous. To move within the Ramlila environments is to experience the city, the forest, the mountains, the sea, the sacred rivers, the battlefield, the gardens, the palaces.

The rasa of this dilation is nowhere better tasting than during sandhya puja, the evening prayer celebrated by the maharaja each day at around 6 p.m. The puja interrupts the dramatic action even while continuing the lila. As Rama's story disconnects for an hour or so, people unpack their suppers, gossip, enjoy the mela. Or they sit in meditation; or read the *Manas*; or dance and sing to ecstasy. The actors rest, their masks set aside, the buttons on their costumes undone to catch a little air. The swarups, uncrowned, with a devotee or two squeezing their feet, stare off into space. Children cry, sleep, play. People go to the toilet. Even the police seem to relax. But during Ramlila all these ordinary happenings are charged with a special sensitivity. The values of the lila infiltrate the most common actions.

This is especially so during the extra-long three-hour sandhya puja of dasahara. The maharaja is back at the Fort. On Lanka's great field there is peace if not quiet. Ravana has been defeated, his effigy atop his four-gated fort awaits cremation. To the north, Rama is in camp on Suvel Mountain. To the west in the ashoka garden Sita sits, her kidnapper dead but she not yet liberated. At this climax of the story the many antipathies of Ramlila are in suspension. Good/evil, ever-present/evanescent, gods/demons, people/super-beings, commoners/rulers, mela/bhakti. For a few hours, as darkness filters into Lanka, all is in unresolved balance, the great struggle neutralized, the principal players pausing prior to their next doings. Ravana, of insatiable appetite, is dead but not cremated. Rama and Lakshman, incarnations of absolute good, are victorious but still in exile. Sita, mother of the world, waits patiently under the ashoka tree. Many in the crowd circulate in an informal circumambulation among these great figures who triangulate Lanka. Of the swarups they take darshan. More boldly they peer up at Ravana's effigy or gleefully climb in it. The great figures are immobile, but lesser performers, in loosened costumes, drink tea and chat. A demon next to a monkey next to a businessman next to a sadhu next to a beggar next to Schechner next to a one-armed vendor of roasted peanuts next to a crying child next to a blind man next to Hindi scholar Linda Hess next to a tourist next to an itinerant singer next to a student dressed in polyester slacks and shirt next to a mother nursing her infant daughter next to three men on camels. "Where do you come from?" I ask them, imagining a long dusty journey from the deserts of Rajasthan. "We are the men who come on camels," one answers. "Each year we come for this day only." Drumming

Plate 5.14 A sadhu in 1978 who has danced with such energy that sweat has soaked through his saffron *kurta*. Often sadhus will sing and dance their devotion to Rama and Sita for hours on end. (Photo: Richard Schechner)

and singing swirl through the evening as nearby a sadhu dances so fiercely that sweat soaks his saffron shirt from shoulders to hips (plate 5.14). Where else does theatre, or religion, as generously dilate time and space so that people can clearly, easily, and fully play their various roles?

Plate 5.15 In the winter of 1981, cows quietly roam the area near where, during Ramlila, the Chitrakut tent will be erected. The tower in the mid-background is where Vishnu and Lakshmi appear on Ramlila's first day. (Photo: Richard Schechner)

Quiet time, waiting space

In January 1978, and again in January 1983, I visited Ramnagar to survey and photograph the Ramlila environments when they were not in use. Not only did I gather "objective data" concerning the size, the architecture of the permanent installations, the distances between stations, and a feel for the overall spatial deployment of Ramlila, I also wanted to walk undisturbed through Janakpur and Ayodhya, up the little hill near Kishkindha, across the grassy field of Panchavati, past the small Shiva temple at Rameshwaram, and into the vast open space of Lanka. I sat where the Chitrakut butterfly-winged tent was raised across from the Durga temple and its deep pool and where now, in winter, cows quietly grazed (plate 5.15). I walked the paths that Rama, Sita, and Lakshman walk when, barefoot, they go into exile. Atmaram – Ramlila's longtime technical director, constructor of the effigies, and keeper of the environments – took me to Agastya's small ashram and to where Rama restored Ahalya to her human form. The Ramlila environments, though silent and deserted in chilly January, still released to me their actions. At Chitrakut my mind's eye followed Jayanta, Indra's son, who took the form of a crow biting Sita's toe sharply enough for it to bleed a little stage blood in a test of Rama's might and Sita's human "reality." Rama's angry arrow pursued Jayanta through "every sphere" until, terrified and remorseful, he fell at Rama's feet crying, "Protect me!" Half-forgiving, half-vengeful, perhaps ironic, Rama's arrow puts out one of Jayanta's eyes, sparing the other. At Ayodyha I once again saw Dasaratha keel over backwards in a deathly swoon of remorse when he realizes his beloved son Rama must enter the forest for fourteen years of exile. In Lanka I felt the heat and saw the light of the cremation fire consuming Ravana's giant bamboo and papier-mâché body. There in the middle of January's chill and emptiness I recalled how the maharaja told Linda Hess and me that "We don't look down on Ravan[a]. We don't burn his effigy but cremate him with respect. In Delhi they kill Ravana by burning him. Here we cremate him." Even stronger than evocations of splendid presence, was the absence of the Ramlila. Bereft of nemis and chat-walas (sellers of snacks), sadhus and ramayanis; without darshan of the swarups; lacking the maharaja on his elephant; failing the crowd's powerful surge at arati – in short, with neither theatrical action nor religious devotion, the Ramlila environments – some in need of repair, some simply waiting, some more or less permanently overgrown – lay fallow. In winter the Ramlila ground was the world between *yugas*, the cosmic cycles of creation–destruction, awaiting its season of activity.

Notes

1. In the age of the *Rgveda*, India's oldest religious document (c.1200–1000 BCE), Vishnu must have already been a more important divine figure than it would appear from his comparatively infrequent appearances in the texts. . . . He is celebrated in a few hymns, of which stanzas 1.22.16–21 came to be a sort of confession of faith. . . . These stanzas eulogize the essential feature of the character of the Vedic Visnu: namely, his taking, from the very place where the gods promote man's interests, three steps [as the dwarf Vamana], by which he establishes the broad dimensional actuality of the earthly space in which all beings abide. . . . *Viraj*, the idea of

extending far and wide the female principle of creation and the hypostasis of the universe conceived as a whole, came to be one of Vishnu's epithets. . . . To the sacrificer, who ritually imitates Vishnu's three strides and so identifies with him, the god imparts the power to conquer the universe and attain "the goal, the safe foundation, the highest light" *Satapatha Brahmana* 1.9.3.10. Vishnu's pervasiveness also manifests itself in the central cosmic axis, the pillar of the universe, whose lower end is visibly represented by the post erected on the sacrificial ground. This axis reaches the earth in the center or navel of the universe, putting the cosmic levels into communication with each other; it thus provides a means of traveling to heaven as well as a canal through which heavenly blessings reach man. In this navel is located the sacrifice with which Vishnu is constantly identified.   (Gonda 1987:288–9)

2. In one of those paradoxes that tease scholars without troubling practitioners, Vishnu's seventh incarnation is not mathematically plausible. King Dasaratha, unhappy because he has no son, performs a sacrifice in the midst of which the fire god Agni appears bearing an offering. As told in the *Ramcharitmanas*, Agni says: "Go, king, divide this offering and distribute the parts in due proportion [to your three wives]". Rama's mother Kausalya gets half; Kaikeyi, Bharat's mother, gets one-quarter; and Sumitra, mother of Lakshman and Shatrughna, gets two fragments of one-eighth each. All the boys are incarnations of Vishnu, sharing in the divine offering, but Rama alone is considered *the* incarnation. All the boys are of equal age, but Rama is represented as the eldest, performed by a boy who is several years older than Shatrughna and Bharat and at least one year older than Lakshman. Lakshman and Shatrughna are twins but in performance Lakshman is several years older than Shatrughna. It happens that a boy who has played Shatrughna or Bharat later plays Lakshman or Rama. Sita, equal to Rama in holiness, the incarnation of Vishnu's wife Lakshmi, has no human mother. She is born from a furrow her father King Janak ploughs. The question of whether Vishnu's seventh avatar is one or four (Sita being of Lakshmi) troubles no one at Ramlila. Of Vishnu's ten avatars, nine have already appeared: Matsya, the fish; Kurma, the tortoise; Varaha, the boar; Narasimha, the man–lion; Vamana, the dwarf; Parasurama, Rama with an Ax; Rama; Krishna; Buddha. Each of these avatars is the locus of many stories. Kalki, the tenth avatar, will come to destroy the world at the end of the Kali Yuga, the dark age in which we now live.

3. There are obvious parallels with both the *Iliad* (war fought over an abducted queen) and the *Odyssey* (adventurous travels of a hero). The similarity of these Indian and Greek tales of far-ranging warful travels should not surprise us: their authors were people of the horse, they rode far in several directions – south, west, east – from their "origins" in the Caucasus region; and they were poets.

4. *Ramcharitmanas*:

Raghunayak's [Rama's] arrows sped forth like great serpents of doom. One arrow dried up the depths of Ravan's navel; the others furiously smote his heads and arms and carried them away with them. The headless, armless trunk danced upon the ground. The earth sank down, but the trunk rushed violently on. Then the Lord struck it with an arrow and cut it in two. Even as he died, he roared aloud with a great and terrible yell, "Where is Rama, that I may challenge him and slay him in combat?" Earth shook as the Ten-headed fell; the sea, the rivers, the mountains and the elephants of the quarters were troubled. Spreading abroad the two halves of his body, he fell to the ground, crushing beneath him crowds of bears and monkeys. The arrows laid the arms and the heads before Mandodari [Ravana's wife] and returned to the Lord of the world; they all came back and entered his quiver. The gods saw it and beat their drums. His spirit entered the Lord's mouth; Sambhu [Shiva] and Brahma saw it and were glad. The universe was filled with cries of triumph.

(Tulasi Das 1971:418–19)

5. Actually four weddings take place simultaneously, for not only is Rama married to Sita but his brothers are also married. Only the Rama–Sita marriage is dramatized in Ramlila.

6. At Varanasi the Ganga loops so that for some miles it flows south to north instead of in its general easterly direction. This means that in Varanasi the sun rises over the sacred river, making early morning bathing very spectacular. Furthermore, Rama is widely celebrated as a solar king, and to a degree it is his radiance that rises over Banaras, the city of Shiva. But Ramnagar is on the eastern (southern), the "bad side" of the river, the inauspicious, polluted side. Not wishing to pollute sacred Kashi (another name for Varanasi), many Varanasi residents journey across the Ganga each morning before dawn to defecate on the river's far bank.

7. All quotations from the *Natyasastra* are from Bharata-muni 1967.

8. Calling a post-Vedic text a "fifth Veda" is a common way of saying how important a text is. The *Natyasastra* is far from alone in being so represented.

9. The Ramlila must start on the fourteenth day of the month – as the moon is waning. Dasahara must be the middle of a waxing moon, on the tenth day of the lunar month. Ramlila must end on a full moon. These requirements can cause some peculiar adjustments to be made. In 1982, for example, because of the insertion of an extra half-month in the lunar year, the Ramlila had to be calculated backward from the full moon, and so it did not begin on the fourteenth day.

10. One vyas trains the swarups, the other oversees the rest of the performers. The vyases are present during all lilas, holding big books which contain the samvads and stage directions. Often they whisper dialogue in the ears of the swarups or other performers. They are not shy about making corrections during the performance: the important thing is for everything to be done correctly.

11. This token is supplemented the next day when in a private audience held in his office at the Fort the maharaja pays each swarup Rs 440 (as of 1978). Other Ramlila performers are also paid, though less.

12. "Deep play" is a concept from Jeremy Bentham elaborated on by Clifford Geertz (1973:412–53). It suggests a level of playing "in which the stakes are so high that it is irrational for men to engage in it at all" (432). Ramlila is deep play in the sense that what is enacted is "realer than real," an experience of Vishnu–Rama presence that transcends the very theatrical practices that bring the Rama of Ramlila into existence.

13. Rasa is not easy to explain. I have tried to do so in Schechner 1985:136–42. See also Kale 1974.

6

Wayang kulit in the colonial margin

People who stay up all night know that the different periods of the night feel very different, give rise to different moods. . . . This experience is an important part of the theatre of Southeast Asia, a part of its message as well as a theatrical medium: the withdrawal into a spiritual wilderness which is enacted in the play and simultaneously experienced as the darkness deepens and the world changes. . . . I have discussed this point with several Javanese musicians and actors. Most of them agreed with me that the periods of the night are very important to the proper presentation of the wayang. . . . Can a permanent, indoor, quiet, nine to eleven urban theatre ever mean the same thing as the theatre I have been writing about? I don't think it can: it can only be an extension of the day, reflecting rational daytime concerns and sunshine magic.

A. L. Becker (1974:161–4)

. . . where the west must face a peculiarly displaced and decentred image of itself . . . at once a civilizing mission and a violent subjugating force. It is there, in the colonial margin, that the culture of the west reveals its "differance", its limit-text, as its practice of authority displays an ambivalence that is one of the most significant discursive and psychical strategies of discriminatory power – whether racist or sexist, peripheral or metropolitan.

Homi K. Bhabha (1986:148)

Sunshine magic in Ann Arbor

At 8 p.m. on 1 April 1988 an audience of more than 1,000 took their places in the large semicircular hall that is the University of Michigan's Rackham Auditorium to see/hear *The Marriage of Arjuna*, a Javanese leather shadow puppet play performed by guest *dalang* (puppeteer) Widyanto S. Putro, the university's Gamelan Ensemble, and "visiting artists" Minarno, Sumarsam,

R. Anderson Sutton, and Richard Wallis.[1] The program lists all of them, giving the Gamelan Ensemble top billing. The play's Javanese title, *Arjuna Wiwaha*, is not in the program, although much of the text was recited or sung in Javanese. A. L. Becker, noted linguist and wayang expert, listed only as translator, sang songs (*suluk*) and narrated the story in English. The performance lasted about four hours with about half the audience remaining throughout. Because of the semicircular seating, many spectators could not see the shadows the puppets threw on the rectangular screen. And because the stage was a small elevated semicircle there was no room for spectators to view the show from behind the dalang, a vantage many Javanese prefer because from there one can watch the dalang manipulate the flat, intricately cut, multicoloured puppets as he (rarely she) recites dialogue and directs the gamelan (an orchestra consisting largely of gongs and xylophones).

In many ways the Michigan performance was different from wayangs done in Java. But it is not possible to compare "American" wayang to "Javanese" wayang because in Java, at present, there is no performance style dominant in practice – although reading the literature you would think there was. From the mid-nineteenth century, Dutch scholars imposed on Javanese court artists a style that was later propagated by dalang schools established in Jogjakarta and Surakarta in the 1920s. This kind of wayang kulit I call the "normative expectation." Most Western scholars and many practitioners use this normative expectation as a baseline for understanding and evaluating all kinds of wayang kulit, even those that blatantly diverge from it.[2]

> In the villages the tradition changes and thrives as it responds to the current wave of modernization overtaking Javanese life. Motorcycle puppets, colored lights, Western style drums, and English expressions are increasingly woven into all-night performances. The clowns make fun of the respected heroes, materialistic values replace those of village solidarity, and female characters demand new rights and new visibility. Restraints on format and characterization are loosening in the villages, and this mirrors the loosening of those restraints in modern Javanese life. (Sears 1989a:124)

So strongly embedded is the normative expectation that even a progressive like Laurie J. Sears anchors her comparison in it. "Change" is the distance between the normative expectation and what some of today's dalangs do. Sears hints at the possibility of what I consider certain: that the inventive responses of today's village dalangs to changing social circumstances are a resurfacing of the kind of wayang that preceded wayang's codification by the Dutch-controlled courts of the nineteenth and early twentieth centuries.

A reassertion not of specific performance details – who drove motorcycles back then? – but of the core process of wayang, the reason for its long history and loved place in Java: its ability to reflect, absorb, criticize, and transform contemporary Javanese life in relation to sustaining myths and values.

In other words, before Dutch intervention, wayang was important not only aesthetically, ritually, and socially but also politically. Wayang was able to incorporate and propagate Hindu and then Islamic values and themes. Why then are the Dutch absent from the normative wayang even though their dominance in Java extended over centuries and their effects stuck deep? Perhaps it was the Dutch themselves who arranged their own absence from wayang. The "purity" of the normative expectation is a strategy not only to drain the politics from wayang, to freeze it in "authenticity" and nonmodernity, but to conceal the Dutch colonial presence and the Javanese responses to it. The Dutch intervention into wayang prevented dalangs from depicting the struggle of the Javanese against the Dutch (the Java War of 1825–30 was not the only local resistance during the nineteenth and early twentieth centuries) and from representing the many changes taking place in the "Dutch East Indies" during the long colonial epoch. The Dutch stripped wayang of its politics and historicity, its ability to relate contemporary events, and tried to invent it in a form emphasizing its basis in ancient "myths," its "timeless" aesthetics and its "mystical" functions. In tying wayang to the supine courts, the Dutch wanted to keep such a strong weapon out of the hands of the emergent revolutionary nationalists. What a service to Dutch colonial exploitation such a program provided.

The normative expectation, a living fiction whose history I intend to trace (to some degree), is held up to Westerners and to many Javanese as "the" wayang. Arguments concerning this construction are entwined not only with the Javanese experience of (Dutch) colonialism but also with the reactions of Westerners to that experience.[3] In this chapter, my focus is on these reactions, colonialism's backflow, and their effects on Western, especially American, scholars and artists.[4]

The Michigan performance was surrounded by accounts of what wayang was ("in Ann Arbor") and what it represented ("in Java"); these accounts constitute a narrative of normative wayang. Although written by journalists, the accounts published before the performance were authored by scholars (who in person or through their articles instructed the journalists in what to write). Take, for example, Martha Keller's article in the 27 March *Ann Arbor News*:

Javanese painted puppets cut from leather cast shadows on a small 4 x 7 screen:
Sounds simple enough, but this is sophisticated shadow painting, a "moving
visual display," a great art form. . . .

The symphonic magic can be watched from either side of the screen over a
time span of several hours to all night. . . . Members of the audience can come
and go as they please during the four-hour performance and can, in fact, check
out both sides of the split realm, the bifurcated world of the shadow screen.
. . .

Javanese shadow theater, *wayang kulit*, presents nothing short of a world
view, the physical and spiritual, the sacred and profane: a miniaturized total
theater. . . . The density, the chaos, of this theater, this "conceptual briar patch
of Br'er Rabbit," as translator/performer and U-M professor emeritus of
linguistics A. L. Becker puts it, gets unified by one performer, the puppeteer.
The lone puppeteer directs everything: the shadow play of the puppets, their
voices (except for Becker's participation as clown/"chorus"/"outsider" in
English) and the music. Javanese puppeteers can be male or female; and the
skill is passed from generation to generation within families.[5] Judith Becker,
advisor to the gamelan and professor in the School of Music says, "Puppeteers
are special people of tremendous endurance, intelligence, and dramatic ability.
. . . The puppeteer always meditates before a performance to invoke the
spiritual power of the world, to control the forces let loose by having the
event, to strengthen his own spiritual power."

A young Javanese, Widyanto S. Putro, who teaches at Lewis and Clark
University in Portland, Ore., and the University of California, Berkeley, will
be puppeteer for this performance. His father is a well-known puppeteer in
Java and so Widyanto began acquiring his skills from childhood. His repu-
tation is based upon his beautiful voice; he has performed seven times in
America.

"The Javanese have far more theater than we," says A. L. Becker. "It is old
and continuous, yet lively and politically free. . . . It's full of vitality, yet it's
high art, not folk art or archaic art; it's one of the world's great art forms. . . .
Composers such as Steve Reich, John Cage, and Philip Glass have obviously
been listening to gamelan music.   (1988:1)

What might happen in Ann Arbor is conflated with what is presumed to
happen in Java. People can move about freely (as in Java), but Rackham's
architecture precluded such flow – many settled deep in their seats listening
to the gamelan with closed eyes, ignoring the puppets which were hard to
see from the back rows and sides. Spectators could come and go (as in Java),
but over time Rackham slowly emptied: I saw no one leave and later return.
Keller makes no comment about the fact that the Javanese all-night show
will be cut to four hours, excising what A. L. Becker once argued was a key

quality of wayang – the "spiritual wilderness" one enters as "the darkness deepens and the world changes." Still, Keller implies that wayang in Ann Arbor will come close to the "real" wayang in Java.

A lot is being said, all of it praising. Wayang is high art, total theatre; it is old and "traditional" (passed down through generations); it is important worldwide (influencing composers such as Reich, Cage, and Glass). The Javanese have "far more" theatre than "we" do – a "lively," "politically free" theatre (tell that to artists jailed in Indonesia). The dalang is "special" (more so than a Western artist), a ritually powerful person who in Widyanto's case straddles two worlds: Javanese-traditional and American-academic. Yet there are tantalizing gaps in Keller's restatement of what she got from the Beckers. Is Widyanto really to be received by those in Rackham as someone able "to invoke the spiritual power of the world?" Or should they concentrate on the beautiful voice his reputation is based on? Is Widyanto "just himself" or does he represent (simulate without quite being) the idealized dalang still "full of vitality" back in Java? What irreducible distance remains between Widyanto performing in Ann Arbor and Widyanto performing in Java? Why do the Beckers and the press want to mediate or elide this distance? Are both the distance and the desire to eliminate it shadows of colonialism giving to Widyanto in Michigan the color of an "exotic other?" How many kinds of dalangs are there? Can a single person, performing in different circumstances and contexts, change the kind of dalang he is?

Later in the article Keller quotes A. L. Becker on wayang's narrative structure. In his canonical "Text-building, epistemology, and aesthetics in Javanese shadow theatre" (1979), Becker stresses wayang's multivocality – how shadow theatre combines different languages, narrative strategies, and characters. He told Keller much the same thing he wrote in 1979, "It's as though you were to put on a play in which Charlie Chaplin, Hamlet, Godzilla, Agamemnon, and Gatsby all appeared as characters. Their stories are all told together in a world containing all as one" (Becker, in Keller 1988:2, after Becker 1979:219). In these ways, the journalist and the scholars who informed her helped create not only the audience's expectations of what the University of Michigan wayang would be but also a vision of Javanese wayang.

A. L. Becker is a person of authority, and his presence before, during, and after the Ann Arbor performance was so palpable that he was almost, I would say, a second dalang – not Javanese, of course, but in many other ways senior to Widyanto. Becker does not claim to be able to "invoke the spiritual power of the world," etc. but his authority and his performance not only split the theatrical focus but gave the spectators a chance to see a leading wayang scholar perform as a wayang artist. While young Widyanto clanged out the rhythms, manipulated the puppets, and spoke the dialog, emeritus Becker narrated the plot in English and sang poetic sections (*suluk*) in old Javanese, a language, scholars delight to inform us, that today's Javanese know as little of as Americans do of Beowulfian English. Becker and Widyanto confirmed each other's authority by publicly sharing the Rackham stage. The young dalang allowed the American to narrate and sing; the older scholar modestly followed the lead of the dalang.

At next morning's public discussion of the performance, I told Becker that I felt his participation was so effective and deeply felt (he wept sometimes as he spoke and sang), that it distracted spectators from what the dalang was doing. In August 1988 Becker wrote me a letter in answer:

> I think your remark was perceptive and accurate: those words (mine) were far too prominent – and even more damaging esthetically, they shattered many viewer fantasies – the wayang they were shaping – and did violence esthetically. I would argue they have a parallel effect in Javanese – but I have no convincing evidence for that. What the carios [recited in English translation] did was to keep more people there to the end. . . . At the post-mortems I was – as you could see – very moved, still, the next morning, for I had thought about the backgrounding of killing and the foregrounding of love and affection which Mas Midyanto (against a little resistance by me) insisted on. I didn't know if that was "Javanese" or "Java-in-Americanness" – but he convinced me that was a change in Java. More sentimental, but very individualizing.

Becker is referring here to a shift of emphasis in the story. Usually battle scenes are played up, but at the Ann Arbor performance the love scenes were given priority. Becker worries that this might not be very Javanese. He is reassured when Widyanto tells him that a similar change of tone has occurred in Java. Becker does not believe in a fossilized or static tradition – he welcomes the process of change. But he wants the changes in wayang kulit to originate in Java or at least be corroborated by Javanese practice (except in Java most spectators do not stay "to the end"). Is authorizing changes by referring them to Javanese practice a sustainable desire? Later in his letter, Becker notes that Widyanto was very busy during the performance: "changing things continually, pressing his teacher, Pak Minarno, for details – getting it right."

"Changing things continually – getting it right." This processual tension is very important to Becker. But who is authorized to make changes; and right for whom? For the particular performance at hand? For Minarno, the teacher? For the dalang? For the – may I call it "tradition"? – back in Java? The dedication to maintaining this link binding Ann Arbor to Java is so strong that one can ask, I think, exactly where did the 1 April 1988 performance take place? Who were its authors? From whom and how did they derive their authority?

The normative expectation

What happened at Rackham did not fit the expectation, exactly; nor was the show analogous to a "traditional" Javanese wayang, exactly. The differences were mediated by the various discourses in and around the performance – the publicity, the presence of the visiting Javanese artists, the next-morning public discussion, the statements of the Beckers. It all added up to most people agreeing that they had seen and/or participated in an "authentic wayang kulit" despite discrepancies and gaps between what they were told and what they experienced. The "normative expectation" is a collation of desires and expertise sustaining a performance and its reception not only in Ann Arbor and elsewhere outside Java but in Java too; a performance said to embody "the tradition" (another slippery idea suggesting a stable trans- mission from past to present). The normative expectation is an agreement, spoken and unspoken, among artists, scholars, publicists, bureaucrats, patrons, students, and spectators (some individuals belong in more than one category) to maintain a specific kind of performance. The Rackham wayang was a powerful example of such an agreement; all concerned were invested in demonstrating a correspondence between what they presumed to be an "authoritative Javanese original" and the University of Michigan performance.

European and American scholars generally agree on what a "traditional" wayang kulit performance is. This wayang is based on the court style though it is played in the villages too. It consists of a nine-hour show beginning in the early evening and ending just after daybreak. For the whole time the dalang sits cross-legged facing the rectangular screen, neither eating nor rising from his place (drinks are brought to him). Behind him is the gamelan. Spectators are on both sides of the screen. In most contemporary perform- ances invited guests are seated on chairs watching the shadows, while uninvited guests and passers-by observe from the dalang's side. How much crossing back and forth there is depends on the circumstances of a given show. (Earlier, some scholars say, the situation was different: women and children were on the shadow side, men on the dalang's side [see Rassers 1959].) Known stories are performed and familiar puppet characters appear. The show depends very much on the dalang who is the only one to manipulate the puppets and enunciate the dialog. He also sings, as does the *pesindhen*, a female vocalist whose popularity has grown since the late 1940s. The dalang controls the gamelan, which he cues by rapping on the puppet storage box and small bronze plates, using a wooden mallet in his left hand and a small mallet held between his toes. All the puppets used in the performance are arranged in order of size at the sides of the screen, with the smallest nearest the screen. What the dalang performs are various *lakons*, roughly speaking, "plays" – though these usually were not written out before wayang came under increasing Dutch influence in the nineteenth century. Even today most dalangs do not learn their lakons by reading them but through oral transmission. There are different kinds of lakons – some dealing with legendary Javanese figures, some based on the *Ramayana*, some on the *Mahabharata*.

Describing the normative wayang means understanding many other details of puppet arrangement and manipulation, vocal styles, language conventions, music, narratives and plot construction, character hierarchies and relationships, reception, social and ritual functions. But even with the immense accumulation of detail there are no clear guidelines for what can be changed or omitted before a performance is no longer traditional. For example, the puppets are supposed to be kept in place when not in use by having their handles stuck into a banana tree bough; the screen is supposed to be illuminated from a single source, a flickering oil lamp (now almost always either a kerosene lantern or an electric bulb); the puppets are supposed to be made from parchment formed out of water buffalo hide, horn, and bone; there are specified grips and movements for different classes of puppets and different actions (see Long 1982). The behavior of the audience is also specified, as are the various ritual, social, and aesthetic functions of wayang (see Keeler 1987).

In Ann Arbor polystyrene stood in for the banana tree, an electric bulb for the flickering oil lamp, the entire audience, genders mixed, sat in a semicircle on the shadow side of the screen, and the performance took about four hours. Still the impression given was of a traditional performance, modified to fit Ann Arbor circumstances, but not deconstructive or experi-

THE FUTURE OF RITUAL

mental. There are performances in Java, however, where dalangs and other artists play around with, update, change, and propose alternatives to the normative wayang – some of these I will discuss later.

The normative expectation was developed from the last half of the nineteenth century to the eve of World War II. Victoria M. Clara van Groenendael (1985, 1987) summarizes the process which began with Dutch scholarship, led to the establishment of schools for dalangs at the royal courts in Surakarta in 1923 and Jogjakarta in 1925, and continued with the dissemination of the normative style of wayang into the Javanese countryside and beyond. Sears tells the same story. In the nineteenth century:

> The Western privileging of written texts and documentation slowly began to erode the traditional authority of the shadow theatre for Javanese puppeteers and their audiences. The Dutch scholars, as bearers of these Western attitudes, helped to displace the Indic/Islamic authority of the wayang tradition by their concern with texts, schooling, and accuracy. They sought to establish "correct" versions of the stories and tended to discount the dynamic ability of the puppeteers to create new stories. . . . Pigeaud (1967–68, vol. 1:257) noted that the Dutch scholars Gericke, Winter, and Wilkens, who took an active part in the literary activity of the mid-19th century Javanese courts, had a great influence on the Javanese authors of that period. The Dutch colonial scholars encouraged Javanese authors to produce written prose and poetic versions of the shadow theatre plays complete with puppeteers' songs, descriptions in rhythmic prose, and dialogs. . . . The Dutch scholars helped to set in motion a process by which the domains in which the wayang stories were meaningful began to narrow. By their efforts to standardize and improve the tradition, the Dutch slowly undermined the world in which oral epic traditions passed on meaningful information. . . . The effects of these Dutch attitudes on the shadow theatre appear in the efforts of the Javanese themselves to upgrade the tradition, especially in Surakarta in the 19th and early 20th centuries. Puppeteers from the villages were called to the courts for upgrading sessions and the stories had to be performed in ways which enhanced the power of the Javanese courts. (1989b:2, 6–7, 9–10)

Western scholars, then as now, "improve a tradition" by privileging early or presumed originary elements. There is an investment in singularity and hierarchy, a denial of multiplicity and equivalence. Plural styles or traditions are reduced to one "best," "original," "primary" model or ideal from which the others derive or deviate; a tradition is invented (see Wagner 1981; Hobsbawm and Ranger 1983) or is restored (see Schechner 1985). In terms of wayang kulit, the situation is complex. Dutch colonials had contradictory opinions regarding the Javanese. These orientals were too refined ("effete") to succeed in the rough and tumble modern world – even as they were primitive, simple, childlike "natives" with limited conceptual horizons inhabiting a fragmented island world. Some Dutch scholars argued that wayang kulit originated in Java, absorbing Indian texts and then Islamic mysticism into an already established indigenous genre (Hazeu 1897). But when shortly after the turn of the century the existence of shadow puppets in Sanskritic India was indicated (Pischel 1906), many scholars argued that wayang was brought from India to Java. This had the advantage not only of explaining the use of *Ramayana* and *Mahabharata* characters and stories, but also of linking wayang to Europe via Indo-European ur-culture. If the "real wayang" could be proven very old and not by origin Javanese, it would be "great" even as its court practitioners were decadent and its village dalangs ignorant primitives. The task of the scholars was clear – to codify, restore, and invigorate court wayang by collecting texts and educating dalangs in "correct practice."

Wherever wayang came from, most colonialists felt the whole system of Javanese culture, no matter how "high" it once had been, no matter how beautiful its living relics could be made to appear, was below the European standard. Even Snouck Hurgronje, the distinguished Dutch scholar of Islam, felt that "The Indonesians had lost whatever of distinctively indigenous and cultural life they had possessed . . . [and] it could not be revived" (in Vandenbosch 1941:72). Such an attitude fostered a duplicitous tendency: to restore wayang while making certain it was only ornamental; to entrust Javanese high culture to the courts while stripping locals of political and economic power. The Dutch paid lip service to "the native leaders" while treating them as little more than "performers of given orders" (Schrieke 1955:283). The *priyayi* (rural aristocrats) were enrolled as overseers of the exploitation of the peasants while the royal courts were made into living museums of dance, theatre, and music.

The normative wayang so beloved today by connoisseurs both Javanese and Western is a product of the collaboration between the courts and colonial Dutch scholars; to be even more precise, this "ancient tradition" in the form so many now imagine, is a rather recent creation of the courts under the guidance of the colonialists. As mentioned before, in order to disseminate into the countryside what the scholars and court artists developed, schools were founded in the 1920s in Surakarta and Jogjakarta and in the 1930s at Mangkunagaran. Clara van Groenendael writes:

At school the dalangs learned not only techniques of puppetry but the written literary tradition of wayang as it was expressed at the courts. . . . Initially these court schools attracted mainly popular dalangs who hoped to increase their popularity via these schools. In later years their students also came from other than dalang circles. At these schools the students came into direct contact with the canonized court tradition, which they now began to help disseminate. The crucial role of the acquisition of esoteric knowledge in the traditional informal dalang training was replaced at these schools by the dalang's intellectual and artistic development. The court schools were nevertheless not aimed at renewal in the art of the dalang, but rather at the transmission of the court art of their specific area (Surakarta, Yogyakarta, or the Mangkunagaran) in as pure a form as possible, towards which end the supposedly corrupt popular tradition was corrected.   (Clara van Groenendael 1985:32, 200)

Sears has a somewhat different interpretation.

It was in the court schools that were established in the 1920s that the court wayang tradition was really created, and the creation of this tradition can be seen as a Javanese response to Western scholarly attitudes and the increasing respect for accurate texts. It was also in this period that the court tradition was sealed off from the popular tradition, as village dalangs were called in or chose to study at the court schools. These dalangs often discovered that the styles they were learning in the courts did not necessarily appeal to their village audiences; thus a court style and a popular style could be said to have existed in the 1930s and 1940s. I suggest that 1923 [founding of the first wayang school] symbolizes for elite Javanese a loss of faith in their own traditions. They succumbed to the Dutch views of wayang – it needs to be cleaned up, the stories need to be organized, the correct versions need to be taught – which they had absorbed from the Dutch scholars in the late 19th and early 20th centuries. Javanese elites began to perceive power and prestige to lie in the mastery of new kinds of scientific and literary knowledge. For the Javanese elites and their Dutch rulers and colleagues, the schools were also a way of controlling the power of the puppeteers.   (1989b:27–8)

Sears makes colonialism appear almost benign. The Javanese didn't "succumb" as if to an unknown disease or "absorb" ideas from "colleagues" like graduate students. The courts knew they couldn't defeat the Dutch so they tried to join them even as the Dutch reduced these masters of puppet theatre into puppets. And Sears and Clara van Groenendael both ignore the Indonesian independence struggle which began early in the nineteenth century: nationalism doubtlessly affected wayang – though Western scholars have taken no notice.

Three basic strains of wayang coexist, influencing each other: the normative expectation; village wayang whose history is not known with any
certitude; and modern wayang, drawing on village and court traditions,
nationalist ideology, and modern popular culture and media. Within these
three kinds are at least fourteen particular styles ranging from wayang
purwa, gedog, and madya, supposedly the "most traditional," to wayang
buddha which "deliberately oversteps traditional boundaries and aims for
the international stage" (Clara van Groenendael 1987:10).[6]

The tension among these strains is reflected in some scholars' desire to
itemize wayang's performative details down to the minutest gesture even
while insisting that the art's real life and delight lies in the dalang's freedom
to improvise, playing to the audience at hand, seizing the moment for
unexpected theatrical coups. The long-submerged struggle between the
rigidity of strict codification and the fluidity of a "tradition behind the
tradition" haunts the scholarship. Neither the plethora of rules developed by
the Javanese court artists of Jogjakarta and Solo nor the five-year plans
Indonesian nation-makers in Jakarta said dalangs were supposed to tout to
the masses, suit the subversive and slippery thing wayang was and may be
once more becoming. The relationship between wayang and the Jakarta
governments has been uneasy at best, while the codified court brand of
puppet theatre flourishes partly because of Western enthusiasm for
aestheticization.

After Indonesian independence Western scholars could appear to be
supporting "authentic native culture" by continuing the operation formed
during the colonial period. Since 1947 the axis of this alliance shifted from
Java–Holland to Java–America (where the money is), though plenty of
Europeans are still involved in Indonesia. A double circle of artistic–
scholarly exchange links Java to the West. Javanese come to America to
study and perform; when they return to Indonesia their reputations are
enhanced by their experiences and their academic degrees. For the most part,
these Javanese do not study Western culture or arts in order to master them
to the level of becoming internationally known experts in them. Could this
be at least in part because in the West they are regarded as experts in
"traditional Javanese arts," typecast as "natives," and almost required to
"speak for" their cultures of origin? Some remain in the West on this basis –
a few of this type were in the Ann Arbor wayang performance. Americans
go to Java on a different basis – to study Javanese arts and culture, to learn it
"from the inside," to become experts (like me), writing about Javanese

culture or applying what they've learned to their own artistic work as, say, John Emigh and Julie Taymor have done.

An imbalance results. In general, Westerners can be scholars of Javanese arts at least equal to the Javanese themselves, but not master practitioners, while Javanese can become practitioners of Western arts but not scholars of them at the highest level. What Javanese is regarded as expert in, say, modern or Elizabethan theatre as the Beckers or Keeler or Sears are about wayang? Western methods dominate both the scholars working in Java and the Javanese in America – but the subject of the studies, the "colonized" or "appropriated" object, remains Javanese culture. An old, colonial pattern remains strongly operative.

Reading representative Western texts on wayang kulit shows how dominant the normative expectation is. Until Ward Keeler's 1987 book on village wayang, all monograph or book-length studies dealt with the court-derived normative style.[7] Aside from Sears (1989a), sections of Clara van Groenendael (1985), and Mylius (1961) there are no studies of city-based, Indonesian government-sponsored, experimental, or other non-normative kinds of wayang. Dalangs using multiple screens (or none at all), introducing new characters and lakons, and in other ways modernizing wayang are thought to deviate from correct practice; they are regarded by scholars as threats to the "tradition." Even more despised is wayang used as propaganda or to incite political action either for or against the government. "Deviant" styles are attacked or ignored, not analyzed with a care approaching that lavished on "traditional" wayang. Why? Is it because such analysis might validate functions of wayang these scholars, like their Dutch predecessors, wish to prevent?

Sears sees the Dutch intervention as recuperative:

> As modernizing Javanese elites began to lose interest in the wayang tradition as a source of power and turned their energies to the accumulation of Western or scientific knowledge, the Dutch-influenced overseers of the tradition responded to this threat by applying Western values to the evaluation of the tradition. If the stories were developed and organized, if the musical pieces were written down, if the aesthetic standards were raised, if the obscene jokes and allusions were removed, perhaps the power of the tradition could be regained. . . . The Dutch scholars in central Java in the late 19th and early 20th centuries had great respect for Javanese literary and performing arts, but they wanted to purify these traditions of the unnecessary cultural accretions that they felt had sedimented around the core of ancient classical tradition. . . . The performance tradition of the shadow theatre was brought into the Solonese

courts, and the invented court performance tradition was given a long and respectable history by court scholars. (1989b:30–1)

But why would representatives of a colonial power want to help a faltering elite regain power? A more plausible reason for the scholars' work is at hand. The emergence of the court tradition is in fact a side-effect, a practice for those of the courtly elite not likely to be of use to Dutch enterprise; a harmless diversion; and a convenient cultural "ornament" preserved, even enhanced, for display in Java or for export back to Europe (where "expositions" hungered for "Orientals" and other exotics). With the examples of the Java War and the Indian "Mutiny" of 1857 reminding them of what can happen when the customs of local people are too rudely disregarded, the Dutch shrewdly shunted the Javanese courts "into art" which the capitalists who were in charge of the Dutch East Indies counted of negligible economic value (how could they guess the tons of cash tourists in the next century would spend on such things?). Turning the courts into art shops opened wayang to "development" by Western academics: before as well as after independence professors came in search of the stuff careers are made of. Foreign scholars and Javanese royals may to this day feel more at home with each other than either do with the generals ruling from Jakarta. From this mixed bag came many results, some not so bad. In any event, the court wayang tradition now exists – it is the wayang most seen, studied, and respected in the West; a version of it was presented in Ann Arbor.

Westernizers, modernizers

Java, from ancient times a source of goods wanted in Asia and Europe, has long been a focus of interculturalism. Up until the Dutch, Java was shaped by successive slow waves of arrivals, resulting both in transformations of Javanese culture and in the assimilation of the newcomers. Indians established themselves by 132 AD when an Indian king ruling in Java "sent an embassy to China" (Majumdar 1973:22). Although many wayang stories are of Indian origin, whether shadow puppetry came from India or was already in Java cannot be known. Eleven centuries after Hinduism, and eight centuries since Buddhism, Islam entered Java, becoming dominant by the end of the sixteenth century. Yet even as Islam was soaking into Java, and being assimilated by it, the Europeans arrived. The Dutch, like the English in India, began as exploiting traders and ended as masters of a colonial empire. Unlike earlier arrivals in Java, the Dutch did not mix in or assimilate and, after a presence of 350 years, were expelled as unwanted foreigners. Yet many Western cultural traits became part of Javanese daily life, government and military organization, and economic planning. This fits global circumstances where colonized peoples attaining independence sought new means of sociopolitical organization (see Anderson 1983; Dube 1988).

Here I distinguish "Westernization" from "modernization." Westernization was the policy of creating "a thousand happy Englands" (as one colonialist exclaimed). Westernizing policies ranged from mission education, requiring instruction in the colonizing language and the imposition of political and judicial systems, to genocide accompanied by massive immigration from the "mother country" as in the Americas, Australia, and New Zealand. In India and the "East Indies" Westernizers eschewed immigration and genocide, possibly because there were so many "natives" already in place, concentrating instead on employing Europeanized native elites to exploit "subject peoples" within a global imperial system. The British Commonwealth of Nations is an afterglow of this approach. Early advocates of Westernization – Arthur Wellesley in India and H. W. Daendels in Java – opposed the rajas, nawabs, and sultans on ideological grounds. These Europeans, admirers of the French Revolution, wanted to eradicate "oriental despots" who, like the Bourbons, ruled neither by reason nor law nor in the interest of the common people but from religious "superstition," greed, and whim. The Europeans saw the immense private wealth of the native rulers not as "earned" but amassed by tribute – and wasted because this capital was not "invested" in industry. Worse even, many rulers lived what the Europeans considered lives of unbridled slothful sensuality. In short, these "swarthy natives" – even if kings – were everything a hard-working man of the Enlightenment hated. So much the better if destroying them meant bigger profits for the Europeans.

But the Java War and the Indian Mutiny discredited the policy of Westernization, which was succeeded by a policy of collaboration with and manipulation of the native rulers. What remained constant was the goal of colonization: wealth for the homeland. At the start of the twentieth century more than 600 local kings remained in place in India. Even after independence the Indian government awarded privy purses to 284 of these princes – not until 1971 were princely privileges revoked. Many Indians, however, continue to honor, even revere, certain maharajas (see chapter 5). In Java, the sultans of Jogjakarta and Surakarta were allowed to stay in place – but as

C. A. Bayly states, "the descendants of the Sultans of Mataram were transformed into equals of low European officials even more abruptly [than their counterparts in India]" (1986:117). Deprived of their power to wage war, collect revenues, and control who lived in their realms, the sultans were left with mostly religious, ceremonial, and artistic duties. These overlapped, as they had for centuries. They attracted some Western scholars who saw in them a compact, coherent, beautiful, and pleasant panoply of activities. But because the sultans had no more actual power, their ceremonial life was a sham, it referred to nothing beyond itself.[8] If the activities were not transformed into "art" in the Western sense, into objects of aesthetic pleasure, they would surely perish. It was the scholars' job to instruct the kings in effecting such a transformation.

Modernization turns Westernization on its head: the slave seizes the master's sword and uses it to her own advantage. Modernizers take ideas and techniques regardless of source. In earlier epochs, Westerners used to their own advantage Chinese techniques for the manufacture of paper and movable type, the Arabic numeral system, and the Indian digit "0" – but this did not make the emergent European culture of the Renaissance Chinese, Arabic, or Indian. In the same way, more recently, various non-Western modernizers have taken techniques from the West. But modernization is no panacea: "Whose modernization? Modernization for what?" asks S. C. Dube (1988:27). He goes on:

> The principal reasons for the failure of the paradigm of developmentalism [modernization] are easy to identify. Both in the global and the national contexts the developmental process was bound to be unequal. In the international setting, it was weighted in favour of the rich and powerful nations who sought to maintain a barely disguised colonial relationship with the underdeveloped countries. The contemporary North–South formulation raises the issues of inequality of resources and power. . . . In the Third World countries themselves small centres have grown at the expense of a large periphery, which has remained impoverished and anaemic. The dominant centres of power – economic and political – favour pockets of prosperity and deal with underdeveloped areas as if they were their internal colonies.
>
> (1988:105)

Dube also questions the modernizers' antagonism to tradition.

> Nor is it easy, or perhaps necessary, to demolish tradition. It survives not because the people in the less developed countries love social and cultural

antiquities, but the functions performed by its different elements – from customs to institutions – render its continuation both necessary and desirable.

(1988:28)

But of this assertion, too, one can ask, whose tradition? Tradition for what? The modernizers who won nationhood for Indonesia have often had a very different opinion of wayang's history, essence, and uses than did the Dutch scholars. And more and more dalangs are acting independently of both the courts and the central government. These dalangs are modern and traditional simultaneously.

Under the Dutch canopy

In Java, Dutch intentions were different from those of the Hindus, Buddhists, or Muslims, each of whom desired a kind of amalgamation with the Javanese. The Dutch wanted an efficient transfer of wealth from the Indies to Holland. The lengthy, hot debates among the Dutch – sometimes brutal and cynical, sometimes humanist – are reducible to one subject: how best to move Indonesian wealth westward. Throughout the nineteenth century, Dutch colonial higher-ups insisted that Europeans treat local rulers with respect, even deference. But in the field these regulations were ignored. Local rulers suffered many humiliations. In 1928, B. Schrieke, perhaps the most sophisticated and humanist of Dutch colonial apologists, saw the pattern clearly:

> Here, then, we have come to the guiding principle of our colonial policy, which is to leave the native population under the leadership of its own rulers, a principle which has been recognized by conservative statesmen, but also by liberals. . . . Viewed in the light of the lessons of practical experience, this principle of government had all the appearance of being a mere slogan, at best a piece of self delusion. [Local authorities] are tools without a will of their own, and their fitness for office is judged accordingly. (1955:188, 190)

The Dutch East India Company, interested in maximizing profits, relentlessly brought a large territory under

> a Dutch canopy. With this the mechanical state of the Dutch East Indies comes into being. As a result the upper class in the native society automatically loses what up to that time had constituted the essential factor determining its position. Its function – and with it its social status – has changed. (1955:189)

Indeed, the Europeans turned the Javanese world topsy-turvy. Former colonizers, be they Hindu or Islamic, never spoke with such contempt concerning Java's kings and aristocrats as did Governor General J. Van den Bosch in the 1830s:

> Although generally speaking the native rulers possess many good qualities, their intellectual development is by no means on a level usually met with among the upper classes in a civilized society. They must therefore be discreetly guided and when they abuse their authority, as they are often inclined to, this must be prudently counteracted. (in Schrieke 1955:282)

Or R.M.A.A. Hadiningrat, regent of Demak, in 1899:

> Now owing to this great difference in education, the native officials recede into the background. On the whole they are not much better than the performers of given orders, than *mandurs*, overseers. (in Schrieke 1955:283)

Among administrators these attitudes were rife. Why should we expect the Dutch scholars of wayang to view the Javanese princes and dalangs any differently?

When speaking for the record (and to themselves) about "the natives," the Dutch spoke in three related but distinct voices. The first (already sampled) uttered by "men in the field," dripping with contempt for the "natives" they were "guiding," is pompous, self-satisfied, and patronizing: the colonialist carrying the "white man's burden." The second voice theorizes the rationale for and advantages of colonial empire. This voice originates "back home," and although sounding kinder and gentler than the first, it raises to the level of social organization and "world history" both the contempt for the "natives" and the need for indefinitely extending the domain of European "civilization" (forgetting about Europe's awful history of murderous internecine wars). This kind of theorizing continued through the 1930s, when surely even the Dutch should have been able to read the handwriting on the wall. Listen to A.D.A. de Kat Angelino, in his day a most respected Dutch theorist of colonialism:

> One sees adult Western state organisation in the midst of primitive divided Eastern communities of which the miniature spheres disappear into nothingness compared with the gigantic dimension of the social horizon with which a similar Western state organisation would correspond. (1931:259)

Granting de Kat Angelino his metaphor, what are we to make of the boast that "adult" Holland (13,000 square miles) has reduced to "nothingness" its big baby Indonesia (620,000 square miles)? Or listen to another Dutchman writing just before the collapse of the Dutch empire:

> The administrative penetration, the Western industries, the extension of Western education – these and other forces were laying native society wide open to Western influences. . . . Christianity battled for mastery over Islamism, Hinduism, and animism; a dynamic world was lashing a static world into action; a secular, urban, science-exalting life and world view invaded a society ruled by a rural, dreamy, intuitive, religious, superstitious outlook on life. (Vandenbosch 1941:316)

Penetration, laying wide open, mastery, lashing a static, dreamy world into action – how else to interpret such rhetoric but as national policy represented by a (sadistic) fantasy of male desire? To say nothing of the outright lies concerning what the Dutch did "for" Indonesia.[9]

Augusta de Wit's voice and pictures

Colonialists spoke also in a third, more personal voice: that of people who were "out there" and who recorded their "impressions" or "glimpses" – their feelings about native peoples and their customs. One of these voices belongs to Augusta de Wit who in 1906 published *Java Facts and Fancies* in Holland and America. I don't know who de Wit was nor what brought her east. She doesn't tell us how long she remained in Java or under what auspices. She is aware of the Dutch colonial enterprise – in the closing pages of her book she describes the processing of cane into syrup into sugar. In doing so, de Wit articulates the colonialist's paradoxical wish to preserve the "legendary" (art, myth, religion) even while exploiting the "reality" of local labor and resources:

> Even now, whilst in the factory yonder fires roar, engines pant, and human beings sweat and toil, to change the dew drenched glory of the fields into a marketable commodity some hamlet in the plains is celebrating the Wedding of the Rice with many a mystic rite. Some native chief, celebrating the birth of a son, welcomes to his house the "dalang," the itinerant poet and playwright, who on his miniature stage, represents the councils of the Gods, and the adventures, in war and love, of unconquerable heroes, and of queens more beautiful than dawn. . . . It is this, I believe, this constant intrusion of the poetic, the legendary, the fanciful into the midst of reality, which constitutes the unique charm of Java. (1906:290–1)

Java Facts and Fancies is lavishly illustrated. There are 139 photographs and 18 paintings/drawings. Eighty-seven illustrations, de Wit tells us, were taken either from the Leyden Ethnographical Museum or the Haarlem Colonial Museum. Others, mostly uncredited photographs, I assume are her own; in any case, she is responsible for them and their telling captions.

De Wit sees the Javanese as carefree, "thoughtless," "childlike":

> Under the gaudy kerchiefs picturesquely framing the dark brows, their brown eyes had that look of thoughtful – or is it thoughtless? – content, which we of the North know only in the eyes of babies, crooning in their mother's lap. And, as they answered our questions, their speech had something childlike too, with its soft consonants and clear vowels, long drawn-out on a musical modulation that glided all up and down the gamut. . . . The native boats appeal to merrier thoughts . . . they remind one irresistibly of grotesque fishes for those big children, the Javanese, to play with. (1906:4, 42)

They are "natural," whether wild (male) or domestic (female):

> Among the squares of Batavia, the largest and most remarkable by far is the famous Koningsplein. It is not so much a square as simply a field, vast enough to build a city on, dotted from place to place by pasturing cattle, and bordered on the four sides of its irregular quadrangle by a triple row of branching tamarinds. . . . Now and then a native traverses the field, slowly moving along an invisible track. He does not disturb the loneliness. He is indigenous to the place, its natural product, almost as much as the cicadas trilling among the grass blades, the snakes darting in and out among the crevices of the sun-baked soil, and the lean cattle, upon whose backs the crows perch. . . .
>
> All day long, the native nurse carries her little charge in her long "slendang," the wide scarf, which deftly slung about her shoulders, makes a sort of a hammock for the baby. . . . She plays with it, not as a matter of duty, but as a matter of pleasure, throwing herself into the game with enjoyment and zest, like the child she is at heart. . . . And, at night, when she has crooned the little one to sleep . . ., she spreads her piece of matting on the floor, and lies down in front of the little bed, like a faithful dog guarding its master's house. (1906:30, 72)

And like wildlife existing seamlessly from generation to generation, world without end, the Javanese are senselessly happy:

> They seem perfectly happy without any visible and adequate cause for such content. As long as they are not dying – and one sometimes doubts if Javanese die at all – all is well with them. The race has a special genius for happiness. (1906:45)

Plate 6.1 "Here they are: plaything-less, naked, and supremely happy."

Do de Wit's photographs support her prose? None depict carefree "children" or "naturals." One, captioned "Here they are: plaything-less, naked, and supremely happy" (plate 6.1) shows seated, clothed, somber-faced young boys overlooked by an adult. The contrast between de Wit's caption and the photograph shows her deep investment in regarding the Javanese as happy primitives. Primitivism is represented in a different way by the handsome "seller of fruit and vegetables" (plate 6.2) and the bare-breasted "Girl from the Preanger Country" (plate 6.3), both posed in front of painted backdrops of jungle foliage barely contained by a frail wood fence. But the higher the class of Javanese, the more they are presented within a European setting and therefore the more "civilized" they appear. The royal "Pangeran Adipati Mangkoe Boemi (Djokjakarta)" (plate 6.4) and a "Javanese Lady," clearly Eurasian (plate 6.5), sit on European chairs with European tables to their left in front of painted backdrops of a European landscape (his) and a European interior wall (hers). His bare feet – an orientalist touch – are akimbo on a fine carpet while hers – only the toes showing – are settled on a Victorian footrest. The "Native nobleman and his wife" (plate 6.6) are posed next to the same kind of table in front of a blank backdrop with only a

Plate 6.2 "A seller of fruit and vegetables his baskets dangling from the ends of a bamboo yoke."

corner of drapery showing. His feet are sandaled. Contrast these with "A village couple" (plate 6.7) or "A brownie of the enchanted garden that men call Java" (plate 6.8) – one of two photos identically captioned, as if certain Javanese were interchangeable. The "village couple" stand on a woven straw mat before a blank backdrop while the "brownie" stands on raw straw in front of a rustic fence and a straw thatch wall. Of course, these people are barefoot. One Javanese scholar is depicted (plate 6.9) in a painting or retouched photo showing him seated on a carpeted floor in front of a blank backdrop or wall with one unopened book before him. From the nineteenth-century European perspective, this man is a poor version of a scholar. He has but one book, and it's closed. All in all, different classes and ages, city and rural dwellers, Javanese, Chinese, and Eurasians are displayed.

De Wit's pictorial colonialist taxonomy of the Javanese is mostly deliberately staged according to turn-of-the-century European conventions of romantic realism. Never are the subjects of the camera "happy naturals."

Plate 6.3 "Girl from the Preanger Country."

Even given the technical necessity for posed shots, how can the pictures be reconciled with de Wit's prose? The problem can be resolved if we comprehend the narrative implicit in the relationship between the prose and the pictures. De Wit's writing speaks of happy "naturals" while her pictures

Plate 6.4 "Pangeran Adipati Mangkoe Boemi (Djokjakarta)."

show an ascending scale from primitives standing in front of painted jungles to orientals ("almost but not quite" civilized) seated at their ease in European-like parlors. The writing is *about* the Javanese while the pictures are made *of* them. For de Wit, the camera stands for what the Dutch did to/for the Javanese: capture, pose, frame, tame, and elevate them – while always holding them at some distance, pinned down within a European sphere of discourse.

De Wit's book is out of date. No author today writes as she did. Yet surprisingly there is a part of her book that reads well – and whose

Plate 6.5 "Javanese Lady."

photographs appear appropriate even now (plates 6.10 through 6.14) – the section about wayang wong and wayang kulit:

There are several kinds of "wayang," each having its own range of subjects and style of acting; the most ancient as well as the most popular however, is the "wayang poerwa," the miniature stage on which the lives and adventures of Hindoo heroes, queens, and saints are acted over again by puppets of gilt and painted leather, moving in the hands of the "dalang," who recites the drama. . . . A puppet show to those in front of the screen . . . it is a Chinese lantern to those on the other side, who see the shadows projected on the luminous

Plate 6.6 "Native nobleman and his wife."

canvas. . . . In fully equipped wayangs, as many as two hundred of these puppets are found, each with its own particular type and garb. . . .

The "dalang" should be called the "showman" of the wayang. But he is a showman on a grand scale. Not only does he make his puppets act their parts

Plate 6.7 "A village couple."

of deities, heroes, and highborn beauties according to the strict canons of Javanese dramatic art, observant at the same time of the exigencies of courtly etiquette; but he must know by heart the whole of those endless epics, the recitation of which occupies several nights; sometimes he himself dramatizes some popular myth or legend; and he must always be ready at a moment's notice to imagine new and striking episodes, adapt a scene from another play to the one he is performing, and improvise dialogues in keeping with the character of the dramatis personae. He should have an ear for music and a good voice, and possess some knowledge of Kawi to give at all well the songs written in that ancient tongue. . . . Moreover, he conducts the "gamellan," the native

Plate 6.8 "A brownie of the enchanted garden that men call Java."

orchestra which accompanies every representation of the wayang. . . .
Manager, actor, musician, singer, reciter, improvisator, and all but playwright,
he is, in himself, a pleiad of artists. . . .

At the same time that it is the chief national amusement, the wayang-show
is, in a sense, a religious act, performed in honour of the deity, and to invoke
the blessing of the gods and the favour of the "danhjan dessa" and all other
good spirits upon the giver of the entertainment. The baleful influence of the
Evil Eye, also, is averted by nothing so surely as by a wayang-performance,
wherefore no enterprise of any importance should be entered upon without
one of these miniature dramatical representations being given. . . .

Plate 6.9 "A scholar."

> Wayang-plays . . . consist of fourteen, fifteen, or even more acts. The
> number of dramatis personae is practically unlimited; new heroes and heroines
> constantly appear on the scene; and to render confusion still worse con-
> founded, they again and again change their names. Time is annihilated. . . .
> Generally, too, no trace of any regular plan is discoverable. Incident follows
> incident, and intrigue disconnected intrigue; and, at every turn, fresh dramatic
> elements are introduced.   (1906:128–9, 130–3, 134, 149)

De Wit's twenty-three-page account of wayang – from which I've quoted a
fair sample – seems to set aside the colonial bias so blatant in the rest of her
book. Her prose is respectful, her appreciation not patronizing.

How can the artful, sophisticated wayang she describes be the theatre of
"thoughtless . . . big children," "natural products" of the jungle, "faithful
dogs" who are "perfectly happy" serving their "masters"?

De Wit's description is in accord with what many of today's scholars
write, her experience of shadow puppetry close to what the Beckers told

Plate 6.10 "The miniature stage on which the lives and adventures of Hindoo heroes, queens and saints are acted over again by puppets of gilt and painted leather."

Keller the audience at Rackham Auditorium could expect. Was de Wit ahead of her time regarding wayang while remaining staunchly colonialist in her other views of Java? Or has wayang – or the Western opinions regarding it – remained frozen for more than four generations, a period of far-reaching change in Indonesia? Questions like these can be asked differently. Did de Wit read nineteenth-century Dutch scholars with the same care as Ann Arbor journalist Keller listened to the Beckers? By the time de Wit saw it, had wayang already been restored according to the constructions of the scholars "guiding" the Javanese court artists? In the years just before de Wit wrote, dalangs were learning the "right way" to perform. For example, in the 1870s–80s Ch. te Mechelen prepared what amounted to manuals for dalangs including scripts and instructions on how to perform (1879a, 1879b, 1882).

De Wit's writing about wayang appears current (while the rest of her book is dated) because the normative wayang taking shape in her day still holds sway over scholarship. It is not that de Wit's account of wayang is at

Plate 6.11 "The native orchestra which accompanies every representation of the wayang."

odds with other aspects of her glimpse of Java – rather, today's construction of normative wayang remains colonial because it was formed by the Dutch when they were masters in Java. Looking carefully at some of de Wit's photographs of wayang shows clearly the Western impositions. "The Regent of Malang's Wayang-Wong" (plate 6.12) is performed on a raised platform stage framed by Western-style draperies. The "Scene from a Wayong-Wong play" (plate 6.13) shows actors posed in front of a backdrop of a European interior. "A Wayang representation" (plate 6.14) is of dancers on the porch of a sumptuous Western-style house. There are other photographs showing a gamelan and a wayang wong outdoors in what may be more "natural" settings (plates 6.11, 6.15) – or further examples of de Wit's primitivizing. Clearly many performances were adapted to suit colonial tastes and circumstances.

These circumstances, with few exceptions, continue to dominate today's Western scholarship where attention remains focused on the wayang that had taken shape by de Wit's time, the normative expectation. This wayang is the "subject" of scholarship in much the way that the posed Javanese were

Plate 6.12 "The Regent of Malang's Wayang-Wong."

the subjects of de Wit's photographs. The normative expectation is first invented and then positioned as the "baseline" for understanding and evaluating all other types of wayang – if any of these are discussed at all. And when wayang is performed in the West, the normative expectation, the "traditional" wayang, is the one that always represents "Javanese culture," allowing Westerners to "glimpse" this culture the way de Wit "took" Javanese life for her book. Thus the privileging of the normative expectation is a way of maintaining a colonial relationship under the aegis of modern liberal scholarship.

Modernizing wayang

The normative expectation is not the only wayang. Nor is the Western view the only one. The modernizers who won independence for Indonesia, no angels to liberal Westerners, promoted their own vision of wayang. In 1951 the Indonesian government issued *The Cultural Life of Indonesia* (*CLI*) in which wayang is called "the oldest form of dramatic art" (Embassy of Indonesia 1951:36). After describing wayang purwa (the normative expec-

Plate 6.13 "Scene from a Wayang-Wong play."

tation), wayang krutjil (flat wood puppets), and wayang golek (three-dimensional wood puppets), *CLI* goes on:

> During the revolutionary period a new form of puppet play, the *wajang suluh*, was developed. These plays portrayed the national leaders and the *pemudas* (young guerrilla soldiers) in their struggle to obtain independence for their country. The puppets were cut from leather, as in the *wajang kulit*, but their features were shaped to resemble more closely the human visage and they were dressed in the modern conventional style. These plays were extremely effective in clarifying for the Indonesian people the spirit and the goal of the revolutionary movement. After independence was won, the success of the *wajang suluh* as a medium of political information, gave rise to the development of the

216

Plate 6.14 "A Wayang representation."

wajang Pantja Sila, based on the five basic principles, or *Pantja Sila*, of the Constitution. In order to maintain the artistic value of the *wajang*, however, this play has been conceived within the traditional framework of the *Mahabharata* epic. Ardjuna, the most famous of the Pandawa heroes of the *Mahabharata*, represents *Nusantara Putra* or "Indonesia," who comes to the aid of "Freedom." The forms of the puppets in this play have been only slightly modified so that while their contemporary significance is indicated by the use of modern headdress and equipment such as cartridge belts, instead of the traditional *kris*, they can be easily identified with the original characters. One of the important characteristics of the *wajang* plays has been their moral implications and philosophical tone. In this modern form, therefore, the traditional quality is maintained, while the story and characters have been adapted to illustrate the principles of a modern democratic society.

(1951:36–8)

Is it because modern Western scholars – like the Dutch before them – wish to see wayang as "art" and not as "propaganda" that styles such as suluh or pancasila (Pantja Sila) are disparaged or ignored?

Clifford Geertz, doing fieldwork in Java at about the same time the wayangs described in *CLI* were being performed, places wayang in the *alus* or high art complex (1960:261). Geertz was aware of wayang's complexity,

Plate 6.15 "The dancers stand listening for the music."

its double life as "part of the abangan ritualistic–polytheistic–magical religious pattern . . . [and as] part of the *prijaji* mystical–pantheistic–speculative
religious pattern" (1960:268). Geertz was also aware of *kasar* or popular arts
as well as what he called the "national art complex" of modern genres. Surely
somewhere in these categories there is room for at least a passing mention of
suluh or pancasila? Not a word. James Brandon spends a few pages on
wayang suluh and pancasila which he says was "a new form of wayang" that
its creators hoped "would retain the mystic appeal and artistic excellence of
traditional wayang kulit while conveying a modern social and political
message" (1967:287). After briefly describing pancasila Brandon concludes
that:

> Like wayang suluh and the dozen wayang forms created by Javanese princes in
> past centuries to glorify themselves, wayang Pantja Sila never caught on with
> the public. . . . Wayang Pantja Sila is very seldom performed any more. It
> disappeared as quickly as new propaganda needs pushed it aside.
>
> (1967:288–9)

More recently, Roger Long introduces his technical study of wayang puppet manipulations and characterization in the normative style by stating that:

> wayang is a vital art form that has for centuries influenced and mirrored Javanese society, and, in an age of increasing technological and social change, it continues to play an important role in Javanese life. As a seminal theatre form, *wayang kulit* has contributed to the development of related genres.   (1982:2)

Yet Long also is silent regarding modern wayang. So is Keeler, even though he notes that "wayang's influence goes beyond the arts and beyond conventional gestures" (1987:15).

In 1971 Barbara Hatley was explicit concerning what many Western experts past and present believe (or want to believe): "The possibilities for innovation in Wayang are limited. . . . Shadow theatre seems to be too deeply rooted in traditional morality and religion to survive major changes in its symbols and ethos" (1971:92–3). What Hatley says about wayang's deep roots in tradition is consistent with the colonialists' construction of wayang as "ancient," "mystical," "high art," "resistant to change," "religious," "conservative." But this view does not accurately reflect what Indonesia's modernizers desire – be they officials in Jakarta or experimenters in central Java. Recognizing wayang's authority and popularity, its connection to religion and mystical beliefs, in short, its power, these people see wayang as an instrument of social change as well as open to changes in itself. Recent writings by Clara van Groenendael (1987) and Sears (1989a) underscore this – as well as open a new phase of wayang scholarship.

Clara van Groenendael reports a village performance in the late 1970s – surely not the only one? – carrying forward the modernizing tendencies of suluh and pancasila.

> The dalang made allusions to different kinds of abuse of power, such as corruption, intimidation, and false reporting, as well as to the coming re-election of the president in 1978. . . . He fitted his allusions in the traditional framework of the story by having Dhastharastra make the relevant comments in the form of a homily by an elder to a younger brother. . . . Another interesting feature was the propaganda made by Dhastharastra for participation in sports, an issue which is strongly stimulated by the Indonesian government.   (1985:176)

This dalang introduced other national and local issues such as family planning, the financial status of his host, his other performances in the region, and the interest of white foreigners in Javanese culture. These matters were not restricted to the comic scenes, as the normative expectation dictates, but were part of the performance from the very first scene. Most villagers liked what they saw and heard:

> On the whole the performance was praised as providing a good example of the new, more dynamic wayang style, which allegedly better met the needs of contemporary Indonesian society than the traditional style with its long, didactic expositions. According to proponents of this view, the performance was proof that the wayang theatre need not lag behind modern developments.
>
> (1985:178)

As I indicated earlier, maybe this style is not new but is like what wayang kulit was before Dutch intervention.

Long after wayang suluh and pancasila were officially dead, the government continued to influence, control, and use wayang.[10] In December 1966, shortly after the bloody coup of 1965 terminated Indonesia's move toward communism, sixty dalangs were gathered in Surakarta by General Suharto's new government. There they heard F. Soetrisno, head of the Central Javanese Regional Cultural Affairs Inspectorate, lecture them on "The new order and the art of the dalang." Soetrisno asserted that "The artist should be aware of his responsibility towards society and be sure not to lag behind the social developments" (in Clara van Groenendael 1985:141). The dalangs' tasks were explicitly laid out during a series of meetings in Jakarta on 10–14 April 1969 attended by fifty-nine dalangs from Bali (three), East Java (twelve), Central Java (fourteen), Jogjakarta (seven), West Java (three), Jakarta (eighteen), and Lampong and Medan (one each). President Suharto took part in the meetings along with his ministers of information–education and culture.

> The President described at length how the Five-Year plan had come about. He asked the dalangs to help arouse the masses and make them aware of their obligations. It was his firm conviction that it would be possible for the dalangs to interweave the necessary information for arousing the consciousness of the masses with the material dramatized by them without having to change the presentation of the story or deviate from the basic principles of dalangship.
>
> (1985:144)

The dalangs voiced support of Suharto's openly political program – what choice had they? (But do we as easily see through the equally transparent Dutch interest in "preserving" and "restoring" nineteenth-century wayang?) Dalangs who actually followed through were rewarded by Jakarta by being selected to represent their art at regional and national workshops and conferences. Shortly thereafter the government organized Ganasidi, a dalang guild, designed to keep puppeteers from "erring" politically. In 1971 Ganasidi issued its "six ethical rules for dalangs," based on the role of the dalang as the "servant" of the people, the nation, and Indonesian culture.

Since 1965 this program has been advanced through the Akademi Seni Karawitan Indonesia (ASKI), the government arts academy in Surakarta. Padat wayang, developed at ASKI, is a kind of wayang where artistic decisions are shared by a team consisting of a stage director, a musical director, a script writer, and one or more dalangs. It is short, sometimes less than an hour, and follows written texts – in Indonesian as often as in Javanese. "The padat plays . . . promulgate new ideas and values that often conflict with the interpretations of puppeteers of earlier generations" (Sears 1989a:132). As Clara van Groenendael notes,

> The aim at ASKI . . . is to train its students to become artists capable of making a critical contribution and giving direction to the national policy. . . . The main emphasis lies on theoretical subjects, with the place of art and of the artist in present-day Indonesian society and the different conceptions of art, in particular Western ones, constituting subjects of study and discussion.
>
> (1985:43; see also Pekan 1969 and Pekan Wayang Indonesia II 1974)

Thus, in the 1980s and early 1990s not only has wayang been changing due to political and social pressure, it is also being drawn into the international art world – not just as an exotic item (as might be expected) but as a "form" to be experimented with. Sears discusses both padat and rebo legi (Sweet Wednesday) performances held monthly at the Surakarta home of the well known dalang, Pak Anom Surata. Rebo legi is "traditional," "political," and "experimental" all at once. Because Surata "has made the pilgrimage to Mecca and is a member of Golkar (Golongan Karya, the political vehicle of the present government), the unspoken authorities at these performances are strict Islam and the Indonesian government" (1989a:123). Surata invites different dalangs to perform, many from villages. At rebo legi all spectators are regarded as professionals closely following the dalang's techniques, sharing and transmitting new ideas. The screen is against the wall so that everyone watches the puppeteer, no one the shadows (opposite to the setup in Ann Arbor). Indonesian and English words are mixed with Javanese. Puppets

> are thrown off the screen or onto the screen in unconventional and abrupt ways. Fights take place between characters who would never fight in more traditional performances . . . and jokes often begin in the first audience hall scene, a place where all humor is traditionally banned.   (1989a:129)

In short, "puppeteers are breaking the rules that were codified by the Dutch-influenced central Javanese courts in the early 20th century" (123). But are they (as Sears acclaims) "even more Javanese than the Dutch-influenced court styles of the late colonial era" (131)?

The underlying function of the dalang schools has not changed since they were established in the 1920s. Now as then they serve the existing powers. The older schools crystallized and disseminated the Dutch-determined court style; today's government schools promote modern wayangs that advance Jakarta's visions of Indonesia (even as these might change as regimes change). In the villages potpourri wayangs thrive. Most Western scholars – and many artists in Java training in wayang – prefer the older court style or village wayang to rebo legi or padat. But the newer styles seem to be gaining popularity. Is there any sense in trying to determine what is the "most Javanese" in all this? Is the quest for what's "most Javanese" still more evidence of colonial thinking?

Isn't it *all* Javanese – the normative expectation, the rebo legi, the padat, the wildly eclectic village shows, the government attempts to control wayang? There are dalangs loyal to the court style, dalangs using whatever works (makes them popular), dalangs toeing the government line, dalangs bent on experimentation, dalangs exploring political expression opposed to Jakarta's. Probably most dalangs combine approaches – bending with the wind, suiting particular performances to immediate circumstances:

> Students from ASKI bring Western ideas to the villages which are incorporated into village performances. Rebo legi puppeteers mingle with puppeteers from the academy and are invited to the academy to take part in the series of conferences and workshops that form part of ASKI's curriculum. The academy uses respected traditional puppeteers to teach the first years of courses to aspiring puppeteers, and innovative puppeteers at the academy are often the sons of famous traditional puppeteers. The existence of all this mixed up activity argues for the continued popularity of wayang projecting its rich and complex legacy into succeeding generations. (Sears 1989a:29)

But can wayang sail off so happily into the intercultural sunset?

The colonial bath

There are things "wrong" with history – events that in a better world humans would not have let happen: slavery, the Holocaust, and colonialism for examples. But having happened, the question is how to go on making history in the aftermath of such events. We have *all* – everyone in the world – taken a colonial bath. The violent exportation–importation of people, religion, values, political systems, technology, and theory has troubled world history for half a millennium, and the story is far from over. Colonialism comes in at least two brands – genocidal–expansionist as in North America, and "let the natives live"–exploitative as in the Dutch East Indies. There is such misery and violence in South Africa because it effectively combines the two brands under the joint authorship of the Dutch and British, more recently underwritten by the USA and its allies. One of the lessons of historiography is that different versions of historical events (or tales) are possible according to whose voices are heard; and telling these different stories opens the possibility of different futures – in fact the concrete desire to live different futures is the motor driving the construction of different pasts. This also is the dynamic performative process of my "restoration of behavior" theory (see Schechner 1985). Seen this way, the persistence in scholarship of the dominance of the normative expectation is a colonialist story written first by the Dutch and later by liberal-thinking Western scholars. But instead of seeing the construction of the normative expectation as a colonialist story, we – Javanese as well as Westerners – have been trained to see it as a model of the "truly Javanese."

Many scholars who prefer the normative expectation take an anticolonialist stance. This "pure" wayang ought not be corrupted; it needs to be preserved. Some, like Keeler, might argue that the "most Javanese" is the wayang played in the villages where ritual and social matters overlap and are as important as aesthetic ones. Until Clara van Groenendael and Sears, no Western scholar gave detailed attention to, no less praise for, styles like suluh, pancasila, rebo legi, padat – or any other non-normative wayang. But is "purity" of any kind obtainable or even desirable? Could not such a desire be an apology for what cannot be undone, namely colonialism? And, in possibly more cases than wayang kulit, in more places than Indonesia, is not this apology, far from a correction, a continuation of colonial thinking? The modernizing forces reshaping the world are not slackening. This complex situation includes a set of double standards extremely difficult to rectify. Within Indonesia (and all other third world nations) is what Dube calls an "oppressive minority which stands to gain from the maintenance of the status quo and would lose many of its advantages if a critical consciousness developed among the poor" (1988:111). At the same time, between the third world and the industrialized nations a widening gap demotes even third world elites to the relatively low status of "other." Only when a nation achieves economic and political par vis-a-vis "developed" nations – Japan for example – can it effectively decide for itself how to preserve whatever it defines as its traditional culture or cultures. This is because prior to achieving par, what constitutes "traditional culture," even how to define it, is determined by forces whose centers of manipulation lie beyond national and cultural boundaries. For many third world nations, what is decided at the 42nd Street New York headquarters of the Ford Foundation, or on a stage in Ann Arbor, counts more than what local people want or do. In other words, the notion of "traditional" is itself a product of colonialism.

The struggle between Western scholars and Indonesian officials over defining and developing wayang is an example of this complex situation. The scholars denigrate the officials as "corrupters" of an "ancient tradition" while the officials cast a wary, maybe even contemptuous but still envious eye on the Westerners. Most Javanese dalangs, operating in the difficult energy field radiating from these contending forces, yet trying also to make wayang on their own and their immediate clients' behalf, more or less subversively seek alternatives suiting local situations.

In September 1987, before beginning research for this chapter, I arranged for Sumarsam and a gamelan from Wesleyan University to perform for my New York University Asian performance theory class. I wanted a "traditional" performance – audience on both sides of the screen, an all-night show performed outdoors, a purwa story, and so on. I wanted my class to see the "real" wayang kulit insofar as it could be hoisted to Manhattan from Java (via Middletown). Except for duration, I got most of what I wanted – a lovely example of the normative expectation. Were I again to arrange a wayang would I seek a pancasila or padat or rebo legi – not because they are "better" than the normative expectation, but because they represent Indonesian responses to colonialism less often heard in the West? Whatever the answer to that question, I am only too well aware that my desire in this matter is, to paraphrase Homi Bhabha, a practice of authority displaying its ambivalence . . . confronting a peculiarly displaced and decentered image of itself.

Notes

1. The presentation of Javanese names in the West is not so simple. Widyanto S. Putro is referred to as Widyanto or, as A. L. Becker calls him, Midyanto or Mas Midyanto. I follow the program and call him Widyanto. Sumarsam avoids the first name/last name dilemma by using one name only. Minarno is called Pak Minarno by A. L. Becker.

2. In Indonesia, there are five kinds of wayang (puppet) shows – only one, wayang kulit, uses flat leather puppets. Other wayangs use three-dimensional wood puppets (*golek*), flat wood puppets (*klitek*), figures painted on a scroll (*beber*), and human actors (*wong* or *orang*). In this essay, whenever I say "wayang" alone I mean "wayang kulit." As will become clear, wayang kulit itself has many subcategories.

3. From 1811 to 1815, the Interregnum, the English were masters of what was to become Indonesia. The Japanese occupied the archipelago during World War II. Since independence the American and then the Japanese economic presence has been strong. For more than 1,000 years a large Chinese population has lived in Indonesia without either being assimilated or expelled. The Dutch were there in force for upwards of 400 years.

4. I do not recount many Javanese reactions not only because I am illiterate in Indonesian languages but also because I am uneasy with how scholars are "giving voice" to the "subjects" of anthropological fieldwork. I very much support the proclaimed intentions of multivocality but worry about the self-righteousness and hypocrisy of the practice. Can voice be "given"? Is it a gift, a right, or a function of power? As an editor myself, I know the hand on the tape recorder, transcribing the "material," editing the manuscript (or tape or video) – however "fair" or "invisible" – is always biased towards itself. What might issue from these well-meaning efforts is the appearance of polylog, its simulation ("almost but not quite," as Homi Bhabha has it). Multivocality means sharing – or having wrenched away through struggle – the means of theorizing, gathering, editing, publishing, and disseminating. Is this happening or are people feeling good about their intentions while practicing a new, maybe more subtle, but still plain paternalism?

5. I've heard of only two Javanese women dalangs (Sears 1989a; 1989b:16–18) – though presumably today there are no gender barriers at the Akademi Seni Karawitan Indonesia (ASKI) in Surakarta or other schools. In the "old days" perhaps there were a number of women dalangs. In any case, at present women dalangs in Java are rare. Does Keller (1988) write as if they were common so that wayang will appear nonsexist?

6. In her 1987 annotated bibliography Clara van Groenendael lists 72 varieties of wayang, most of which are wayang kulit of one kind or another.

7. Clara van Groenendael's bibliography of writings about wayang in Indonesian,

modern Javanese, Sundanese, English, Dutch, and other European languages tells the story. She has 564 entries; but only two, Hadisoeseno (1955) and Mylius (1961), deal mostly with modern and/or "secular" forms of wayang kulit such as suluh, pancasila, padat, perjuangan, or wahana; or with the Catholic or Protestant wayang, wahyu and warta respectively. Hadisoeseno is the originator of wayang pancasila. Mulyono (1979) considers various wayangs, including the rather recent wayang buddha, from an Islamic and mystical perspective. Papers from the First Indonesian Wayang Week held in Jakarta in July 1969 and the Second Wayang Week held in March 1974 have been distributed in stencil. Several of these deal with the modernization process. I have not read these, Hadisoeseno, or Mulyono. Brandon in his influential *Theatre in Southeast Asia* (1967) spends nine pages (45, 286–93) on government wayangs and the reasons for their failure. By contrast, Brandon discusses "classical" wayang kulit from various perspectives, but not critically, in many different parts of his book, spending roughly a total of thirty pages on it.

8. Vandenbosch (1941:155–6) relates what he calls an "amusing incident" that demonstrates all too clearly how powerless the sultans were.

> The degree of the Governor's control [over Jogjakarta and Surakarta] is illustrated by an amusing incident which occurred at the time of the visit of the King and Queen of Siam to Java in 1929. One of the Javanese princes gave a lavish dinner in honor of the King and Queen. The Governor, however, exercised a control over the issuance of the invitations with the result that 250 European guests were invited by the Governor and a mere handful, since there was room for no more, were invited by the prince himself.

Even the colonialists knew this was going too far. As Vandenbosch notes, "The incident was criticized in European circles and played up in Indonesian nationalist circles."

9. Statistics and Indonesian opinion both contradict Vandenbosch's assertions. During Dutch hegemony, and since, Christianity made but tiny dents in Indonesia's Islamic and Hindu populations, next to none in central Java. At the end of Dutch colonial rule, the Indonesian population was 4 percent Christian, most of whom resided on islands that were previously neither Islamic nor Hindu. Concerning education, the authors of *The Cultural Life of Indonesia* in 1951 spoke of the

> totally inadequate educational policy followed by the Dutch colonial government during their long period of rule. As a result of this policy the rate of illiteracy in Indonesia at the beginning of World War II was estimated at ninety percent, one of the highest illiteracy rates in the world.
> (Embassy of Indonesia 1951:56)

Vandenbosch actually represented a widely held Dutch view regarding their "permanent" presence in Indonesia – leading ultimately to "the reconciliation of East and West . . . in a synthesis of their cultures. This synthesis has the best chance of success under the colonial relationship. . . . The idea of a Netherlands East Indian empire underlies the argument" (Vandenbosch 1941:72). Of course the high-sounding "synthesis" is nothing other than indefinite continuation of Dutch dominance.

10. My information regarding the Indonesian government's relation to wayang in the 1960s–1970s is from Clara van Groenendael (1985).

7

The future of ritual

Even to say it in one word, ritual, is asking for trouble. Ritual has been so variously defined – as concept, praxis, process, ideology, yearning, experience, function – that it means very little because it means too much.[1] In common use, ritual is identified with the sacred, another slippery word. But scholars have long discussed "secular ritual" (see Moore and Myerhoff 1977). Current opinion holds that the barriers between sacred and secular, like those between work and play, are both extremely porous and culture-specific. Rituals have been considered: 1) as part of the evolutionary development of animals; 2) as structures with formal qualities and definable relationships; 3) as symbolic systems of meaning; 4) as performative actions or processes; 5) as experiences. These categories overlap. It is also clear that rituals are not safe deposit vaults of accepted ideas but in many cases dynamic performative systems generating new materials and recombining traditional actions in new ways.

Whatever the future of ritual, its past is pedigreed. Ethologists, observing animals performing rituals, use the word without quotation marks.[2] Ethologically speaking, ritual is ordinary behavior transformed by means of condensation, exaggeration, repetition, and rhythm into specialized sequences of behavior serving specific functions usually having to do with mating, hierarchy, or territoriality. In animals, ritualized behavior is often set in "fixed action patterns" elicited automatically by certain kinds of stimuli. These patterns are augmented and highlighted by conspicuous body parts that have evolved over time for use in "ritual displays" – the moose's horns, the peacock's tail, the red rump of a baboon in estrus, the brilliant colors of any number of fish species. Other animals have the ability to dramatically change size or color. The evolution of ritual from an ethological perspective can be diagrammed as a tree (figure 7.1). The further up the tree,

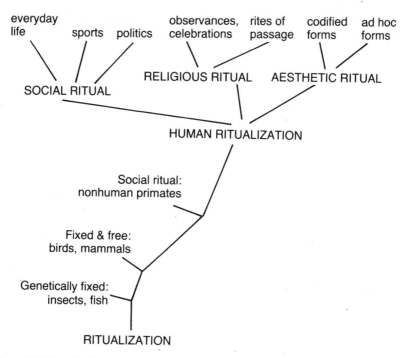

Figure 7.1 The ritual tree.

the closer to human. Nonhuman primates such as chimpanzees and gorillas behave in some respects very much like humans. Some of their actions closely resemble human performance.[3] Even if nonhuman primates cannot speak as humans do (lacking not only the muscular formations necessary for the articulation of speech but also a well-enough developed brain) they can express and communicate feelings. Such expressive behavior, communicating and sharing feelings, might be closer to human ritual and its associated "behavior arts" (theatre, dance, music, some kinds of painting) than anything rational or cognitive the "higher apes" are capable of.

But if there are homologies between animal behavior and human rituals and arts there are important differences also. The patterned "waggle dance" of bees may look like dancing to a human observer predisposed to see such an analogy, but the bees are not dancing in the same sense as a kathakali dancer or the performers in *A Chorus Line* are. For the bees everything is genetically determined. There is no learning or improvisation, no composition classes where new behaviors are invented and tested. Nor are there rehearsals where behaviors are revised, taking into account the particular individual "talent" of this or that bee. The most that can happen is the accidental occurrence of some advantageous genetic variation that will then be passed on. Nor can any bee make a mistake or lie or be resistant. A ballet dancer can choose one night simply not to go up on point though the choreography tells her to do so. She might lose her role, or even her job, but she won't be examined to determine what genetic mutation caused her to go flatfoot. Not so with the "dancing" bees. If they go wrong, or change their basic pattern of behavior, scientists will look into their screwed-up DNA. Human performance is paradoxical, a practiced fixity very hard to achieve because it is founded on contingency. What a weird delight it is for people to go up on point, or recite words written hundreds of years earlier, or perform choreographed ineptitude as clowns do. Even weirder for other people to pay good money (or its equivalent) to watch and savor such behavior. And what is true of ballet or Shakespeare or clowning is true also of the Mass, an initiation rite of Australian aborigines, a Hindu puja, or a World Cup soccer match.

Are ethologists begging the question? Do they call some animal behavior "ritual" because it looks like what people do? Or are there true homologies based on genetics? Is there an evolution of behavior connected to the evolution of the body, especially the brain? It is not easy to settle this question – one which anthropologist and philosopher Victor Turner was wrestling with when he died suddenly of a heart attack in 1983. I will discuss Turner's speculations later.

In both animals and humans rituals arise or are devised around disruptive, turbulent, and ambivalent interactions where faulty communication can lead to violent or even fatal encounters. Rituals, and the behavior arts associated with them, are overdetermined, full of redundancy, repetition, and exaggeration. This metamessage of "You get the message, don't you!?!" (a question surrounded by emphasis) says that what a ritual communicates is very important yet problematic. The interactions that rituals surround, contain, and mediate almost always concern hierarchy, territory, and sexuality/mating (an interdependent quadruple). If these interactions are the "real events" rituals enfold, then what are the rituals themselves? They are ambivalent symbolic actions pointing at the real transactions even as they help people avoid too direct a confrontation with these events. Thus rituals are also bridges – reliable doings carrying people across dangerous waters. It is no accident that many rituals are "rites of passage."

Both animal and human ritual actions are very close to theatre. In theatre, too, behavior is rearranged, condensed, exaggerated, and made rhythmic. Theatre employs colorful costumes and masks as well as face and body painting every bit as impressive as a peacock's tail or a moose's antlers. In theatre, perilous journeys and deadly conflicts are acted through. Even farces and comedies barely hide their violent subtexts. The violence of ritual, like that of theatre, is simultaneously present and absent, displayed and deferred. The ritual actions are displayed even as the "real events" are deferred. Two wolves fight and at a certain point one animal gets the better of the other. The vanquished wolf suddenly offers his throat to his opponent but the winning wolf does not – cannot – slash the jugular. Surrender defers death. After the ceremony of offering the throat, the winner allows the loser to slink away. Or in Jewish circumcision an 8-day-old boy's penis is cut, his foreskin violently taken, as a direct and permanent bodily proof of God's special arrangement with the Jews: the deferral granted to Abraham who was willing, on God's word, to sacrifice his son Isaac for whom, at the last minute, a lamb was substituted. Or, following the same theme, when the Christian priest elevates the Eucharistic bread and wine, the grain and liquor are masks for flesh and blood, the real human body, God's lamb and first son, sacrificed on the Cross (God was not as lucky as Abraham). As the way to celebrate Christ's redemptive *sparagmos*, communicants are offered a cannibal feast once removed.

Violence, sexuality, and theatre converge in the two main Western traditions, the Greek and the Hebraic-Christian. These traditions combine Middle Eastern, northern European, and Eurasian elements – fertility rites, human and animal sacrifice, sun worship, and shamanism. Even a cursory look at Christian iconography and painting as it developed through the Middle Ages into the Renaissance reveals the orgasmic, not to say orgiastic, qualities of martyrdom as imagined and depicted. This display of violence against the body is not limited to bygone epochs. Violence against the body is a strong theme in contemporary art and popular culture. Chris Burden specialized in assaulting his own body, even going so far as to have himself shot; Stelarc exhibits his body suspended by hooks and cords. The violence of certain kinds of rock-and-roll is well known. American football, boxing, and especially professional wrestling celebrate a highly theatricalized violence. Special automobile shows called "demolition derbies" feature high-speed car crashes and "monster trucks" whose specialty is crushing other vehicles beneath their gargantuan wheels. With the exception of wrestling, these events – as distinct from the extraordinarily graphic scenes of violence in the movies (often in slow motion in order to emphasize the spectacularity and bloody detail of the violence) – are not simulated. A close look at these violent displays cannot but disclose their erotic content.

If not universal, the connections between violence and sex are character-istic of Indo-European arts and literature. The classic Sanskrit epics, *Ramayana* and *Mahabharata*, like their Western counterparts, the *Iliad* and the *Odyssey*, are full of extremely bloody and erotic episodes. The *Ramayana* pivots around the lust of Ravana, the ten-headed demon-king of Lanka who kidnaps and attempts to seduce/rape Sita, the wife of Vishnu incarnate, Rama. The epic includes a great war of Rama and his allies against Ravana and his demon hordes (see Chapter 5). The *Mahabharata* turns on the lust and greed of the Kauravas who cheat their Pandava cousins of their kingdom and wealth. One of the key scenes of the *Mahabharata* is how the Kaurava Dusassana tries to strip and rape the Pandavas' joint-wife, Draupadi, who is saved only by the intercession of Krishna. The story goes through many adventurous turns (there are literally hundreds of side-tales absorbed into the *Mahabharata*) before climaxing in the bloody battle at Kurukshetra. One of the most frequently performed scenes of the epic is the Pandava Bhima's revenge against Dusassana. As played in kathakali, Bhima with his great war club smashes Dusassana's thighs. Then with his bare hands he rips open Dusassana's stomach, drinks his blood and eats his intestines. Finally, as he had sworn, Bhima washes Draupadi's hair in the bloody bowl of Dusassana's stomach. Bhima and Draupadi laugh wildly as they accomp-lish this absolute revenge. Only then is Dusassana permitted to die.

What of all this violence, examples of which could be multiplied many times over from different cultures around the world? It is not part of "real life." The first-time or "original" violence of real life is anything but redemptive. Humans need to "make something out" of the violence of real life, if at first only by repetition. The rebroadcasting of events like the assassination of John F. Kennedy or the explosion of the Challenger space shuttle are kinds of low-level ritualizing, an attempt to absorb and transform the violence of the event itself into something redemptive. When official real-life violence approaches the absolute, as at Auschwitz-Birkenau, the memorials and museums meant to commemorate seem almost to parody. The Polish schoolkids bused to Auschwitz in May 1985 were more inter-ested in the T-shirts imprinted with Michael Jackson's face displayed at the tourist kiosk than in any confrontation with Polish–Jewish–German history. Perhaps this is as it should be. The ritual of going-to-Auschwitz-as-part-of-school erases the pain of seeing what was/is there. For me, part of no group, walking alone the mile or so from Auschwitz to Birkenau, standing among the wild grasses growing over the rail line terminating between the wrecked but recognizable twin gas chambers–crematoria, watching the bees work the spring flowers while a couple of Polish boys on bikes rolled down the rail path, stopping to talk, then casually turning around and pedaling out again, I felt a stunning void and heard only the wind in my ears.

Until very recently when work on animal cognition began to be taken seriously, it was assumed that animals have no Oedipal choices to make. They act without entertaining either skepticism, irony, or subjunctive negativity ("Ought I do that?" "What will happen if I don't do that?"). Animals suffer no wedges driven between impulse and act. Perhaps a splinter of subjunctivity annoys the so-called "speaking animals": chimpanzees, gorillas, dolphins. But even if there were a gorilla Oedipus wondering if he should leave his forested Corinth to avoid his awful doom, he would be a far cry from Sophocles' character.

But human ritual, too, might be said to short-circuit thinking, providing ready-made answers to deal with crisis. Individual and collective anxieties are relieved by rituals whose qualities of repetition, rhythmicity, exaggeration, condensation, and simplification stimulate the brain into releasing endorphins directly into the bloodstream yielding ritual's second benefit, a relief from pain, a surfeit of pleasure. In saying that religion was the opium of the people, Marx may have been right biochemically speaking. But ritual is also creative because, as Turner showed, the ritual process opens up a time/space of antistructural playfulness. And whereas in animals the non-cognitive is dominant, in humans there is always a dialectical tension between the cognitive and the affective.

René Girard in his *Violence and the Sacred* (1977) asserts that real violence always threatens the social life of a group:

> Inevitably the moment comes when violence can only be countered by more violence. Whether we fail or succeed in our effort to subdue it, the real victor is always violence itself. The mimetic attributes of violence are extraordinary – sometimes direct and positive, at other times indirect and negative. The more men strive to curb their violent impulses, the more these impulses seem to prosper. (1977:31)

Girard links this violence to sexuality:

> Like violence, sexual desire tends to fasten upon surrogate objects if the object

233

to which it was originally attracted remains inaccessible; it willingly accepts substitutes. And again, like violence, repressed sexual desire accumulates energy that sooner or later bursts forth, causing tremendous havoc. It is also worth noting that the shift from violence to sexuality and from sexuality to violence is easily effected, even by the most "normal" of individuals, totally lacking in perversion. Thwarted sexuality leads naturally to violence, just as lovers' quarrels often end in an amorous embrace. (1977:35)

Girard believes (and I agree) that ritual sublimates violence: "The function of ritual is to 'purify' violence; that is to 'trick' violence into spending itself on victims whose death will provoke no reprisals" (1977:36). All this sounds very much like theatre – especially a theatre whose function is cathartic, or at least a theatre that "redirects" violent and erotic energies. Cathartic or not, theatre always manufactures substitutes, specializing in multiplying alternatives. Is it accidental that so many of these alternatives combine the violent with the erotic?

The "sacrificial crisis," as Girard sees it, is the dissolution of distinctions within a society – from the erasure of the reciprocal rights/responsibilities of parents to/from their children, to the elision of all hierarchy. Incest and regicide are radical attacks on differentiation. Girard, a dyed-in-the-wool advocate of differentiation, says: "Wherever differences are lacking, violence threatens" (1977:57). The enactment of ritual death – whether the victim is actually or theatrically killed – restores distinctions by emphasizing the difference between the victim and the rest of society:

> The surrogate victim plays the same role on the collective level as the objects
> the shamans claim to extract from their patients play on the individual level –
> objects that are then identified as the cause of the illness. (1977:83)

In theatre the substitutions are more complex than in shamanism. In theatre the actor is a substitute for a surrogate. The actor who plays Oedipus or Lear or Willie Loman is not that "character" who itself is not a "real person." There may be no "real person" at all behind the scenes, but only the play of embodied representations:

[victim]→character→actor::audience←[society]

At the place where the actor meets the audience, that is, in the theatre place, society faces the sacrificial victim twice-removed. The individuals who comprise an audience "leave" society and "go to" the theatre where they play the role of society, responding more as a group than as discrete individuals. The actor performs the character behind whom is the victim. The actor's performance is a representation of a representation. But in a ritual like the Eucharist, a layer of representation is stripped away from the actor's side. There is no character. The priest, an actor on behalf of Christ, faces the congregation which, like the theatre audience, represents society, in this case the society of Christians (of the same denomination).

[victim]→actor::congregation←[society]

Still there is no direct meeting between society and victim. The priest performing the Eucharist "elevates" Christ while the congregants "stand for" the Christians they are. In some rituals, an animal takes the place of a human victim. And in other rituals a person faces the representatives of society directly and an actual sacrifice takes place:

victim::celebrants←[society]

This is very rarely the sacrifice of a human life. It may be a cutting or scarring or burning, etc.; or the exchange of rings, the giving of a thread, an immersion, or some other irrevocable act. Is it proper to use the term "victim" to describe a person who is not only not harmed but often celebrated? In these cases is there even the shadow of a sacrificial victim? Take the exchange of wedding rings. Certainly there is a suggestion of bondage. The gold ring is a master's gift marking and enclosing she (or he) who wears it. Before the custom of the double ring ceremony, it was the bride who was "given" to the husband and she alone who wore the ring. And the failure to live up to the arrangement of submission still does, in some cases, lead to violence and death. Or what can the burning candles on a birthday cake blown out by the celebrant signify if not the brevity of life and the temporary reprieve granted to one whom death will someday claim?

There are ways other than Girard's to explain the widespread association of violence, sexuality, ritual, and theatre. In *Totem and Taboo* (originally published in 1913) Freud proposed an analogy between the thought of animists, neurotics, children, and artists.

> It is easy to perceive the motives which lead men to practice magic: they are human wishes. All we need to suppose is that primitive man had an immense belief in the power of his wishes. (1962:83)

> Children are in an analogous psychical situation. . . . They satisfy their wishes in an hallucinatory manner, that is, they create a satisfying situation by means of centrifugal excitation of their sense organs. An adult primitive man has an

alternative method open to him. His wishes are accompanied by a motor impulse, the will, which is later destined to alter the whole face of the earth in order to satisfy his wishes. This motor impulse is at first employed to give a representation of the satisfying situation in such a way that it becomes possible to experience the satisfaction by means of what might be described as motor hallucinations. This kind of representation of a satisfied wish is quite comparable to children's play, which succeeds their earlier purely sensory technique of satisfaction. (1962:83–4)

This "omnipotence of thoughts," as Freud called it, makes a world where "things become less important than ideas of things" (1962:85). Neurotics also live in this "world apart" where "they are only affected by what is thought with intensity and pictured with emotion, whereas agreement with external reality is a matter of no importance" (1962:86). Freud notes that neurotics undergoing psychoanalysis are "unable to believe that thoughts are free and will constantly be afraid of expressing evil wishes, as though their expression would lead inevitably to their fulfillment." In this way, neurotics reveal their "resemblance to the savages who believe they can alter the external world by mere thinking" (1962:87).

Freud, a social Darwinist, argues for a progression from an animist view of the world to a religious view to a scientific view.

At the animistic stage men ascribe omnipotence to themselves. At the religious stage they transfer it to the gods but do not seriously abandon it themselves, for they reserve the power of influencing the gods in a variety of ways according to their wishes. The scientific view of the universe no longer affords any room for human omnipotence; men have acknowledged their smallness and submitted resignedly to death and to the other necessities of nature. None the less some of the primitive belief in omnipotence still survives in men's faith in the power of the human mind, taking account, as it does of the laws of reality. (1962:88)

Each successive stage credits "external reality" with more autonomy. Too bad that Freud did not know that even as he was proposing this evolutionary scheme, Niels Bohr and Werner Heisenberg were developing ideas of indeterminacy – a theory that categorically denies to "external reality" its independent existence while also denying to the human mind any claims of omnipotence.

Freud notes one mode of "civilized thought" that remains unreconstructed.

In only a single field of our civilization has the omnipotence of thoughts been retained, and that is in the field of art. Only in art does it still happen that a man who is consumed by desires performs something resembling the accomplishment of those desires and that what he does in play produces emotional effects – thanks to artistic illusion – just as though it were something real. People speak with justice of the "magic of art" and compare artists to magicians. But the comparison is perhaps more significant than it claims to be. There can be no doubt that art did not begin as art for art's sake. It worked originally in the service of impulses which are for the most part extinct today. And among them we may suspect the presence of many magical purposes.

(1962:90)

Extinct impulses? Looking at Freud through a contemporary lens means throwing out the notion that some humans are more "primitive" – or "aboriginal" – than others. Biologically and culturally speaking, all homo sapiens have been on earth for the same amount of time and all have undergone continuous historifications. Although, as Freud believed, the child might be the parent to the adult, the so-called primitive is not the child to the so-called civilized. Nor is the neurotic an unreconstructed child/primitive/artist – or vice versa. What we have is a diversity of cultures none of which is closer to the "beginning of human history" than any other. Each culture embodies its own system of organizing experience.

Crediting Freud with extraordinary insight, how can it be restated to suit today's view of things? Perhaps we should say that certain systems are more porous in relation to the unconscious than other systems. But the ways in which this porosity is encouraged or repressed, guarded, regulated, and used, differ vastly not only from culture to culture but within every culture, and even within each individual. Children, crazies, and "technicians of the sacred" each encounter and filter differently what Anton Ehrenzweig (1970) calls "primary process." Children are porous to the unconscious because they have not yet learned how to repress material streaming into consciousness; their egos are in the process of formation. Neurotics are by definition people whose defenses are weak or wrongly positioned – but behavior that might be "neurotic" in one culture, or one setting within a given culture, might prove normal and effective in other contexts. Extremely neurotic people have not only been great artists, but royalty, saints, presidents, tycoons, dictators, and war chiefs. Shamans, artists, and others who perform the "omnipotence of thoughts" seek out teachers and/or techniques to help them master the powerful impulses streaming into consciousness.

Account after account tells the story: a future shaman is "called" but resists the call. But s/he cannot control the experiences "coming" in the form of dreams, visions, uncontrollable impulses, and sickness. After a period of doubt and often terror, the neophyte submits, and finds someone to teach her/him the tricks of the trade.[4] Becoming an artist, even in the West, is not unlike learning to be a shaman. The techniques and ambivalent social status of artist and shaman approximate each other. In modern Western cultures it might be said that the impulses from which art is made – the experiences of the artist (the shaman's "call," the artist's "raw material") – originate in difficult confrontations between daily life and the unconscious. In many cultures such impulses are said to originate with gods, ancestors, demons, ghosts, etc. I believe these represent relatively unmediated material streaming into consciousness, Ehrenzweig's "primary process." The impulses manifest themselves in dreams, visions, obsessive thoughts, trance possession, speaking in tongues, and half-hidden, feared yet irresistible violent and erotic wishes. Sometimes these impulses and their manifestations make the recipient feel ecstatic, happy beyond the power of description, and sometimes the recipient is terrified.

Ehrenzweig's theories fit nicely with those of Girard and Freud. Girard believes that lack of differentiation brings about the "sacrificial crisis" which is remedied by the mimetic violence of ritual. Ehrenzweig celebrates what he calls the child's "global vision"

> which remains undifferentiated as to its component details. This gives the younger child artist the freedom to distort color and shapes in the most imaginative and, to us, unrealistic manner. But to him – owing to his global, unanalytic view – his work is realistic. (1970:22)

Ehrenzweig sounds like Girard when he says that "the truly unconscious and potentially disruptive quality of undifferentiation" threatens to introduce "the catastrophic chaos which we are wont to associate with the primary process" (1970:37–8). But that which terrifies the neurotic the artist seeks to play out publicly. Or, as is frequently the case, the artist–neurotic (or shaman–neurotic) is compelled to explore the very process that terrifies her/him. It is fashionable today to say that artists are healthy while neurotics are sick – that ten years of art are equivalent to a psychoanalytic cure (Sartre on Genet 1963:544). Maybe. But from an operational perspective, art and neurosis are closely linked because both behaviors are generated by a porous and shifting boundary between the unconscious and the conscious. And what art manipulates on an individual basis, ritual does collectively. Ritual gives violence its place at the table of human needs. As Kafka noted:

Leopards break int, the temple and drink to the dregs what is in the sacrificial pitchers; this is repeated over and over again; finally it can be calculated in advance, and it becomes part of the ceremony. (1954:40)

Humans need to perform rituals. Where is this need located? Eugene d'Aquili *et al.* place it in the brain (1979). As Turner put it in one of his last writings:

> What is the role of the brain as an organ for the appropriate mixing of genetic and cultural information in the production of mental, verbal, or organic behavior? . . . If ritualization, as discussed by Huxley, Lorenz, and other ethologists, has a biogenetic foundation, while meaning has a neocortical learned base, does this mean that creative processes, those which generate new cultural knowledge, might result from a coadaptation, perhaps in the ritual process itself, of genetic and cultural information? (1983:225, 228)

Or as d'Aquili *et al.* say:

> Human ceremonial ritual is not a simple institution unique to man but rather a nexus of variables shared by other species. . . . One may trace the evolutionary progression of ritual behavior from the emergence of formalization through the coordination of formalized communicative behavior and sequences of ritual behavior to the conceptualization of such sequences and the assignment of symbols to them by man. (1979:36-7)

D'Aquili *et al.* propose what they call a "cognitive imperative." A human being "automatically, almost reflexly, confronts an unknown stimulus by the question 'What is it?' Affective responses such as fear, happiness, or sadness and motor responses are clearly secondary to the immediate cognitive response" (1979:168). If their thesis is true, then humans work from the top down, from the present to the past (evolutionarily speaking). Furthermore, narrativity – the need to construct a plausible story – is not only hard-wired into the brain but dominant. This contradicts what I said earlier – that ritual short-circuits thought.

The contradiction can be resolved by supposing that ritualizing – the performance of ritual – is not a simple, one-step, one-way operation. My own experience from running many performance workshops during the past twenty-five years, is that rhythmic activities – especially if movement and sound-making are carefully coordinated and maintained for long periods of time – invariably lead to feelings of "identical opposites": omnipotence/vulnerability, tranquility/readiness for the most demanding physical action. In other words, the narrative–cognitive stimulus works from the cerebral cortex down while the movement–sonic stimulus works from the lower brain up. Performing a ritual, or a ritualized theatre piece or exercise, is both narrative (cognitive) and affective. These work together to form the experience of ritualizing. If d'Aquili et al. are right, the affective states aroused by ritual are necessarily nested within a narrative frame. But from within – the experience of a person performing – the narrative frame dissolves, the action is just "done," not thought about.

Barbara Lex, another of d'Aquili's associates, proposes that trance, and other supremely affective states of flow, result from the extreme stimulation of both the ergotropic and trophotropic systems of the brain.[5]

> Exposure to manifold, intense, repetitive, emotion-evoking stimuli ensures uniformity of behavior in ritual participants. . . . Rituals properly executed promote a feeling of well-being and relief, not only because prolonged or intense stresses are alleviated, but also because the driving techniques employed in rituals are designed to sensitize or "tune" the nervous system and thereby lessen inhibition of the [neocortex's] right hemisphere and permit temporary right-hemisphere dominance, as well as mixed trophotropic–ergotropic excitation, to achieve synchronization of cortical rhythms in both hemispheres and evoke a trophotropic rebound.
>
> (in d'Aquili et al. 1979:120, 144–5)

Or, as Turner put it:

> the rhythmic activity of ritual, aided by sonic, visual, photic, and other kinds of "driving," may lead in time to simultaneous maximal stimulation of both systems, causing ritual participants to experience what the authors [d'Aquili et al.] call "positive, ineffable affect." They also use Freud's term "oceanic experience," as well as "yogic ecstasy," also the Christian term unio mystica, an experience of the union of those cognitively discriminated opposites typically generated by binary, digital left-hemispherical ratiocination. I suppose one might also use the Zen term satori (the integrating flash), and one could add the Quakers' "inner light," Thomas Merton's "transcendental consciousness," and the yogic samadhi.   (1983:230)

People seek experiences that provide a "rebound" or "spillover," simultaneously exciting both left and right hemispheres of the forebrain (see Fischer 1971, Turner 1983, Schechner 1988a).

The ethological and neurological theories answer some questions but what they don't explain are the creative and playful aspects of ritual. Direct investigation of these aspects has been undertaken by some anthropologists and artists. Felicitas D. Goodman, founder of the Cuyamungue Institute,

New Mexico, guides workshop participants in making masks and performing dances.

> What distinguishes our performance from other similar ones is that our ideas and imagery do not come about by "rational" planning, but originate in a nonordinary dimension of reality, to which we gain access via a particular kind of change of consciousness – the religious trance. . . . Received wisdom used to hold that there were a number of different religious trances, but since the early 1980s, researchers have come to realize that there is only one neurophysiological change which underlies a number of different religious experiences.
>
> (Goodman 1990:102)

Goodman's own research was the anthropological investigation of glossolalia, speaking in tongues (1972).

> I discovered that these nonordinary utterances, often but not always without any semantic content, shared certain remarkable properties. These traits, such as accent and intonation patterns were not related to the native tongue of the speaker: Americans, Japanese, and Maya Indians, for instance, all exhibited them in the same way. I came to the conclusion that they were nonlinguistic in origin and instead of obeying rules of language, most probably were caused by the striking bodily changes that I observed in speakers in tongues. (1990:103)

Goodman soon saw that not only were the "tongues" patterns unrelated to specific languages, they were not "religious" in the ideological sense. That is, content and belief did not cause a person to speak in tongues. Quite the contrary, the "tongues" were driving religious belief. At first, Goodman thought that "tongues" and other trance phenomena were induced by rhythmic stimulation. But her four years of work (1972–6) with students at Denison University were "somewhat disappointing."

> Then, almost by accident, I stumbled on a remarkable observation. If I had my students assume ritual postures known from native art, certain seemingly stereotypical ways of standing or kneeling and holding their arms and hands, and then induced the trance, these postures in a predictable way shaped not merely the somatic perceptions, but even more impor tly the contents of the visionary experience. In other words, in a certain posture, my participants might feel cold and leave the body to travel to the Lower World; in another one, feeling very hot, they reported turning into an animal, a plant, or an insect; while in still another one, important divinatory insights were mediated.
>
> (1990:103)

Goodman identified the postures by researching ethnographic literature and photographs.[6] Examining photos of a "singing shaman," "a shaman with bear spirit," and the well-known Lascaux rock painting of a man with an erection falling backwards, Goodman charted the postures. Her measurements were very precise. The Lascaux figure, according to Goodman, was reclining at a 37-degree angle, with a relaxed right arm slightly bent at the elbow, thumb pointing up, while the left arm is rigidly straight with the thumb pointing down. Goodman instructed her students to stand or recline exactly as in the paintings or sculptures. Working with Andrew Neher at the University of Munich in 1982, Goodman found that the postures induced trances characterized by physiological changes.

> The heart rate of the subjects increased dramatically and blood pressure simultaneously dropped considerably. . . . In the blood serum the stressors, namely adrenalin, noradrenalin, and cortisol, initially rose slightly, then dropped below normal levels, while beta-endorphin, the brain's own painkiller and opiate, made its appearance and stayed high even after the conclusion of the experiments, accounting for the euphoria so often reported after a religious trance experience. EEG tracings indicated a predominance of theta (5–7 cps) waves, with very little activity in the other bands. During later experiments in the laboratory of the Institute of Psychology of the University of Vienna in 1987, using DC rather than AC current, even more striking processes were recorded in the brain. Instead of a negative potential change of only about 250 microvolts during learning tasks, there were changes of up to 2,000 microvolts during trance.
> (1990:106)

Goodman continued her research at the Cuyamungue Institute where she "contemplated the possibility of using the trance postures in conjunction with a ritual dance performance" (1990:107). She rejected the idea of imitating an existing ritual because "such rituals are anchored in their social contexts, something we could not create." Also the trance postures were all stationary and Goodman wanted to make a dance. She did what so many Westerners have been doing – put together from several cultures a way of working in order to create new rituals.

> We had discovered a number of divining postures. Why not pose the question concerning the general theme and the details of the ritual while doing one of those? And if we wanted to create masks, why not go to the Lower World in a trance session and see which being may want to be represented in a mask and what that mask should look like? We tried this approach during our first masked trance dance in Austria in 1985 . . . and it was so successful that we have continued with the same method ever since.
> (1990:107)

The dances that Goodman and her students make deal with generalized themes – "spring and initiation," "the sorrow of fall," "the struggle between order and chaos." Goodman is forthright in describing her recipe, which never varies:

> There is a) an initial ritual in the kiva; b) a dance drama on the dance court; c) a metamorphosis dance, where everyone dances the movements of his/her animal spirit and eventually experiences turning into it; and d) a brief conclusion, a farewell to the Spirits and return to ordinary reality back in the kiva.
>
> (1990:107)

The kiva is the semiunderground classroom at the Cuyamungue Institute, modeled after the sacred ritual rooms of the Pueblo native Americans. The Institute is

> situated on a rough spread of hilly desert country endowed with great natural beauty, facing the Sangre de Cristo Mountains to the east, and the west the Jemez Range, where, according to local Pueblo Indian tradition, humans emerged from the third to the present fourth world.   (1990:107)

To prepare for the ritual trance experience, Goodman asks participants to make an offering to the spirits, practice five minutes of light breathing exercises, and then, in posture, listen with eyes closed to fifteen minutes of Goodman shaking a rattle at a rapid, even 200–205 strokes per minute. Participants in Goodman's rituals report strong effects.

> I sank down very fast, all was black, then a bear appeared. At first he was threatening, but then I checked him out. I could not only see him but also felt his fur, and he wore a necklace of natural things, like bones, stones, and berries.

> At first I only saw abstract shapes, but then a bird emerged. . . . It had luminous eyes, feathery legs, immense black talons, and a beak.

> I went down into a cave in a swirling, multicolored cone. The sky lit up as if with strobe lights and I saw a regal white ram. I decided to search for something else and saw a tiger, a fish, a whale, but all said no. . . . There were eagles, hawks, even Walt Disney's Woody Woodpecker, but they all rejected me. It was clear I was supposed to stay with the ram. (Goodman 1990:108–9)

This first exploratory session identified the participants' tutelary animals. At another session, using a different posture, they explored what kinds of masks to make. In order to find out what kind of dance to do, Goodman arranged her students in the posture of "the Tennessee diviner " (plates 7.1

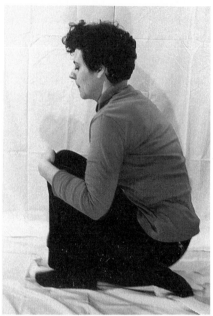

Plate 7.1 and 7.2 On the left, Felicitas Goodman adjusts Belinda Berkowitz's posture to that of the "Tennessee diviner." On the right, a side view of the pose. (Photos: Noe Farfan)

and 7.2) derived from "a beautiful stone effigy found in Tennessee, about 700 years old" (1990:110). This figure, Goodman says, "is particularly useful when we need advice concerning ritual matters" (1990:110). The Tennessee diviner showed one of the trancers a line of people, "weaving in and out, also doing somersaults, whirling, dancing in a circle, six in the middle in one direction, others in the opposite direction" (1990:110). Another saw two circles joined in a figure 8, another saw them all dancing up to the ridge of a hill. One woman saw the clouds part and a huge scaly serpent appear; others saw the serpent too. A threatening mushroom cloud appeared; people needed to be healed and protected. Using such divining techniques the masks and choreography took shape during the six-day workshop. Goodman helped the participants make a feathered serpent – a symbol in the southwest of blessings, rain, and fertility: the antidote to the mushroom cloud. Various images received during divining trances were put into material form. Goodman herself "set about composing the dance, which to me always seems like a religious drama, a mystery play" (1990:111).

It is not necessary to describe in detail the dance itself – Goodman does so in her article. But it is worth noting that while earlier in her essay Goodman recognizes that the classroom at Cuyamungue is "modeled after" the Pueblo kiva, later on she erases any difference between the Pueblo and Cuyamungue kivas. She says the dance started around the *shipapu*, "the sacred center of the world in local pueblo tradition" (1990:111). The kiva is lit by candles, the masks hang from pegs on the wall. After performing rituals, "they left the kiva . . . changed from beings of ordinary reality into denizens of the alternate world" (1990:111). The dancing took place in the "dance court" in the hills. Clearly, the workshop–ritual–dance is meant to have an effect on the participants' lives. It is not anything like going to the theatre or performing in an ordinary play or dance.

> The participants clearly perceive a change in themselves after going through the trance dance experience. They speak about not seeing their own life as they had before, of having gained a different view of life. They report a strong identification with the role that goes beyond their participation in the performance. The experience reaches into their inner life. This is facilitated by the religious altered state of consciousness, the trance, which not only opens up the alternate reality, but also affords access to hidden personal recesses. . . . What the participants describe is, of course, catharsis. Since the masked trance dance is a performance without audience, this catharsis is shifted from the audience to the players. (1990:113)

Goodman says the effect of the trance ritual is parallel to what occurs in many "non-Western therapeutic dances" and in ancient classical Greek theatre.

Jerzy Grotowski's work since he "left the theatre" in the late 1960s, and especially during his recent "objective drama" and "ritual arts" phases, starting in the 1980s and continuing to the present, can be compared to Goodman's investigations. Grotowski has never been open about his work. He is a reclusive person, and increasingly so. Unlike most theatre workers who seek a home in the capitals – New York, Tokyo, Paris, London, Warsaw, Moscow – Grotowski works in out-of-the-way places: Opole and later Wroclaw, a barn in a far corner of the Irvine campus of the University of California, a village outside Pontedera, Italy. Along with this reclusivity is a reticence in speaking directly about his work. Nothing comes from Grotowski approaching the facticity of what Goodman writes. But from what Grotowski says in talks or interviews (his favored modes, placing him in an oral tradition) as well as from the writings of participants in his recent

work, a fairly consistent picture of his recent work emerges.[7] Like
Goodman, Grotowski is interested in making not-for-a-public ritual performances whose sources are almost totally "traditional" – that is, non-
Western – cultures. Grotowski works through intermediaries. For objective
drama these were "master teachers" from Haiti, Bali, Korea, and Taiwan as
well as a short-term visit from a sufi dancer and a Japanese martial artist.

Grotowski's method is to sift through many practices from different
cultures for what is similar among them, searching for the "first," the
"original," the "essential," the "universal." These are then synthesized into
repeatable sequences of behavior. Grotowski described the goal of objective
drama as:

> To re-evoke a very ancient form of art where ritual and artistic creation were
> seamless. Where poetry was song, song was incantation, movement was dance.
> . . . One might say – but it is only a metaphor – that we are trying to go back
> before the Tower of Babel, and discover what was before. First to discover
> differences, and then to discover what was before the differences.
>
> (in Osinski 1991:96)

Grotowski's goals are very different from Goodman's though he is playing
with the same fire.

> We can hope to discover a very old form of art, art as a *way of knowledge*. But
> we live *after* the Tower of Babel, and the attempt will not be to form a new
> synthesis. We cannot say: "Now we will create a new form of ritual." Maybe it
> is possible to do this, but one has to have 1,000 years. Nor is the intention to
> discover new ways of manipulating the consciousness of people. . . . The effect
> of our work must be indirect. . . .
>
> [Grotowski's work is driven by] a desire to reach the deepest layers of
> human existence – the depths of one's inner, spiritual environment, where
> creative silence reigns and where the experience of *sacrum* occurs.
>
> (in Osinski 1991:96–7, 99)

Grotowski's work sessions are famous for their duration, especially overnight. The master sleeps by day, or hardly at all, and work continues
routinely for ten hours, often for fifteen or sixteen hours. The workspaces
for objective drama in Irvine were a barn and a yurt-like round house, both
quite small. In Pontedera the work takes place in two rooms of an old
farmhouse. In both cases some renovations were made – adding a wood
floor in Italy, stripping the barn to bare walls and wood floor in Irvine.

Sometimes the work takes place outside. The workgroup is always small, twenty or less, and except for special occasions there are no spectators.

It's not necessary to describe many details of the work here (for that see Lendra 1991, Osinski 1991, Winterbottom 1991, and Wolford 1991). It is physical, grueling, and psychologically demanding. "Accuracy and precision are crucial. The steps must be precise, the body is 'flowing' the entire time" (Osinski 1991:101). There are nine basic exercises that each participant performs and individual songs and dances worked out over time. But this work is prepatory for "the Action."

> Every day the ritual is evoked anew. Always the same and yet each time not just the same. This ritual is . . . not just a theatre creation, or an imitation or reconstruction of any of the familiar rituals. . . . Nor is it a synthesis of rituals which, in Grotowski's opinion, would be impossible in practice. . . . Grotowski's work . . . has elements related concomitantly to several traditions which are archetypal. These elements are set into a composition. . . . Grotowski defines the technical difference between a theatre production and a ritual in relation to "the place of montage." In the production, the spectators' minds are the place of montage. In the ritual, the montage takes place in the minds of the executants. The connection with old initiation practices is very subtle. . . . Grotowski would not ask anyone, "Do you believe?" but "You must do well what you do, with understanding." The Action is evoked and accomplished each day in its totality. Sometimes it is executed every few days if the technical work on details or the search for some elements from scratch take up too much time. (Osinski 1991:101–2)

Osinski was an observer of the work – one of the people Grotowski invites periodically to witness (and celebrate) what he is doing. I Wayan Lendra, a trained Balinese dancer who has studied and taught in the West, participated in the Irvine objective drama project.

> The work itself was very rigorous. It required not only physical dexterity and stamina but also mental perseverance. Grotowski imposed uncompromising discipline. There was a change of consciousness and awareness, a change of physical impulses and behavior, and an intensity which developed. . . . There seemed to be a close similarity with the trance situations I had seen in Bali, or the trancelike quality of Balinese performing arts. (Lendra 1991:115)

What Osinski and Lendra describe at some emotional distance, Philip Winterbottom recorded immediately in his journal. Winterbottom agrees concerning the precision, duration, and difficulty of the work. "Whatever was worked on was done with precision, concentration, and duration. If we danced, we danced for hours; if we chanted, we chanted for hours" (1991:141). Once Grotowski told Winterbottom that

> I should observe my own breath and what is happening internally. With the inhale, observe the outer world, with the exhale, the inner. Do not identify. Observe the inner as if it were the outer. Find a route and walk for about 20 minutes [every day]. He said this was a very old device. . . . Jerzy addressed us in the yurt. . . . We should not speak of the work but hold it inside as a personal possession. If we talk about it, we will kill it. (1991:142)

During the year Winterbottom and the others learned songs and dances from Korea, Egypt, Bali, and Poland. They developed their own "mystery plays . . . structures that allowed the subconscious to appear and operate" (1991:147), worked on improvisatory exercises like "Sculpturing and Diving" where the actors stood

> overlooking the rolling pastureland and internally sculpt the body to the environment. . . . The next step was to physically relate by walking through the terrain. . . . Third stage was for participants to run through the terrain letting the lay of the land show the way, determining pace, posture, and direction and also sensing temperature, flow of air, wind gusts, and any other energy draws or repulsions. . . . A person might head into the wind or weave in and out of warm air currents or seek out disturbing areas or tranquil ones. (1991:148)

Later in the year, Grotowski told Winterbottom to search out Gnostic and Maronite practices; he said:

> to concentrate on searching for a Syriac church. He felt their mass which was in Aramaic was probably the closest to the original movements and chant quality. I was to watch the "shaman" closely. I presumed from this Grotowski meant for me to regard the priest as someone extraordinary. . . . If he contained "life," . . . when the time was right I was to approach him and ask him about the meaning of the movements. When I connected with something deep I was to learn that segment and perform it as if I were the shaman. (1991:153)

In reading Winterbottom's journal, one sees that Grotowski's rhetoric is spiritual while his practice combines "ancient ritual techniques" (or ones foreign to most Europeans and Americans) with theatre exercises long known to students of Konstantin Stanislavski or Vsevelod Meyerhold. Grotowski, like Goodman, clearly has two goals: the development of some kind of ritual performance (public or not) and, perhaps more importantly, a way for the people he works with to develop their spiritual, personal, and

Plate 7.3 The primary position for the Motions. *Plate 7.4* The *agem*, or basic body position, for Balinese dance theatre, as demonstrated by I Wayan Lendra. The similar torso placement in these two positions gives a sense of locomotive movement, of alertness and readiness. For a full set of photographs, description, and analysis of the Motions, see Lendra 1991:129–39. (Photos: Leslie S. Lendra)

perhaps professional (though that is less obvious) abilities. Maintaining a group mystique is very important to Grotowski. He wants the work to be more or less secret and he wants its secrets kept. In this, he joins a long list of Europeans including the Rosicrucians, Masons, and mystics (like Gurdjieff).

One of Grotowski's key exercises in his objective drama and art as vehicle phases is "the Motions." Lendra detects strong similarities between the Motions and Balinese dance theatre (plates 7.3 and 7.4). According to Winterbottom:

The Motions evolved out of the Theatre of Sources from 1977–82. They were developed and coordinated with a cross-cultural group: Mexican–Americans, an American, Sufi dervishes, Western Europeans, Gnostic Christians, Japanese Buddhists, Hindu Indians, and Poles. The movements were first developed by the Poles and then passed on to the next group who discarded those aspects that did not work for them. They were passed on again. In the end they were presented to a Mexican Indian tribe [the Huichols], then a group of Catholics, then a group of Hindus. This was done to verify the Motions. They all accepted the Motions in one way or other. They either recognized them as part of their own ritual or as prayer, meditation, etc.   (1991:152)

Lendra says that the Motions awaken the "sleeping energy" (*kundalini* in Sanskrit), the serpent at the base of the spine; this the Haitians working with Grotowski call the serpent Damballah whose dance is the *yanvalou*. The kundalini fits the biology of the brain as modeled by neuroanatomist Paul MacLean. The human brain, MacLean theorized, is really three-in-one, a "triune brain" evolutionarily speaking, consisting of a "recent" frontal cortex, the seat of thought, a subcortical or "old mammalian" brain, the seat of emotions, and the oldest part of the brain, the "reptilian." According to Turner's reading of MacLean, the reptilian brain is:

> the brain stem, an upward growth of the spinal cord and the most primitive part of the brain, which we share with all vertebrate creatures and which has remained remarkably unchanged throughout the myriads of years of evolution. . . . What MacLean did was to show that . . . the reptilian brain, whether in reptiles, birds, or mammals, is not only concerned with control of movement, but also with the storage and control of what is called "instinctive behavior" – the fixed action patterns and innate releasing mechanisms so often written about by the ethologists, the genetically preprogrammed perceptual-motor sequences such as emotional displays, territorial defense behaviors, and nest building.   (Turner 1983:226)

Turner felt that human ritual was founded in the "reptilian brain" and he saw in MacLean's model of the triune brain a possible unifying theory:

> How does [MacLean's model] fit with Freud's model of the id, ego, and superego, with Carl Jung's model of the collective unconscious and archetypes, with neo-Darwinian theories of selection, and especially with cross-cultural anthropological studies and historical studies in comparative religion? . . . To what extent is it true that human feelings, hopes, and fears of what is most sacred are a necessary ingredient in generating decisions and motivating their implementation? . . . If ritualization, as discussed by [Julian] Huxley, [Konrad] Lorenz, and other ethologists, has a biogenetic foundation, while meaning has a neocortical learned base, does this mean that creative processes,

those which generate new cultural knowledge, might result from a coadaptation, perhaps in the ritual process itself, of genetic and cultural information? We also can ask whether the neocortex is the seat of programs largely structured by the culture through the transmission of linguistic and other symbol systems to modify the expression of genetic programs. How far, we might add, do these higher symbols, including those of religion and ritual, derive their meaning and force for action from their association with earlier established neural levels of animal ritualization? (Turner 1983:228)

Whether or not MacLean's key unlocks the mysteries of the brain thereby disclosing the biogenetic sources of ritual (and the odds are against it, the triune brain hypothesis is no longer accepted by most brain neurologists), the idea shows how strong the desire is to connect the ethological and neurological, the "scientific," with the imagery of "old" cultures. There is a wish for validation and mutual confirmation. Ritual is given several faces – that of the very "oldest" behavior rooted in what the "reptiles" do; that of "old cultures" who intuit what Western scientists such as d'Aquili, Lex, and MacLean find in their researches; that of a repository of "higher symbols" and religion. Activating what Turner theorizes, Goodman and Grotowski say they have found (or synthesized or invented) precise

> practices – rituals – drawn from or invented to be like the wisdoms of old cultures, wisdoms that answer the needs of "modern people." At the end of his life, Turner believed the patterns underlying these wisdoms were genetically based. MacLean's triune brain satisfies the desires of city dwellers to return to the kiva of received knowledge.

Goodman and Grotowski aren't the only ones working the field. What is to be made of advertisements in magazines like *Shaman's Drum: A Journal of Experiential Shamanism*? Any issue will do, but these are from issue 16, mid-spring 1989. Under the picture of a partly concealed wizened face, readers are told that "Elf, assisted by Maia, guides & journeys with initiates seeking personal/planetary transformation in [the] timeless, multi-cultural web of full spectrum shamanism." Above the photo, in larger type, buyers are warned, "Strong Medicine . . . Not quick Not easy." Earth Path offers persons the chance to "create a personal shield from traditional rawhide and willow. The workshop includes: How to vision for the shield; hands on instruction in shield making and decorating; and sacred ceremony to empower your shield." The Great Round offers "Desert Vision Quests" where (either for women only or in a mixed group) one can "experience 10 days under the desert sky (3 days solo-time & fasting), medicine teachings, singing, drumming, dancing, opening our hearts, weaving our stories, finding our power." Amarok advertises "Shamanic classes & counselling" as well as "vision quest outings" while White Eagle Vision Expeditions combines "wilderness skills along with an awareness of nature and the spirit that moves in all things." Leslie Gray, Ph.D., offers "shamanic counseling for individuals and couples." Oh Shinnah's ad shows her playing a guitar (photo credit Lynn Levy). The text begins with: "Oh Shinnah, born in the Land of Many Snows, in the Moon of Frozen Waters, in the Cycle of Strange Storms, brings to the world a unique blend [is this shamanism or is it coffee?] of many ancient traditions with modern knowledge." Yet later the ad asserts that "Oh Shinnah, despite her many accomplishments, prefers to be known as one without a personal history." Topping her list of workshops is "the Shamanic Quest." Maybe because they are just across the California border in Mexico and recognizably "shamanic," or because Barbara Myerhoff wrote her classic *The Peyote Hunt* (1974) about them, the Huichols are very popular.[8] Prem Das and Silve will help you visit them for $675 a week per person ("profits to go to Huichol families"). The ad lets readers know that "Prem Das has lived among the Huichols since 1970, during which time he completed an apprenticeship with Don José Matsuwa. His wife Silve is a Huichol artist and grand-niece of Don José." Brant Secunda doesn't need to take you to Don José, he's imported the powers of "the renowned 109 year old Huichol shaman" to the Dance of the Deer Foundation in Soquel, California. The photo topping this full-page ad shows a smiling Secunda slightly upstage of serious and shamanically attired Don José and his wife Dona Josepha Medrano. Potential what? – shamans, buyers, the spiritually needy? – are invited to "Discover the Spirit of your Heart with Huichol Shamanism." Secunda, "the adopted grandson and close companion of Don José," his shamanic heir, "will lead people in Huichol rituals and ceremonies, including the sacred Dance of the Deer."

The promise in *Shaman's Drum* (absolutely rejected by Grotowski) is that in a short time a person can access "sacred" knowledge and practices. How can Secunda lead people in Huichol rituals? Goodman's research suggests that belief and cultural context are unnecessary – put yourself in the proper posture, perform the right actions, and the experience will come. But does "experience" equal knowledge? Changing heart rate, blood pressure, and brain wave activity is one thing, learning and knowing is something else. To seek experience without knowledge is to commodify the process. And why is it that ancient and sacred knowledge is restricted to "old souls" from "old cultures?" Why would they want to share what they know with strangers or pass it on to authorized disciples who, living between cultures, dispense priceless timeless knowledge for a price, on a first come, first served basis?

The ads (and many articles in *Shaman's Drum* and like publications) can be analyzed back to their snake-oil and medicine show traditions; they can be used as evidence of culture tourism, an appetite for the exotic, that has long characterized the colonial and neocolonial mind. But they, along with Goodman's and Grotowski's experiments, indicate something else too. There is an awakened desire spawning an exploitable market for religious experiences, for "spiritual knowledge" outside the religious establishments – even outside burgeoning pentecostal, fundamentalist, or orthodox Jewish movements. All but extinct cultures are exoticized and felt to contain people with "ancient" or "original" sacred knowledge that can be taught, transferred, and experienced. This exotification – whatever its political and ideological ramifications – indicates also a certain state of mind, a receptivity, a desire for a change of life, mind, and feelings. In Ehrenzweig's language, many people feel the need to experience primary process.

For those people who are dissatisfied with their religions of birth, this need actively downplays cultural specificity. Grotowski says he was born a Catholic but no longer believes in it or practices it. Goodman studied glossolalia in specific Christian churches, but soon felt that speaking in tongues was only Christian on its surface. Grotowski's work is full of analogies to Polish Catholicism, various Eastern Orthodox rites, and even Hassidism. But these are used to approach a universal or archetypal reality that Grotowski believes underlies specific rituals. The Motions and other exercises and improvisations, whatever their sources, are intentionally drained of their specific cultural meanings. They are devised and experimented with outdoors or in barns or yurts (but with no effort to use these structures in ways derived from agrarian Euro-American or nomadic Mongolian practice). Grotowski sent Winterbottom to the Syriac church to observe the priest (dubbed shaman). But Winterbottom was not asked to buy into Syriac beliefs because these actually hide what is "essential" or "original" in the ritual practice. According to Goodman and Grotowski, what is universal are doable acts of the body; and these acts are nonideological, not culture-specific. The ads in *Shaman's Drum* proclaim both cultural specificity *and* universality. Because the ancient knowledge is universal one can move freely between a Plains Indian shield-making Saturday, a Huichol weekend, a ten-day vision quest, a two-week Inca pilgrimage and full moon ceremony, or a summer-long or a full year's training in "shamanic practices." In each workshop, participants are promised something specific from a definite cultural source. But the implication is that these "ways of power and knowledge" converge, overlap, all participate in the same universal ocean of spiritual stuff. So one can move from one to the next, immersing oneself, sifting out the essential, the universal, from the particular. Learning about one cultural practice will help in learning about the others as deep, governing patterns become clearer and clearer.

All this – from the serious work of Goodman and Grotowski to the flim-flam of some of the *Shaman's Drum* advertisers – can be viewed as more Western reification and appropriation. Goodman, Grotowski, Secunda – all of them – want to control and use what they know is very powerful stuff. Goodman wants to "scientize" what she finds, to explain it rationally as anthropology, neurology, and history. Grotowski, on the other hand, uses a kind of scientific method to pursue nonscience goals. Perfected scientific reductions express themselves as mathematical equations which are supposed to be correct regardless of culture, history, or location. Grotowski's highly disciplined, precise work is designed to find doable actions that "work" (have effects, yield experiences) regardless of culture, etc. As Grotowski wrote in 1988:

> The Performer, with a capital letter, is a man of action. He is not a man who plays another. He is a dancer, a priest, a warrior: he is outside aesthetic genres. Ritual is performance, an accomplished action, an act. Degenerated ritual is a spectacle. I don't want to discover something new but something forgotten. Something which is so old that all distinctions between aesthetic genres are no longer of use. . . . Essence interests me because in it nothing is sociological. It is what you did not receive from others, what did not come from outside, what is not learned. . . . One access to the creative way consists of discovering in yourself an ancient corporality to which you are bound by a strong ancestral relation. . . . Starting from details you can discover in you somebody other – your grandfather, your mother. A photo, a memory of wrinkles, the distant echo of a color of the voice enable you to reconstruct a corporality. First, the corporality of somebody known, and then more and more distant, the corporality of the unknown one, the ancestor. Is this corporality literally as it was? Maybe not literally – but yet as it might have been. You can arrive very far back, as if your memory awoke . . ., as if you recall Performer of the primal ritual. . . . With the breakthrough – as in the return of an exile – can one touch something which is no longer linked

to origins but – if I dare say – to *the origin*? I believe so.

(Grotowski 1988:36–40)

People who have been with Grotowski all agree that the work is highly disciplined, grueling in its physical and psychological demands, not senti-mental. His recent investigations are very closely linked to the *via negativa* of his "poor theatre" phase (1959–67) where Grotowski's method was to eliminate from practice all that was not necessary. By the end of the 1960s, spectators were eliminated. By the late 1980s only the search for Performer remained. The experiences of the performers were evoked by and channeled through rigorous psychophysical exercises. This method of work was called "rendering," a term linked to a "designer's sketch or working drawing", but also evoking another

> meaning of the word as illustrated in the process of rendering butter, the distillation of an object to its essence. The process of rendering is governed by a number of rules: no improvised conversation, no random violence, no stomping on the floor, no imitation of animals, no crawling on hands and knees, no imitation of trance states, and no processions, to name a few.
>
> (Wolford 1991:171)

Turner's speculations at the end of his life closely paralled Grotowski's work. Grotowski begins with "objective" elements – tempo, iconography, movement patterns, sounds. The research is not historical, not how the Sanskrit "om" and English "Amen" (a transliteration of the Hebrew "Aw-main") may be versions of the same ur-mantra; but that the open "uh" sound followed by a "hummed" closure is a sequence found in a number of cultures because it expresses brain structure. If Turner had lived, he would have wanted to find out if a Grotowskian "objective drama" performance shared with the rituals of its source cultures attributes at the level of autonomic nervous system responses, brain waves, and so on.

Like Grotowski, Turner searched for ritual's creative powers (1969, 1983, 1986). He wanted to show how ritual was not just a conservator of evol-utionary and cultural behavior, but a generator of new images, new ideas, and new practices. In reviewing structural and neurological theories of ritual, Turner was troubled by the absence of any consideration of "play," precisely what Grotowski is investigating (in a most serious if not sanctimo-nious manner).

> As I see it play does not fit in anywhere particular; it is a transient and is recalcitrant to localization, to placement, to fixation – a joker in the neuroan-thropological act. . . . Playfulness is a volatile, sometimes dangerously

explosive essence, which cultural institutions seek to bottle or contain in the vials of games of competition, chance, and strength, in modes of simulation such as theater, and in controlled disorientation, from roller coasters to dervish dancing. . . . Play could be termed dangerous because it may subvert the left–right hemispheric regular switching involved in maintaining the social order. . . . The neuronic energies of play, as it were, lightly skim over the cerebral cortices, sampling rather than partaking of the capacities and functions of the various areas of the brain. As Don Handelman (1977) and Gregory Bateson (1972) have written that is possibly why play can provide a metalanguage (since to be "meta" is to be both beyond and between) and emit metamessages about so many and varied human propensities and thus provide, as Handelman has said, "a very wide range of commentary on the social order" (189). Play can be everywhere and nowhere, imitate anything, yet be identified with nothing. . . . You may have guessed that play is, for me, a liminal or liminoid mode, essentially interstitial, betwixt-and-between all standard taxonomic nodes, essentially "elusive." (1983:233–4)

As Turner himself notes, there is a contradiction between his theories of playful liminality and the ethological–neurological propositions. To ethologists and neurologists ritual is central both to behavior and to brain structure/function. But Turner locates ritual "betwixt-and-between," in cultural creases and margins, making it more like play than anything else. The ritual process is liminal–liminoid, unauthorized, antistructural, subjunctive ("if"), and subversive. The contradiction also expresses the difference between Turner's social perspective and the ethologist's–neurologist's biological one. This difference is a version of an old, insoluble argument between determinists and those who assert that humans are free to make their own destinies.

It would be foolish to dismiss out of hand the practice and thought of two such visionaries as Grotowski and Turner – especially where their work converges. From the late 1970s onward the two were aware of each other (though, as best I know, they never met). Turner was fascinated by Grotowski's experiments. Turner wasn't a synthesizer. He was always urging people to look for the "minute particular," to pay attention to the details of cultural performance and individual expression. But in "Body, brain, and culture" (1983), published just months before his death, Turner passionately felt the need to find a global basis for the ritual process. He wrote as if the world depended on it – as well it might.

I am really speaking of a global population of brains inhabiting an entire world of inanimate and animate entities, a population whose members are incessantly communicating with one another through every physical and mental instrumentality. But if one considers the geology, so to speak, of the human brain and nervous system, we see represented in its strata – each layer still vitally alive – not dead like stone, the numerous pasts and presents of our planet. Like Walt Whitman, we "embrace multitudes." . . . Each of us is a microcosm, related in the deepest ways to the whole life-history of that lovely deep blue globe swirled over with the white whorls first photographed by Edwin Aldrin and Neil Armstrong from their primitive space chariot, the work nevertheless of many collaborating human brains.   (1983:243)

Much as I admire Turner, I am uncomfortable with this attempt to relocate and thereby resolve the "problems" of ritual in the workings of evolution or, more specifically, of what he called "the most sensitive and eloquent instrument of Gaea the Earth-spirit – the cerebral organ" (1983:243). I am uncomfortable with Grotowski's Performer and with wisdom that exists before or behind genres, in the "original" times, in the "old cultures." These anthologies of cultures, or the wish for globalism, strike me as premature because they are unavoidably expressions of Western hegemony, attempts to cull and harvest the world's cultures. Maybe later in history, if there is more equality of power, more actual multiculturalism, but not now.

The globalist turn was unusual for Turner who delighted in the peculiar "not-yetness" of human experience, its unfinishedness. Turner saw the ritual process as analogous to the training–workshop–rehearsal process where "givens" or "ready-mades" – accepted texts, accepted ways of using the body, accepted feelings – are deconstructed, broken down into malleable bits of behavior, feeling, thought, and text and then reconstructed in new ways, sometimes to be offered as public performances. In traditional genres such as kathakali, ballet, or noh, people start their training early in life. This training involves learning new ways of speaking, gesturing, moving. Maybe even new ways of thinking and feeling. New for the trainee, but well known in the tradition of kathakali, ballet, and noh. As in initiation rites the mind and body of each performer are returned toward a state of *tabula rasa* (to use Turner's Lockeian image), ready to be written on in the language of the form being learned. When finished with training, the performer can "speak" noh, kathakali, or ballet: s/he is "incorporated" into the tradition, initiated and made one with the body of the tradition. The violence of scarring or circumcision is absent – but deep, permanent psychophysical changes are wrought. A kathakali performer, a ballet dancer, a noh shite each have their genre-specific ways of moving, sounding, and, I would say, being: they are marked people.

257

Turner went far beyond Van Gennep when he said that the the artworks and leisure activities of industrial and postindustrial societies were like the rituals of tribal, agrarian, and traditional societies. He called the arts and leisure activities "liminoid." Liminal rites are obligatory while liminoid activities are voluntary. Workshops of experimental theatre and dance – including Grotowski's and Goodman's – are liminoid laboratories of psychophysical initiation. Some of the transformations accomplished by workshops are temporary, used to make specific performances and that's all. But sometimes workshops effect permanent transformations. An aesthetic–ritual initiation can be as consequential and permanent as anything wrought on an aborigine. The "parashamans" of experimental theatre and dance, Grotowski among them, intend aesthetics to yield initiatory permanence (see Grimes 1982:255–66).

Parashamanism turns orthodox ritual on its head. Ethological procedures are mimicked, neurological responses elicited – but in the service of ideas and visions of society that are anything but conservative. In nonhuman animals ritual is a way of increasing signal clarity in order to mediate crisis. It is often this among humans too – but it is also something else: a means of conserving and transmitting traditional cultural knowledge and individual patterns of behavior. Turner knew this, but he did not emphasize it. He focused instead on how the ritual process is a machine for introducing new behaviors or undermining established systems. This led him away from traditional or liminal rituals toward investigating the way artists work, the techniques of the parashamans, and to his own theatrical work in "performing ethnography" (Turner and Turner 1986).

It is precisely when this creative and/or subversive function of ritual dominates, spills over its usually well-defined boundaries, that art separates from – and sometimes opposes – religion. The maskers of carnival, Hopi mudhead clowns, and Yaqui Chapayekam are also antistructural, but always in the service, ultimately, of reinforcing traditional ways of doing and thinking. A period of license is permitted, even required. Things are "done backwards," excesses are celebrated, promiscuous sexuality and drunkenness flourish. But then Ash Wednesday terminates carnival and the subversive shenanigans of Mardi Gras are put away for another year. Among the Yaquis, the ritual clowning of the masked Chapayekam continues right through to Holy Saturday. This clowning is mixed in with their role as pursuers and persecutors of Jesus. But finally, also, the Chapayekam reinforce Yaqui-Catholicism. There is never an Easter when they are not defeated. The people know what to expect of them, what their actions represent. But in art, experimental art especially, things are different. The subversion is continuous. The avant-garde is art's permanent revolution.

The violence acted out in performance is no mere "symbol," sapped of its ability to wound, frighten, and astonish. Even if work like Grotowski's is not violent in the physical sense, there is real danger and risk in it. This danger is a mortgaged actuality indefinitely postponing catastrophe. Ritual violence is not a remembrance of things past. As outlined in my theory of "restoration of behavior" (Schechner 1985:35–116) the present moment is a negotiation between a wished-for future and a rehearsable, therefore change-able, past. History is always in flux; that is what makes it so like a performance. The mortgaged future is always death; the past is always life-as-remembered, or restaged. Individuals, all of whom will die, are assimilated into families, groups, religions, and ideologies which are putatively immortal. The stories these groups tell, their ritual enactments, concern temporary and uneasy triumphs over death.

The ancient Greeks always sent a messenger on to stage to report the violent acts performed out of sight of the spectators. Actually, of course, these acts were never performed – they existed as reports only. But did the fictitious atrocities inflicted on Pentheus or Oedipus reflect an historical time when such actions were performed? Probably not. Rites come and go, but there is no unilinear pattern leading from ritual to theatre or away from violence to mimesis. The fictive violence of the stage refers not to the past or to elsewhere but to the future – to threats, to what will happen if the aesthetic–ritual project crashes.

Not in the Western tradition alone has there been a big place reserved for a theatre of violence such as on the Elizabethan–Jacobean stage, the Grand Guignol, or today's horror, war, or vengeance movies. Sometimes this violence is participatory. In the sado-masochistic theatres of New York minor violence – spanking, whipping, pinching, dripping hot wax on naked flesh – is not only done to actors but to spectators/participants who pay fancy prices for the privilege. Are these people perverts, initiates undergoing ordeals, or just ordinary people out for kicks? Is *King Lear* less effective than *Oedipus* because Gloucester has his eyes put out on stage? Semiotically there is scant difference between "reported" and "pretended" actions. Spectators at *Lear* know they are seeing tricks, violence deferred. But the minor violence of the sado-masochistic theatre is similarly violence deferred. As Belle de Jour, the stage name of the proprietress of one such theatre told me,

"A good sadist or masochist wants to experience giving/getting pain every night. To do that you have to be careful not to injure yourself or your partner." The violence *imagined* at Belle's theatre is many times more intense than the violence done.

Actual violence is all around, much of it truly horrific. Today's American television news tries to get as close to the action as possible. Everyone has seen video images of the aftermath of gruesome murders and terrorism, or on-the-spot shots of wars, natural disasters, and personal tragedies. The criminals, soldiers, and victims are not actors in the aesthetic sense, even if the reporters are. But these images work on people differently than do the actions presented in the theatre. The real life violence arouses appetites that can't be satisfied by more of the same. Actual violence framed as aesthetics or sport – like the eroticism of pornography – transforms bits of actuality into full-fledged fantasies. The omnipotence of thought is given free rein. What would television be like – that is, what would the public imagination be feeding on – if, as in Greek tragedy, all violence was reported instead of being seen? Or am I crediting videotape with too much "actuality"? How much more "real" is a photograph or a film or a tape of an event than a verbal description or a written report? How long before we reestablish the blood games of the Coliseum?

What about the violence of ritual – human and animal sacrifice, cannibalism, flesh-piercing, initiatory ordeals . . . on through a very long list? Do these practices tame the violence they simultaneously actualize and represent? Girard believes they are homeopathic – that a little ritual violence inoculates a society against more general, and destructive anarchic violence. This is close to what I say about ritual violence mortgaging death. Or is ritual violence a vestige of earlier, bloodier "primal rituals"?[9] Who can identify historically and specify the process transforming such rituals into make believe, into theatre? In Papua New Guinea, intertribal warfare and headhunting have been outlawed. Today PNG tribespeople gather for "sing-sings" to perform for each other and for tourists. Some of the dances are transformations of earlier, bloodier "war dances" or spear-throwing techniques. But this modulation of warfare into theatre, if that's what it is, hardly seems a general model or one that even explains what's going on in PNG.

It is no accident that in Asian all-night performances the demons appear in the hours just before dawn. Demons – like the devils of the great medieval European cycle plays – are both horrific and farcical. Appearing as they do at the "witching hour" they participate in both the theatre and the dream world. Children awaking to the roars of demons stare wide-eyed not really knowing if they are "seeing" or "dreaming." Parents too watch the performances while in a hypnagogic twilight zone. This is not only a matter of clock-time. The Japanese say that the proper way to "watch" noh is in a state between waking and sleeping. Among the noh audience are many whose eyes are closed, or heavy-lidded. These experts are "paying attention" by relaxing their consciousness, allowing material to stream upward from their unconscious to meet the images/sounds streaming outward from the stage. In this state of porous receptive inattention the spectator is carried along in noh's dreamlike rhythms. Often images and sounds are shared by shite, chorus, and musicians so that the principal character is distributed among a number of performers. The spectator's own reveries blend in with what's coming from the stage. As Kunio Komparu notes:

> the viewer participates in the creation of the play by individual free association and brings to life internally a drama based on individual experience filtered through the emotions of the protagonist. The shared dramatic experience, in other words, is not the viewer's adjustment of himself to the protagonist on stage but rather his creation of a separate personal drama by sharing the play with the performer. Indeed, he becomes that protagonist.   (1983:18)

Ehrenzweig called this similarity between liminal half-sleep and artistic creativity "poemagogic." He recognized that it assimilated violence to creativity:

> Poemagogic images . . . of suffering, destruction, and death . . ., in their enormous variety, reflect the various phases and aspects of creativity in a very direct manner, though the central theme of death and rebirth, of trapping and liberation, seems to overshadow the others. Death and rebirth mirror the ego's dedifferentiation and redifferentiation.   (1970:189–90)

In the life of the imagination, dreams are the paradigm of liminality, existing in a world totally "as if." Dreams take place between the clarity of reasoned thought and the confusion of lived and recollected experience.

The dreaming I am talking about is not limited to fantasies of the night. Dreaming can be trained as a technique of the mind partly dissolving boundaries between unconscious and conscious, private fantasy and public representation. Some lived dreams – the enactment of visions, conversations with God, sexual fears and desires, national "destinies" – can be very oppressive and destructive. War has evolved into a complex network of games, contingencies, and scenarios played out in various "theatres." This is not to deny the economic, ideological, and political causes of war. But for males especially, war actualizes dreams of doing harm, of using obsessive order to make chaos, of playing with and inflicting death.

At a certain deep level of dreaming – a level as much cultural as it is individual – strong links connect tragedy, violence, sexuality, and farce. Look at the cartoons children watch on Saturday morning TV. Compare these to the classics of silent film: Chaplin, the Keystone Cops, Laurel and Hardy. Connect this tradition of slapstick clowning to the circus, Grand Guignol, the *commedia dell'arte*, Punch and Judy shows and back to medieval, Roman, and Greek mimes. In the triadic relation of laughter to violence to sex one corner of the triangle often is hidden. Slapstick connects laughter to violence, romantic comedy connects laughter to sex, sado-masochism connects violence to sex. Sometimes all three corners are visible as in Aristophanic comedy or in the antics of Hopi mudhead clowns, who are obscene, cruel, and funny all at once. The Hopi example could be multiplied the world over. Milan Kundera nicely invokes this progression from laughter to arousal to violence:

> There they stood in front of the mirror (they always stood in front of the mirror while she undressed), watching themselves. She stripped to her underwear, but still had the [bowler] hat on her head. And all at once she realized they were both excited by what they saw in the mirror. What could have excited them so? A moment before, the hat on her head had seemed nothing but a joke. Was excitement really a mere step away from laughter? Yes. When they looked at each other in the mirror that time, all she saw for the first few seconds was a comic situation. But suddenly the comic became veiled by excitement: the bowler hat no longer signified a joke; it signified violence.
>
> (1985:86)

What is it that defines the human species? A nexus of circumstances: speech, bipedal locomotion, brain size and complexity, social organization. Let me add another quality to the list, performed dreams. Dreams are desires, erotic and violent. When dreams were first performed – not only dreamed and remembered but spoken, danced, sung, and acted out – a definite threshold was crossed. Performing a dream actualizes what can never be shown. A dream is experienced firsthand only by the dreamer; like the violence of Greek tragedy, it is forever offstage, shared only insofar as it can be represented. Shamans and artists are "dream-trained." They can focus their dreams, retain and retell them. This retelling may be in any medium:

words, actions, pictures, sounds. Dream-trained people are also able to freely combine their dream-images with what they get from ordinary life, tradition, and other sources. Once a dream is performed it changes its character entirely. It enters the social arena, the ritual–aesthetic sphere. It can be taught to others. It can be revised, combined, and transformed to accord with – or radically break from – tradition. The great dreamers are those who are able to combine most effectively what was dreamed with what is drawn from other realms; and who are able to exercise the strictest discipline when it is time to rehearse, perform, and transmit the elaborated dream.

Enacting dreams – or elaborated recollection of dreams – violently ruptures the boundary between the virtual and the actual, a boundary animals (we presume) have no choice but to keep intact. Among people, the "as if" of dreaming is by means of performance transformed into the "is" of bodily actions. And once the boundary between dreaming and doing is ruptured, all kinds of things – conceptual, fantastic, recollected – spill through in both directions. The quantity and quality of dreaming changes as do the kinds of performances enacted – or played. The "playing" which I proposed as the ground of all human experience (see Chapter 2) is truly a dreamfield of unlimited possibilities.

At some point in human history people began performing their dreams and elaborating on them. These were not facts nor were they imaginary. They were performances of events between fact and imagination. These virtual actualities, staged as rituals, shared the authority of recollection with the play of imagination. Artful elaborations, found or invented (there is no way to tell the difference, that is why Grotowski is both right and wrong), have been decisive in human history at least since paleolithic times. These performed dreams appear always to have been erotic and violent. Human creativity still works this playfield betwixt and between the ethological, the neurological, and the social. The future of ritual is the continued encounter between imagination and memory translated into doable acts of the body. Ritual's conservativism may restrain humans enough to prevent our extinction, while its magmatic creative core demands that human life – social, individual, maybe even biological – keep changing.

Notes

1. The writings about ritual are voluminous. Ronald Grimes has done much excellent bibliographic work putting at least the writings in English into some kind of order; see his *Research in Ritual Studies* (1985). Some of the texts that have influenced my thinking are: Armstrong 1981; d'Aquili, *et al.* 1979; Geertz 1973, 1980, 1983; Goffman 1967; Grimes 1982, 1990; Handelman 1977; Kapferer 1983; La Barre 1972; MacAloon 1984; Moore and Myerhoff 1977; Rappaport 1968, 1971; Staal 1979; Turner 1969, 1974, 1982, 1986; Van Gennep 1960. Even this list is painfully partial. For references of a distinctly ethological kind, see note 2 below.

2. The work by ethologists on ritual has been extensive. To begin with, see Darwin 1965; Eibl-Eibesfeldt 1970, 1979; Konner 1982; Lorenz 1959, 1961, 1965, 1967; Tinbergen 1965. For a critique of the way scientists – males mostly – have conducted their research with primates see Haraway 1989.

3. For my own views on the possible relationships between performance and ethology see "Ethology and theater" and "Towards a poetics of performance," both in Schechner 1988a.

4. For surveys of shamanism, see Eliade 1970 and Lewis 1971. In Korea, shamanic practice is still active – see Kendall 1988 and Du-Hyun Lee 1990. For "new age shamanism" see Halifax 1979, Harner 1980, Larsen 1976, Nicholson 1987. For a theory of shamanism as the origin of theatre, see E. T. Kirby 1975.

5. Flow as defined by Mihaly Csikszentmihalyi is

> the merging of action and awareness. A person in flow has no dualistic perspective: he is aware of his actions but not the awareness itself. . . . The steps for experiencing flow . . . involve the . . . process of delimiting reality, controlling some aspect of it, and responding to the feedback with a concentration that excludes anything else as irrelevant.   (1975:38, 53–4)

6. Much more work needs to be done on gesture and movement from an ethological and cross-cultural perspective. An early classic work is David Efron's *Gesture, Race, and Culture* 1941. Paul Ekman and his team of researchers have done much work on the display of emotions in the human face; see Ekman 1972, 1977, 1980, 1985; and Ekman *et al.* 1972. For applications of this approach to the study of dance and other aesthetic performances see *TDR, the Drama Review* 32 (4) (winter 1988), a special issue on movement analysis edited by Ann Daly.

7. Nigerian theatre scholar J. Ndukaku Amankulor noted how closely Grotowski's style of public speaking "followed the ritual structure of an African divination consultation" (1991:156). Over the years, Grotowski has published almost nothing that he has written (I don't know of a single example and would guess that Grotowski does not write, even for himself). When Grotowski appears in print it is what someone has tape recorded from a public appearance or private

interview or written from notes. In this, Grotowski is unique among modern Western performance theorists and practitioners. Stanislavski (reluctantly at first), Meyerhold, Brecht, Artaud, and many others (myself among them) commit to paper. And even those who do not write much for publication, Robert Wilson for example, leave behind a significant paper trail of notes and sketches. Not so Grotowski.

8. If the Yaquis were what Carlos Castaneda invented them as being (see Castaneda 1968, 1971, 1972, 1974), or if they lived nearer the California border – instead of further south close to the Rio Yaqui (with other settlements in Arizona) – they surely would be marketed as the Huichols have been. For a debunking study of Castaneda's works, see de Mille 1976.

9. An early theory concerning the emergence of theatre from a "primal ritual" was proposed in the first decades of the twentieth century by the "Cambridge anthropologists," scholars of ancient Greek culture who followed the lead of Sir James G. Frazer. See Jane Ellen Harrison 1912, 1913; Gilbert Murray 1912; and Francis Cornford 1914; see Schechner 1988a for a critique of their thesis.

References

Agnew, Spiro (1969) "Honolulu address to the Young Presidents Organization, 2 May," in Lee Baxandall, "Spectacles and scenarios: a dramaturgy of radical activity," *TDR, The Drama Review* 13 (4): 52–71.

Alvarado, Anita Louise (1974) *Catalan Holy Week Ceremonies, Catholic Ideology, and Culture Change in the Spanish Colonial Empire*, Dissertation in the Department of Anthropology, Tucson: University of Arizona.

Amankulor, J. Ndukaku (1991) "Jerzy Grotowski's 'Divination Consultation': objective drama seminar at U. C. Irvine," *TDR, The Drama Review* 35 (1): 155–64.

Anderson, Benedict (1983) *Imagined Communities*, New York: Verso.

Armstrong, Robert Plant (1981) *The Powers of Presence*, Philadelphia: University of Pennsylvania Press.

Artaud, Antonin (1958) *The Theatre and Its Double*, New York: Grove Press.

Attwater, Donald (1965) *The Penguin Dictionary of Saints*, Baltimore: Penguin.

Awasthi, Induja (n.d.) "*Ramcharitmanas* and the performing tradition of the *Ramayana*," unpublished MS.

Awasthi, Suresh (1989) " 'Theatre of roots': encounter with tradition," *TDR, The Drama Review* 33 (4): 48–69.

Bakhtin, Mikhail (1981) *The Dialogic Imagination*, Austin: University of Texas Press.
—— (1984) *Rabelais and His World*, Bloomington: Indiana University Press.

Barba, Eugenio (1986) *Beyond the Floating Islands*, New York: PAJ Publications.
—— (1988) "Eurasian theatre," *TDR, The Drama Review* 32 (3): 126–30.

Barr, Donald (1992) "Easter, Keruk, and Wi: gita," in Rosamond B. Spicer and N. Ross Crumrine (eds) *Performing the Renewal of Community: Indigenous Easter Rituals in Northern Mexico and Southwest United States*, Washington DC: University Press of America.

Bateson, Gregory (1972) *Steps to an Ecology of Mind*, New York: Ballantine Books.

Baxandall, Lee (1969) "Spectacles and scenarios: a dramaturgy of radical activity," *TDR, The Drama Review* 13 (4): 52–71.

Bayly, C. A. (1986) "Two colonial revolts: the Java War, 1825–30 and the Indian 'Mutiny' of 1857–59," in C. A. Bayly and D. H. A. Kolff (eds) *Two Colonial*

Empires, Dordrecht, Holland: Martinus Nijhoff.

Becker, A. L. (1974) "The journey through the night," in Mhd. Taib Osman (ed.) *Traditional Drama and Music of Southeast Asia*, Kuala Lumpur: Dewan Banasa Pustaka.

—— (1979) "Text-building, epistemology, and aesthetics in Javanese shadow theatre," in Abram A. Yengoyan (ed.) *The Imagination of Reality*, Norwood, NJ: Ablex.

Bhabha, Homi (1984) "Of mimicry and man: the ambivalence of colonial discourse," *October* (spring): 125–33.

—— (1986) "The other question: difference, discrimination and the discourse of colonialism," in Francis Barker, Peter Hulme, Margaret Iversen, and Diana Loxley (eds) *Literature, Politics, and Theory*, London and New York: Methuen.

Bharata-muni (1967) *The Natyasastra*, ed. and trans. Manomohan Ghosh, Calcutta: Granthalaya.

Bhardwaj, Surinder Mohan (1973) *Hindu Places of Pilgrimage in India*, Berkeley: University of California Press.

Boal, Augusto (1980) *Stop! C'est magique*, Paris: Hachette.

—— (1983) *Jeux pour acteurs et non-acteurs*, Paris: La Decouverte/Maspero.

—— (1985) *Theatre of the Oppressed*, New York: Theatre Communications Group.

—— (1990a) "Invisible theatre: Liège, Belgium, 1978," *TDR, The Drama Review* 34 (2): 24–34.

—— (1990b) "The cop in the head: three hypotheses," *TDR, The Drama Review* 34 (2): 35–42.

—— (1990c) *Methode Boal de theatre et de therapie*, Paris: Ramsay.

—— (1992) *Games for Actors and Non-Actors*, London and New York: Routledge.

Brandon, James (1967) *Theatre in Southeast Asia*, Cambridge, Mass.: Harvard University Press.

Branley, Edward J. (1992) "The Zulu Social Aid and Pleasure Club," e-mail, 19 January.

Bristol, Michael (1985) *Carnival and Theater*, London: Methuen.

Caillois, Roger (1959) *Man and the Sacred*, Glencoe: The Free Press.

Carlson, Marvin (1989) *Places of Performance*, Ithaca: Cornell University Press.

Castaneda, Carlos (1968) *The Teachings of Don Juan: A Yaqui Way of Knowledge*, New York: Ballantine Books.

—— (1971) *A Separate Reality*, New York: Simon & Schuster.

—— (1972) *Journey to Ixtlan*, New York: Simon & Schuster.

—— (1974) *Tales of Power*, New York: Simon & Schuster.

Clara van Groenendael, Victoria M. (1985) *The Dalang Behind the Wayang*, Dordrecht, Holland/Cinnaminson, USA: Foris Publications.

—— (1987) *Wayang Theatre in Indonesia: An Annotated Bibliography*, Dordrecht, Holland/Providence, USA: Foris Publications.

Cohen-Cruz, Jan (1990) "Boal at NYU: a workshop and its aftermath," *TDR, The*

Drama Review 34 (2): 43–9.

Cohen-Cruz, Jan and Schutzman, Mady (1990) "Theatre of the oppressed workshops with women" (interview), *TDR, The Drama Review* 34 (2): 66–76.

Cornford, Francis (1914) *The Origin of Attic Comedy*, London: Edward Arnold.

Csikszentmihalyi, Mihaly (1975) *Beyond Boredom and Anxiety*, San Francisco: Jossey-Bass.

d'Ans, André-Marcel (1980) "Gasparilla: myth and history on Florida's west coast," *Tampa Bay History*, vol. 2: 5–30.

d'Aquili, Eugene G., Laughlin, Charles D. Jr., and McManus, John (1979) *The Spectrum of Ritual*, New York: Columbia University Press.

Darwin, Charles (1965) *The Expression of the Emotions in Man and Animals*, Chicago: University of Chicago Press. First published 1872.

Davis, R. G. (1966) "Guerrilla theatre," *TDR, The Drama Review* 10 (4): 130–6.

de Kat Angelino, A. D. A. (1931) *Colonial Policy*, vol. 2, *The Dutch East Indies*, The Hague: Martinus Nijhoff.

de Mille, Richard (1976) *Castaneda's Journey*, Santa Barbara, CA: Capra Press.

de Wit, Augusta (1906) *Java: Facts and Fancies*, Philadelphia: J. B. Lippincott; The Hague: W. P. van Stockum & Son.

Dube, S. C. (1988) *Modernization and Development*, Tokyo: United Nations University.

Durkheim, Emile (1915) *The Elementary Forms of the Religious Life*, New York: Macmillan.

Efron, David (1941) *Gesture, Race, and Culture*, The Hague: Mouton.

Ehrenzweig, Anton (1970) *The Hidden Order of Art*, St Albans: Paladin.

Eibl-Eibesfeldt, Irenaus (1970) *Ethology: The Biology of Behavior*, New York: Holt, Rinehart, & Winston.

—— (1979) "Ritual and ritualization from a biological perspective," in M. von Cranach, K. Foppa, W. Lepenies, and D. Ploog (eds) *Human Ethology*, Cambridge: Cambridge University Press.

Ekman, Paul (1972) "Universal and cultural differences in facial expressions of emotion," in *Nebraska Symposium on Motivation, 1971*, Omaha: University of Nebraska Press.

—— (1977) "Biological and cultural contributions to body and facial movement," in John Blacking (ed.) *The Anthropology of the Body*, London: Academic Press.

—— (1980) *The Face of Man*, New York: Garland.

—— (1985) *Telling Lies*, New York: W. W. Norton.

Ekman, Paul, Friesen, Wallace V., and Ellsworth, Phoebe (1972) *Emotion in the Human Face*, New York: Pergamon Press.

Eliade, Mircea (1970) *Shamanism: Archaic Techniques of Ecstasy*, Princeton: Princeton University Press.

Esherick, Joseph W. and Wasserstrom Jeffrey N. (1990) "Acting out democracy: political theater in modern China," *The Journal of Asian Studies* 49 (4): 835–66.

REFERENCES

Evers, Larry and Molina, Felipe S. (1987) *Yaqui Deer Songs: Maso Bwikam*, Tucson: Sun Tracks and the University of Arizona Press.

Fischer, Roland (1971) "A cartography of the ecstatic and meditative states," *Science* 174 (26 November): 897–904.

Freud, Sigmund (1962) *Totem and Taboo*, New York: W. W. Norton.

Gallop, Rodney (1936) *A Book of Folkways*, Cambridge: Cambridge University Press.

Geertz, Clifford (1973) *The Interpretation of Cultures*, New York: Basic Books.

(1976) *The Religion of Java*, Chicago: University of Chicago Press.

(1980) *Negara: The Theatre State in Nineteenth Century Bali*, Princeton: Princeton University Press.

(1983) *Local Knowledge*, New York: Basic Books.

Girard, René (1977) *Violence and the Sacred*, Baltimore: The Johns Hopkins University Press.

Goffman, Erving (1959) *The Presentation of Self in Everyday Life*, Garden City: Doubleday.

(1967) *Interaction Ritual*, Garden City: Doubleday.

Gomez-Pena, Guillermo (1991) "A binational performance pilgrimage," *TDR, The Drama Review* 35 (3): 22–45.

Gonda, Jan (1987) "Visnu" in Mircea Eliade (ed.) *The Encyclopedia of Religion*, vol. 15: 288–91, New York: Macmillan.

Goodman, Felicitas D. (1990) "A trance dance with masks: research and performance at the Cuyamungue Institute," *TDR, The Drama Review* 34 (1): 102–14.

Greene, Bob (1988) Title unknown, *Esquire*, July: 29–30.

Grimes, Ronald L. (1982) *Beginnings in Ritual Studies*, Washington, DC: University Press of America.

(1985) *Research in Ritual Studies*, Metuchen, NJ: Scarecrow Press and the American Theological Library Association.

(1990) *Ritual Criticism*, Columbia, SC: University of South Carolina Press.

Grotowski, Jerzy (1968) *Towards a Poor Theatre*, Holstebro: Odin Teatret Verlag.

(1987) "*Tu es le fils de quelqu'un* [You are someone's son]," *TDR, The Drama Review* 31 (3): 30–41.

(1988) *Workcenter of Jerzy Grotowski – Centro di Lavoro di Jerzy Grotowski*, Pontedera, Italy: Centro per la Sperimentazione e la Ricerca Teatrale.

Hadisoeseno, Harsono (1955) "Wayang and education," *Education and Culture* 8 (1): 1–20.

Hair, William Ivy (1976) *Carnival of Fury*, Baton Rouge: Louisiana State University Press.

Halifax, Joan (1979) *Shamanic Voices*, New York: E. P. Dutton.

Handelman, Don (1976) "Re-thinking 'Banana Time'," *Urban Life* 4 (4): 33–48.

(1977) "Play and ritual: complementary frames of metacommunication," in A. J. Chapman and H. Foot (eds) *It's a Funny Thing, Humour*, London: Pergamon.

Haraway, Donna (1989) *Primate Visions*, London and New York: Routledge.

Harner, Michael (1980) *The Way of the Shaman*, New York: Bantam.

Harrison, Jane Ellen (1912) *Themis: A Study of the Social Origins of Greek Religion*, Cambridge: Cambridge University Press.

(1913) *Art and Ritual*, New York: Henry Holt.

Harrison-Pepper, Sally (1990) *Drawing a Circle in the Square*. Jackson: University of Mississippi Press.

Hatley, Barbara (1971) "Wayang and ludruk: polarities in Java," *TDR The Drama Review* 15 (1): 88–101.

Hawley, John Stratton (1981) *At Play with Krishna*, Princeton: Princeton University Press.

Hazeu, Godard Arend Johannes (1897) *Bijdrage tot de kennisvan het Javaansche tooneel*, Leiden: Brill.

Hertel, Bradley R. and Humes, Cynthia A. (eds) (1992) *Living Banaras: Hindu Religion in Cultural Context*, Albany: State University of New York Press.

Hess, Linda (1983) "Ram Lila: the audience experience," in Monika Thiel- Horstman (ed.) *Bhakti in Current Research 1979–82*, Berlin: Dietrich Reimer.

(1988) "The poet, the people, and the Western scholar: the influence of a sacred drama and text on social values in north India," *Theatre Journal* 40 (3): 236–53.

Hobsbawm, Eric and Ranger, Terence (eds) (1983) *The Invention of Tradition*, Cambridge: Cambridge University Press.

Hoffman, Abbie (1968) *Revolution for the Hell of It*, New York: Dial Books.

(1969a) *Woodstock Nation*, New York: Vintage Books.

(1969b) "Media freaking," *TDR, The Drama Review* 13 (4): 46–51.

(1971) *Steal This Book*, New York: Pirate Editions.

Huizinga, Johan (1955) *Homo Ludens*, Boston: Beacon Press.

Inden, Ronald (1978) "Ritual, authority, and cyclic time in Hindu kingship," in J. F. Richards (ed.) *Kingship and Authority in South Asia*, Madison: University of Wisconsin Publication series no. 3.

Indonesia, Embassy of (1951) *The Cultural Life of Indonesia*, Washington: Embassy of Indonesia.

Kafka, Franz (1954) *Wedding Preparations in the Country and Other Posthumous Prose Writings*, London: Secker & Warburg.

Kale, Pramod (1974) *The Theatric Universe*, Bombay: Popular Prakishan.

Kamm, Henry (1989a) "East Berliners march for democracy," *The New York Times*, 22 October: A16.

(1989b) "Words fly on Marx-Engels-Platz," *The New York Times*, 25 October: A14.

Kapferer, Bruce (1983) *A Celebration of Demons*, Bloomington: Indiana University Press.

Keeler, Ward (1987) *Javanese Shadow Plays, Javanese Selves*, Princeton: Princeton University Press.

Keller, Martha (1988) "Shadow dancing," *The Ann Arbor News*, 27 March: G1–2.

REFERENCES

Kendall, Laurel (1988) *The Life and Hard Times of a Korean Shaman*, Honolulu: University of Hawaii Press.

Kenyon, Jim (1990) "Invasion proves profitable," *The Tampa Tribune*, 10 February: 8-A.

Kirby, E. T. (1975) *Ur-Drama: The Origins of Theatre*, New York: New York University Press.

Kirby, Michael (1969) *The Art of Time*, New York: E. P. Dutton.

Komparu, Kunio (1983) *The Noh Theater*, New York: Weatherhill/Tankosha.

Konner, Melvin (1982) *The Tangled Wing*, New York: Holt, Rinehart, & Winston.

Kumiega, Jennifer (1985) *The Theatre of Grotowski* London and New York: Methuen.

Kundera, Milan (1985) *The Unbearable Lightness of Being*, New York: Harper.

La Barre, Weston (1972) *The Ghost Dance*, New York: Dell.

Lannoy, Richard (1971) *The Speaking Tree*, London: Oxford University Press.

Larsen, Stephen (1976) *The Shaman's Doorway*, New York: Harper.

Lee, Du-Hyun (1990) "Korean shamans: role playing through trance possession," in Richard Schechner and Willa Appel (eds) *By Means of Performance*, Cambridge: Cambridge University Press.

Lendra, I Wayan (1991) "Bali and Grotowski: some parallels in the training process," *TDR, The Drama Review* 35 (1): 113–39.

Lesnick, Henry (ed.) (1973) *Guerilla* [sic] *Street Theater*, New York: Avon.

Levine, Mark L., McNamee, George C., and Greenberg, Daniel (eds) (1970) *The Tales of Hoffman*, New York: Bantam.

Lewis, I. M. (1971) *Ecstatic Religion*, London: Penguin.

Lex, Barbara W. (1979) "The neurobiology of ritual trance," in Eugene d'Aquili *et al.*, *The Spectrum of Ritual*, New York: Columbia University Press.

Ley, Graham (1991) "Sacred idiocy: the avant-garde as alternative establishment," *New Theatre Quarterly* VII (28) (November): 348–52.

Lipman, Joanne (1989) "Spring Break sponsors in Florida find too much of a good thing," *The Wall Street Journal*, 21 March: B1, 7.

Long, Roger (1982) *Javanese Shadow Theatre*, Ann Arbor: UMI Research Press.

Lorenz, Konrad (1959) "The role of aggression in group formation," in B. Schaffner (ed.) *Primate Ethology*, Garden City: Anchor.

(1961) *King Solomon's Ring*, New York: T. Y. Corwell.

(1965) *Evolution and Modification of Behavior*, Chicago: University of Chicago Press.

(1967) *On Aggression*, New York: Bantam Books.

MacAloon, John (ed.) (1984) *Rite, Drama, Festival, Spectacle*, Philadelphia: Institute for the Study of Human Issues (ISHI).

McFadden, Robert D. (1989) "The Berlin Wall: a monument to the cold war, triumphs and tragedies," *The New York Times*, 10 November: A15.

McLaren, Robert Mshengu (1992) "Theatre on the frontline: the political theatre of

Zambuko/Izibuko," *TDR, The Drama Review* 36 (1): 90–114.

Majumdar, R. C. (1973) *Hindu Colonies in the Far East*, Calcutta: Firma K. L. Mukhopadhyay.

Mechelen, Ch. te (1879a) *Drie-en-twintig schetsen van wayang-stukken (lakons), gebrukerlijk bij vertooning der wayang-poerwa op Java*, Verhandelingen of the Bataviaasch Genootschap: 40.

(1879b) "Een en ander over de wajang," Tijdschrift van het Bataviaasch Genootschap 25: 72–107.

(1882) *Drie teksten van tooneneelstukken uit de wayang poerwa, voor den druk bezorgd door Ch. te Mechelen en meteen voorede van Professor H. Kern*, Iste Deel, Verhandelingen of the Bataviaasch Genootschap: 43.

Mills, Barbara (1993) "The Boundary Face-Off of New Orleans Civil Rights Law and Carnival Tradition," *TDR* 37(1): in press.

Mok, Chiu Yu and Harrison, J. Frank (eds) (1990) *Voices from Tiananmen Square*, Montreal–New York: Black Rose.

Molina, Felipe and Kaczkurkin, Mini (1980) "A Yaqui folklore map," Tucson: Tucson Public Library.

Moore, Sally F. and Myerhoff, Barbara (eds) (1977) *Secular Ritual*, Amsterdam: Van Gorcum.

Mulyono, Sri (1979) *Simbolisme dan mistikisme dalam wayang*, Jakarta: Sunung Agung.

Murray, Gilbert (1912) "An excursus on the ritual forms preserved in Greek tragedy," in Jane Ellen Harrison, *Themis*, Cambridge: Cambridge University Press.

Mylius, N. (1961) "Wayang Suluh und Wayang Wahyu, zwei moderne Wayang-Arten Javas," *Archive für Volkerunde* 16: 94–104.

Narain Singh, C. P. N., brother of the maharaja of Banaras (1978) Interviews conducted by Richard Schechner and Linda Hess in Ramnagar.

Narain Singh, Vibhuti, the maharaja of Banaras (1978) Interviews conducted by Richard Schechner and Linda Hess in Ramnagar.

Nicholson, Shirley (ed.) (1987) *Shamanism*, Wheaton, Ill.: The Theosophical Publishing House.

Nunley, John W. and Bettelheim, Judith (1988) *Caribbean Festival Arts*, Saint Louis: The Saint Louis Art Museum and Seattle: University of Washington Press.

O'Flaherty, Wendy Doniger (1984) *Dreams, Illusions, and Other Realities*, Chicago: University of Chicago Press.

Osinski, Zbigniew (1986) *Grotowski and His Laboratory*, New York: PAJ Publications.
(1991) "Grotowski blazes the trails: from objective drama to ritual arts," *TDR, The Drama Review* 35 (1): 95–112.

Painter, Muriel Thayer (1971) *A Yaqui Easter*, Tucson: University of Arizona Press.
(1986) *With Good Heart*, Tucson: University of Arizona Press.

Pascua Tribal Council (1982) "Pascua means Easter," mimeographed sheet distributed during Holy Week.
(1985a) "Preface something about the Pascua Yaqui Indians," mimeographed sheet

distributed during Holy Week.

(1985b) "A chronological history of the Pascua Yaqui Indians," three-page mimeographed pamphlet distributed during Holy Week.

(1987) "Pascua Pueblo Giotojame, Cuaresma 87," seven-page pamphlet, introduction in English to the Easter Ceremony as it is celebrated in New Pascua.

Pekan (1969) *Pekan Wajang Indonesia [1] 1969*, Jakarta: Sekretariat Musjawarah Pedalingan Seluruh Indonesia.

Pekan Wayang Indonesia II (1974) *Pekan Wayang II/1974*, Jakarta: Senawangi.

Pigeaud, Th. (1967/68) *Literature of Java*, vols 1 and 2, The Hague: Martinus Nijhoff.

Pischel, R. (1906) "Das altindische Schattenspeil," *Sitzungsberichte der Berliner Akademie*, 3 May.

Poggioli, Renato (1968) *The Theory of the Avantgarde*, Cambridge, Mass.: Harvard University Press.

Protzman, Ferdinand (1989a) "Westward tide of East Germans is a popular no-confidence vote," *The New York Times*, 22 August: A1, 3.

(1989b) "Thousands swell trek to the West by East Germans," *The New York Times*, 12 September: A1, 14.

(1989c) "Broken heart of Berlin is coming back to life," *The New York Times*, 13 November: A10.

Rappaport, Roy A. (1968) *Pigs for the Ancestors*, New Haven: Yale University Press.

(1971) *Ecology, Meaning, and Religion*, Richmond, CA: North Atlantic Books.

Rassers, Willem Huibert (1959) "On the origin of the Javanese theatre," in his *Panji, The Culture Hero*, The Hague: Martinus Nijhoff. First published 1931.

Roach, Joseph R. (1993) "Carnival and the Law," *TDR* 37(1): in press.

Roach, Joseph R. and Reinelt, Janelle (eds) (1992) *Critical Theory and Performance*, Ann Arbor: University of Michigan Press.

Rubin, Jerry (1970) *Do It!*, New York: Simon & Schuster.

Sankalia, H. D. (1973) *Ramayana – Myth or Reality?*, New Delhi: People's Publishing House.

Sartre, Jean-Paul (1963) *Saint Genet: Actor and Martyr*, New York: George Braziller.

Sax, William (1979) "Ramlila as a pilgrimage: preliminary report," unpaginated MS.

(1982) "The Ramnagar Ramlila: a theatre of pilgrimage," unpublished MS.

(1989) "The Ramlila of Ramnagar," unpublished MS.

Schechner, Richard (1969) *Public Domain*, Indianapolis: Bobbs-Merrill.

(1973) *Environmental Theater*, New York: Hawthorn Books.

(1974) "From ritual to theatre and back: the structure/process of the efficacy–entertainment dyad," *Educational Theatre Journal* 26 (4): 455–81.

(1983) "The Performance Group in India," 31–54, *Quarterly Journal* of The National Centre for the Performing Arts, Bombay.

(1985) *Between Theater and Anthropology*, Philadelphia: University of Pennsylvania Press.

(1988a) *Performance Theory*, London and New York: Routledge.

1988b) "Performance studies: the broad spectrum approach," *TDR, The Drama Review* 32 (3): 4–6.

(1989a) "Last exit from Shanghai," *American Theater* 6 (8): 24ff.

(1989b) "Race free, gender free, body-type free, age free casting," *TDR, The Drama Review* 33 (1):4–12.

(1989c) "*PAJ* distorts the broad spectrum," *TDR, The Drama Review* 33 (2): 4–9.

(1990) "Performance studies: the broad spectrum approach," *National Forum* 70 (3): 15–16.

(1991) "Tales of a few cities," *New Theatre Quarterly* VII (28): 315–24.

Schechner, Richard and Appel, Willa (eds) (1990) *By Means of Performance*, Cambridge: Cambridge University Press.

Schmemann, Serge (1989a) "Exodus galls East Berlin," *The New York Times*, 14 September: A14.

(1989b) "Sour German birthday," *The New York Times*, 6 October: A8.

(1989c) "Gorbachev lends Honecker a hand," *The New York Times*, 7 October: A5.

(1989d) "Another big rally in East Germany," *The New York Times*, 31 October: A17.

(1989e) "East Germany opens frontier to the West," *The New York Times*, 10 November: A1, 14.

Schmidt, Peter Clay (1990) *The Fall of the Berlin Wall*: video.

Schrieke, B. (1955) *Indonesian Sociological Studies*, The Hague/Bandung: W. van Hoeve.

Schutz, A. (1977) "Multiple realities," in Mary Douglas (ed.) *Rules and Meanings*, Harmondsworth: Penguin.

Schutzman, Mady (1990) "Activism, therapy, or nostalgia: theatre of the oppressed in New York," *TDR, The Drama Review* 34 (3): 77–84.

Schutzman, Mady and Cohen-Cruz, Jan (1990) "Selected bibliography on Augusto Boal," *TDR, The Drama Review* 34 (3): 84–7.

Sears, Laurie J. (1989a) "Aesthetic displacement in Javanese shadow theatre: three contemporary performance styles," *TDR, The Drama Review*, 33 (3): 122–40.

(1989b) "The invention of tradition in colonial Java: history, schooling, and political control," unpublished MS.

Spence, Jonathan D. (1981) *The Gate of Heavenly Peace*, New York: Viking Penguin.

(1990) *The Search for Modern China*, New York: W. W. Norton.

Spicer, Edward H. (1962) *Cycles of Conquest*, Tucson: University of Arizona Press.

(1974) "The context of the Yaqui Easter ceremony," in Tamara Comstock (ed.) *CORD Research Annual VI: New Dimensions in Dance Research: Anthropology and Dance – the American Indian*, New York: Committee on Research in Dance, New York University.

(1980) *The Yaquis*, Tucson: University of Arizona Press.

(1983) "Yaqui," in Alfonso Ortiz (ed.) *Handbook of North American Indians, Southwest*, vol. 10, Washington: Smithsonian Institution.

Spicer, Rosamond B. (1939) *The Easter Fiesta of the Yaqui Indians of Pascua, Arizona*, Master's Thesis, Department of Anthropology, Chicago: University of Chicago.

Spicer, Rosamond B. and Crumrine, N. Ross (eds) (in press) *Performing the Renewal of Community: Indigenous Easter Rituals in North Mexico and Southwest United States*, Washington, DC: University Press of America.

Staal, Frits (1979) "The meaninglessness of ritual," *Numen* 26: 2–22.

Stein, Bonnie Sue (1986) "Butoh: 'Twenty Years Ago We Were Crazy, Dirty, and Mad,' " *TDR, The Drama Review* 30 (2): 107–26.

Sutton-Smith, Brian (1979) "Epilogue: play as performance," in Brian Sutton-Smith (ed.) *Play and Learning*, New York: Gardner Press.

Tallant, Robert (1948) *Mardi Gras*, Gretna, LA: Pelican Publishing Company.

Taussig, Michael and Schechner, Richard (1990) "Boal in Brazil, France, the USA" (interview), *TDR, The Drama Review* 34 (3): 50–65.

TDR, The Drama Review (1988) Special issue on movement analysis 32 (4).

TDR, The Drama Review editors (1989) "Public demonstrations and secret politics in China," *TDR, The Drama Review* 33 (4): 4–7.

Thompson, Robert Farris (1974) *African Art in Motion*, Berkeley: University of California Press.

Tilly, Charles (1978) *From Mobilization to Revolution*, Reading, MA: Addison-Wesley.

Tinbergen, N. (1965) *Social Behaviour in Animals*, London: Scientific Book Club.

Tulasi Das (1971) *The Holy Lake of the Acts of Rama*, a translation of the *Ramcharitmanas* by W. D. P. Hill, Bombay: Oxford University Press.

Turner, Victor (1967) *The Forest of Symbols*, Ithaca: Cornell University Press.

(1969) *The Ritual Process*, Chicago: Aldine.

(1974) *Dramas, Fields, and Metaphors*, Ithaca: Cornell University Press.

(1977) "Variations on a theme of liminality," in Sally F. Moore and Barbara Myerhoff (eds) *Secular Ritual*, Amsterdam: Van Gorcum.

(1982) *From Ritual to Theatre*, New York: PAJ Publications.

(1983) "Body, brain, and culture," *Zygon* 18 (3): 221–45.

(1986) *The Anthropology of Performance*, New York: PAJ Publications.

(1990) "Are there universals of performance in myth, ritual, and drama?" in Richard Schechner and Willa Appel (eds) *By Means of Performance*, Cambridge: Cambridge University Press.

Turner, Victor and Turner, Edith (1986) "Performing ethnography," in Victor Turner, *The Anthropology of Performance*, New York: PAJ Publications.

United States Senate (1977) "Hearing before the United States Senate Select Committee on Indian Affairs," 95th Congress, first session on S. 1633, 27

September, Washington: US Government Printing Office.

Van Erven, Eugene (1987) "Philippine political theatre and the fall of Ferdinand Marcos," *TDR, The Drama Review* 31 (2): 57–78.

(1988) "Resistance theatre in Korea," *TDR, The Drama Review* 32 (3): 156–73.

(1989) "Plays, applause, and bullets: Safdar Hashmi's street theatre," *TDR, The Drama Review* 33 (4): 32–47.

Van Gennep, Arnold (1960) *The Rites of Passage*, Chicago: University of Chicago Press. First published 1908.

Vandenbosch, Amry (1941) *The Dutch East Indies*, Berkeley: University of California Press.

Vyasa (1986) *The Bhagavad Gita*, trans. Barbara Stoler Miller, New York: Bantam Books.

Wagner, Roy (1981) *The Invention of Culture*, Chicago: University of Chicago Press.

Waldrop, M. Mitchell (1987) "Do-it-yourself universes," *Science*, 20 February: 845–6.

Walker, Barbara G. (1983) *The Women's Encyclopedia of Myths and Secrets*, San Francisco: Harper & Row.

Weisman, John (1973) *Guerrilla Theater*, Garden City: Anchor.

Wenner-Gren Foundation for Anthropological Research (1981) Transcript of tape no. 1 of discussion at the Oracle Conference Center, Arizona, 20 November.

Whitney, Craig R. with Binder, David and Schmemann, Serge (1989) "Party coup turned East German tide," *The New York Times*, 19 November: A1, 27.

Wilkins, W. J. (1975) *Hindu Mythology*, Calcutta: Rupa & Co.

Winnicott, D. W. (1971) *Playing and Reality*, London: Tavistock.

Winterbottom, Philip Jr. (1991) "Two years before the master," *TDR, The Drama Review* 35 (1): 140–54.

Wolford, Lisa (1991) "Subjective reflections on objective work: Grotowski in Irvine," *TDR, The Drama Review* 35 (1): 165–80.

Wright, C. E. (1964) Title unknown, *The New York Times*, section 10: 5.

Yamamoto, Yoshiko (1978) *The Namahage*, Philadelphia: Institute for the Study of Human Issues (ISHI).

Zaehner, R. C. (trans.) (1966) *Hindu Scriptures*, London: J. M. Dent.

Index

Caillois, Roger 47–8

"Cambridge Anthropologists" 265 n.9

Carnivals/festivals 46–8; and revolution 47, 83, 86, 88; and collapse of East Germany 68–71; and official culture 82–4; in anti-Vietnam War movement 64–7; in Chinese democracy movement 57–8

Castaneda, Carlos 265 n.8

Chan, Choi Lai 62

Chapayekam, Chapayeka masks. See Waehma

Chekhov, Anton, Uncle Vanya 12

Chicago 8, trial of 64, 91–2 n.10

China 5, 6; Cultural Revolution 52; democracy movement focused in Tiananmen Square: 17, 21, 46, 52–63, 58, 69–70, 72, 84–5; democracy movement in Shanghai 51–2, 58–62; Goddess of Democracy and Freedom 55–6; model operas 6, 22 n.1

Clarke, Martha 8

Clara van Groenendael, Victoria M. 192, 193–4, 196, 219, 221, 223, 225 n.6, 225–6 n.7, 227 n.10. See also wayang kulit

Colonialism 222–4, 226–7 n.9. See also wayang kulit; Westernization, modernization

Csikszentmihalyi, Mihaly 25, 264 n.5

Cunningham, Merce 8

Cuyamungue Institute 240, 242–3, 245

d'Aquili, Eugene 239–40. See also ritual

Daendels, H. W. 198

Dai Rakuda-kan 15

Daly, Ann 265 n.6

Daly, Richard 64

Davis, R. G. 91 n.8

Davis, Rennie 91–2 n.10

Daytona Beach Spring Break Weekend 46, 78, 80–2, 83, 84, 87; and consumerism 81–2; as carnival 85–6

de Kat Angelino, A. D. A. 201–2

de Wit, Augusta (Java Facts and Fancies) 202–15; analysis of her photos 204–7; Javanese as "childlike," "natural," and "happy" 203; on wayang kulit 208–15. See also wayang kulit

Dellinger, David T. 91–2 n.10

Deng Xiaoping 21, 51, 58, 62, 67, 68, 85

Direct theatre: and television 86–90; dramaturgy of 83–5, 88–90; scenography and choreography of 82, 88

Disequilibrium and performing 39–40

Dreaming and performed dreams 261–3. See also ritual

Dube, S. C. 199–200, 223. See also wayang kulit; Westernization, modernization

Durkheim, Emile 74, 90 n.2

Dutch colonial policies in Indonesia 200–2. See also wayang kulit

East Germany (GDR), collapse of 67–71

Efron, David 264 n.6

Ehrenzweig, Anton: artistic "primary process" 237–8, 253; "poemagogic" revery 261

Ekman, Paul 265 n.6

Emigh, John 196.

Esherick Joseph 53–5, 58

Eurasian Theatre 11, 12. See also Barba, Eugenio; Grotowski, Jerzy

Evers, Larry 103, 128 n.4

Festival of Life 1968. See guerrilla theatre

Flaszen, Ludwig 12. See also Grotowski, Jerzy

Folsom, A. O. 80

Foreman, Richard 8

France 5